NEW PERSPECTIVES IN MANAGEMENT CONTROL

Twenty years after the development of management control theory, it is time for a reappraisal of the state of the art. This book provides a comprehensive synthesis of the different perspectives on management control together with an analysis of their strengths, weaknesses and prospective developments. The book is written by a team of multidisciplinary specialists, the contributors including most of the leading thinkers in the area. The papers are modern, thorough, include excellent bibliographies and have been rigorously cross-referenced. The mixture of cybernetics, sociology, social psychology and epistemology which this book encompasses makes it ideal for the growing interest in management control theory. There is no book which contains survey articles as well as thought-provoking original contributions in the forefront of enquiry. The breadth of scope makes *New Perspectives in Management Control* suitable for advanced undergraduate as well as postgraduate students and, above all, it provides a basis for genuinely interdisciplinary teaching.

Tony Lowe is Professor of Accounting and Financial Management, University of Sheffield.

John L. J. Machin is Senior Lecturer in Management Control Systems, University of Durham Business School.

NEW PERSPECTIVES IN MANAGEMENT CONTROL

Edited by

Tony Lowe and John L. J. Machin

St. Martin's Press   New York

ISBN 0–312–56856–8

Library of Congress Cataloging in Publication Data

Main entry under title:

New perspectives in management control.

   Bibliography: p.
   Includes index.
   1. Management—Addresses, essays, lectures. I. Lowe,
Tony. II. Machin, John L. J. III. Title: Management
control.
HD38.N367   1983   658.4′013   82–23108
ISBN 0–312–56856–8

To the prospect of a civilised, loving, faithful, integrated human society in the lifetime of my children: Anthony, David, Stephanie, Andrew, Christopher.

Tony Lowe

Contents

Preface

This book is designed to stimulate discussion and debate about the theory and practice of management control. It has been written to help managers and students to understand more clearly the major influences in the development of the management control systems currently used in organisations, so that they have enough information to take part in the crucial debate on the kinds of management control systems which managers and their organisations will need in the future.

Such a debate is essential, given the changes that are bound to take place in both the managerial task and the information and control systems which will enable that task to be undertaken effectively during the next decade. These changes are likely to be so great that there is a need for informed discussion of the implications they bring with them for either enhancing or reducing the quality of work fulfilment, which is one of life's basic satisfactions. This book provides the material to generate and sustain important aspects of such discussions.

This book was designed to include contributions from authors with a wide variety of background disciplines and kinds of work experience. All of the contributors are concerned to improve our understanding of the theory of management control, and the practical assistance which the application of such theory can give to managers and organisations. The diversity of background disciplines of the authors enables them collectively to offer new perspectives on a vitally important subject.

Academic specialism in a particular subject is as important as managerial specialisation in a particular function. Equally, however, as both managers and theorists become more specialised, so there is an increasing need for those with the multidisciplinary skill to assist the coordination of those specialisms.

For a number of decades, those who have been concerned to design and develop management control systems have seen their role as facilitating the managerial process – that is, to enable specific and specialised resources within the organisation to be harnessed effectively in line with organisational purpose.

Over the past two decades, however, managerial research has shown that organisational purpose is rarely either clearly or adequately defined. The question has become, 'In an organisation whose purpose includes the stated and unstated, the explicit and the implicit, perhaps in contradiction and conflict in some cases, how can you design and develop a coherent, effective management control system?'

The theoretical challenge is often ignored in practice. Traditional management control systems continue to be used in organisations despite research which shows that their strengths are often undermined by their weaknesses.

This book is intended to help managers, students, and academics to seek better ways of first identifying the weaknesses in present systems, and then finding ways of overcoming those weaknesses through better theories for the better design of management control systems.

CONTENTS OF THE BOOK

None of the material in this book has been published before and all the chapters were written specifically for it. In developing their contributions for the book, the contributors acted as reviewers for their colleagues' submissions. This process enabled contributors to improve the quality and relevance of their material, and has produced a book with a coherent sense of purpose, something which is often lacking in collections of separately-authored chapters.

The process described above whereby the contents were prepared could have produced a collection of bland material reflecting the contributors' desire to avoid contention amongst themselves. In practice, the review process served to sharpen and clarify the key points of disagreement within the subject, and it also enabled contributors to reference their work to those parts of the book where other contributors either share the same views or disagree.

The book is divided into the following parts:

Part I   An introduction to the book and an overview of the history of the development of the subject of management control.

Part II   A study of the purpose of management control systems and the theories that underlie their design and development.

Part III   A review of the influences that are brought to bear on, and the attitudes of, the users of management control systems.

Part IV   An assessment of the relevance of three kinds of information which are carried in management control systems.

Part V   A concluding chapter which sets the topic of management control systems in the context of organisational effectiveness.

The early chapters strive to identify the critical differences in the approaches taken by different people to the design and development of management control systems, whilst the final chapter seeks to identify those areas of consensus that are to be found, and thus closes the ring in the study of the subject.

CONTRIBUTORS TO THE BOOK

The contributors to the book combine managerial and academic experience of management control systems.

All of the contributors are, or have been, members of academic institutions in Europe, mostly as members of multidisciplinary departments whose prime purpose is to teach and research management.

Many of the contributors have first-hand experience of management control systems derived from their employment in industry, commerce or the public sector.

Biographical data about the contributors is presented at the end of the text.

Acknowledgements

The editors and contributors to this book are, or have been, members of academic institutions in Europe. Initially, as management education developed in Europe, specialists in management control systems tended, like specialists in all other functions, to work in multidisciplinary departments such as business schools. In that position they shared a commitment to management with their colleagues in a particular department, but it was often to colleagues in other academic institutions that they turned for specialist discussion and interaction.

In the 1970s two self-formed groups began to emerge – the Management Control Workshop Group in the United Kingdom and the Management Information and Control System Workshop in Europe, centred on the European Institute for Advanced Studies of Management in Brussels.

The editors and a number of the contributors were founder-members of both. In a multidisciplinary subject, interaction and stimulation from others working in the field is, even more than in other subjects, essential for new ideas to be developed which add both to theory and to practice.

All contributors to this book would, therefore, like to acknowledge their indebtedness to members of the above workshop groups, for the many hours of discussion and interaction which have helped to generate and then incubate the ideas presented in this book.

Every chapter in this book was reviewed by two or more members of the Management Control Workshop Group in the United Kingdom. Whilst all contributors were also reviewers, many reviewers were not contributors. This process of review was exceptionally helpful to the contributors as they revised and improved their original submissions. Thanks are particularly due to Simon Archer, Syd Howell, Howard Lyons and Tony Puxty.

The process of critical collaboration described above is being continued in respect of a further book, *Critical Perspectives in Management Control*, which will be published shortly.

The editors and contributors wish to acknowledge the support which the Management Control Workshop Group has received over the years from the SSRC for funding meeting costs. The present book represents a by-product from the regular MCWG workshops held to discuss individual and group research. The contributors hope that this book will help to demonstrate the value of such 'pump-priming' funds as a means of supporting the generation of new ideas and initiatives.

In collaborative work, secretaries become arguably the most important people involved. The editors wish to thank Glynnis Benison for her help with all the editorial work, and contributors would like to acknowledge their indebtedness to those who prepared their material for submission, namely: Glynnis Benison, Marie Boam, Pat Brookes, Lyn Caudwell, Margaret Creighton, Karen Hanson, Rebecca Jackson, Pat Lawson, Joyce Lea, Jean Waring and Val Wilson.

The editors would like to thank the contributing authors for their dedication to the task of improving their chapters, their patience with the editors and their willingness to help with editorial tasks.

TONY LOWE
JOHN L. J. MACHIN

Part I

1 Introduction

John L. J. Machin
Tony Lowe

THE NEED FOR 'NEW' PERSPECTIVES IN MANAGEMENT CONTROL

Mythology and tradition are powerful determinants of both behaviour and thinking patterns. It is important, from time to time, to assess whether the myths and traditions of a particular subject are helping or hindering the pursuit of knowledge in that subject.

Now is an appropriate time to review the myths and traditions of management control systems design and practice, because the subject is rapidly approaching a theoretical and practical watershed. The key elements in the study of such systems are all facing profound changes simultaneously.

The purpose of such systems is in dispute. Societal expectations of employing organisations, and the managerial tasks within them, are changing rapidly. Whilst some causes for that change – increased and better education – can be readily identified, the ultimate effects of the ebb and flow of the debate between individual freedom and organisation man, the debate concerning the environmental impact of the explosive increase in the number of the human species, the environmental impact of the things made by human beings (organisations, nuclear waste, chemical pollutants, etc.) are much harder to forecast. All these debates, however, raise profound questions about the purpose of management control systems.

Within the subject itself there is an increasing recognition of the need to reappraise the demands placed on management control systems' designers. Traditionally, emphasis has been placed upon the demand for efficient management control systems; that is, systems which were simply designed to ensure the efficiency of use of resources without questioning the goals or objectives of the organisation.

3

Increasingly there is a demand for effective management control systems, where the purposes for which the resources will be used become the primary concern and the efficiency in use important but secondary.

Thus a decision about 'the most efficient system to use' should be dependent on the purpose for which the system will be used.

Thus, we would contend that greater emphasis on the definition of *effective* management control systems calls for a greater examination of *their purpose* at the three most important resolution levels of human interaction:

1. as persons, individually;
2. as organisations, collectively;
3. as human society, holistically.

This is turn requires us to review and, if necessary, challenge present enterprise management control practice in terms of its mythology and tradition. Mythology and tradition are powerful values at all social levels: individual and collective. Moreover, they are so pervasively programmed into us in our early life that they are effectively *non-rational* parts of our individual being and of our whole human civilisation. As a result, we quite naturally tend to see bodies of practice such as those constituting enterprise management control systems, as strictly rational, that is, as being formed entirely by the use of reason. We tend to be unaware that culture values determine our particular (subjective) definition of rationality and of rational practices within our society. Our popular common ideas on what is appropriate behaviour and attitude are so much part of our being that it affects the *Weltanschauung* (whole world outlook) of all persons within an organisation. More specifically, they are likely to affect the way in which both practitioners and theorists perceive control procedures and actions. Consequently, the barriers to change in thinking about control procedures and actions, and subsequently in actually trying to change them, are formidable because they are part of the whole culture and ideology of a society. Just this concern led Herbert Simon (1976), for instance, to require that he always qualified the word 'rationality' when he used it as 'objective', 'subjective' or 'conscious'.

It is important to stress at this point that we are not advocating the abandonment of the idea of rationality in a study of management control: we merely wish to emphasise that we must always bear in mind the limitations which must apply, of necessity, to any (human) conception of rationality. Moreover, we consider it especially important to emphasise the overwhelming prevalence of cultural ideology (in terms of mythology and tradition) in a book about management control systems because management control is precisely one of those particular kinds of human activity in which carefully considered, deliberate, rational action is considered to be both necessary and desirable, not least because of its importance in avoiding and resolving human conflict, potentially highly damaging to our whole society. Unconscious fixity of viewpoint and a resultant lack of sufficient conceptual flexibility is, therefore, likely to be one of the most damaging tendencies we are likely to be prone to, given our concern for, and close involvement in, the management of work groups. Indeed, members of the Management Control Workshop Group (Lowe and Puxty, 1979) have argued elsewhere in somewhat more detail concerning such myopic tendencies in orthodox approaches to management control practice.

Thus we feel that in the field of *effective* management control systems (based on the broad assumption that organisational and enterprise purpose must ultimately be to enhance the quality of life on the planet) it is clear that we still have a long way to go before we can claim to understand how to achieve effectiveness.

Social concerns such as unemployment (or enforced leisure), coupled with changing concepts of organisational purpose and form, raise profound questions about the *purpose* of management control systems, which those concerned to develop the theory in the subject – and subsequently to design and develop new systems – cannot avoid.

At the same time as the purpose of management control systems has become a central item for study, developments in information technology have removed most of the traditional constraints on information handling. Sheer volume of information and its useful organisation are no longer problems from a storage point of view. The challenge has become to find ways of accessing exactly the information that is needed for a given decision from the volume that is available; providing access to relevant information presents management control system specialists with both technical and psychological conundrums. For such purposes a (highly complex) model of the decision-maker's and enterprise's needs for information is required, in principle, in order to overcome the technical challenge to access exactly the information that is needed from what can now be virtually an infinite volume of accessible data.

The psychological challenge to management control systems'

designers is whether to lead or to follow societal views concerning access to information. For example, is it the duty of management control systems' designers to design systems where access to organisational information is available to any member of the organisation? If so, the most critical (moral) problem is that of defining organisational membership.

Alternatively, the management control systems' designer could be constrained by the user's specification. The ultimate end of such a system might be to give total power to one individual. Information always confers power, and the fact that we can harness almost unlimited quantities of information if anything reinforces that fact. If the user is the sole determinant of a system's design, then the ultimate user could presumably preclude any others from access to information of importance to them.

Somewhere along that spectrum from universal free access to individual sole access must lie the most appropriate position for management control systems in different kinds of organisations.

The theoretical challenge of designing systems which could give that flexibility is with us now. It is essential that decisions about the appropriate place on the spectrum of access to information should be made after public debate by those who will be affected by the systems, as well as by those who will use them. Despite the complexities of such a process it is therefore evident that we recognise the relevance of legislation in respect of management information and control systems.

The managerial environment itself is also changing rapidly. There has been a progressive shift in the advanced economies of the world from 'goods' production to services creation. Even in 'goods' production industry the importance of design and development services is now much greater than before.

Expressed in traditional accountancy terms, i.e., the terms of the tripartite split of cost between 'engineered', 'managed' and 'committed', the last two decades in advanced economies have seen a major switch from 'engineered' to 'managed'. The percentage of total cost incurred that is 'managed' has rocketed.

The major attribute of managed cost has always been the difficulty of forecasting or measuring the outcome for a given amount of cost incurred. As the volume of gross national product which is devoted to service industries rises, so does the challenge of developing more effective systems for handling uncertain, and in some cases unmeasurable, output in discrete, homogeneous terms. Traditional accounting-based systems have little relevance for measuring the output of managed cost, and can, at best, only tell us whether the input cost we planned to incur has actually been incurred.

Summary

The position the management control system's designer faces in 1983 and after is a healthy one for specialists in the field. There is an explosive growth in the kinds of organisations that need new and better management control systems. There is available at the present moment a much greater, and better documented, understanding of the theories and practice of designing and developing management control systems than was available twenty years ago. At the same time this healthy, essential development raises profound moral and legal problems at all levels: personal, organisational, societal and humankind.

Teaching, researching and working in the field of management control systems now are specialists drawn from a wide range of disciplines. Many of them bring to the subject a very much greater understanding of the workings of society, and the motivation of individuals and groups, than was available at the beginning of the 1960s.

In such circumstances, the work of such specialists becomes not a question of upgrading 'manual' systems, but of opening up new perspectives on the most appropriate theory for the next generation of management control systems and then designing and developing them in practice.

One of the strongest myths in the field of management control systems is that 'management control' is synonymous with 'management accounting'. Nothing could be more misleading, but the mythology has been supported by the tradition, particularly in the United States, that it was 'accountants' who tended to leave their early discipline to move into the field. The contributors to this book are all acknowledged experts in the field, but their range of early qualifications (see Notes on the Contributors) shows that the American tradition is now a European myth.

Management control systems – a multidisciplinary subject

The management control system specialist must seek to understand what it is that managers do when they are planning and controlling the use of resources within an organisation, and then seek to design and develop more effective systems for enabling that process to be carried out.

Management is known to be a complex activity. Sometimes it is carried out by people who are actually called managers, though most of the time all individuals within an organisation carry out some managerial activities.

A number of approaches have been taken to developing theories and models which enable us to approach the complexity of the managerial task in a sufficiently structured manner to be able to understand it a little more clearly and, therefore, to be able to design ways of helping people to deal with the complexity more effectively.

That is the paramount purpose of management control system specialists. They are the individuals who produce the systems which enable both specialists and integrators to combine to achieve organisational effectiveness.

At the theoretical level such a task is presently doomed to failure. At the present moment there is no universally accepted definition of the phrase 'organisational effectiveness', let alone the phrase 'managerial effectiveness'. It necessarily follows, therefore, that no effective management control system can be demonstrated to exist, given the present state of our knowledge and understanding.

At the practical level, however, organisations exist and the people within them are clearly capable of generating a range of outputs from the inputs that are supplied. Equally clearly, the people involved in those processes use management control systems in the course of their work and are able to describe the ways in which those systems help or hinder them.

Thus, we have the dichotomy that whilst the present theory does not enable us adequately to understand what is going on, practical observation of what is going on shows that there is considerable dissatisfaction both with the results achieved and with the systems used to achieve them.

Part of the problem undoubtedly lies in the fact that many of the key terms in the study of employing organisations are insufficiently defined. The very word 'system' is a prime case in point.

Many disciplines have been brought to bear on the study of organisations and the individuals who work within them. Some of those disciplines are functional – marketing, production, finance – some of the disciplines are concerned with the process within the organisation, irrespective of function, such as psychology, sociology, general systems theory and cybernetics.

There has been much discussion of the most appropriate discipline with which to tackle the practical problems associated with designing and developing management control systems and in Chapter 2 Machin seeks to identify the key strands that have gradually become interwoven into the body of knowledge currently subsumed under the words 'management control systems', when used to denote a field of academic study and research.

Why study management control?

The contributors to this book represent a wide spread of interest and purpose in studying management control. Some seek to produce a progressively clearer *definition* of the process called 'management control'. The thrust of their research is based on the assumption that until you can define what you are studying sufficiently clearly, you are likely to be ill-placed to comment on what constitutes a more, rather than a less, effective implementation of that particular process. Such research is aimed, *inter alia*, at producing ways of evaluating in a progressively more objective manner the effectiveness with which different managers are controlling what they do.

Others are seeking to identify the *purposes* of those undertaking the management control process within organisations. Some approach research on this topic from a normative stance based on their assumption of what the goals of organisations *should* be. They carry beliefs about the purpose of society, and thus of organisations within society, and seek to develop systems that will enable those beliefs to be supported. Other researchers on the purpose of the management control process in organisations seek only to ascertain, rather superficially, in a non-problematic manner, what the goals of that process actually *are in practice*. Their work has already shown that it is exceptionally difficult to develop an understanding which is in any sense meaningful about what the goals of any given organisation are, since there is significant debate about whether organisations can have goals. Many would argue that an organisation, being a non-sentient entity, cannot have goals. Thus in the same way that a table does not have goals (that is, the purpose for which a table is used is specified in the manifest behaviour of the person owning or using the table) they would argue that an organisation does not have goals.

A third group of researchers is concerned to try to develop ways of assessing the effectiveness and efficiency of the systems which managers currently use to enable them to carry out the management control process. Managers themselves are well able to express their views on the extent to which current systems help them in their managerial control activity, and much practical research and development has undoubtedly helped to improve current systems.

A fourth group of individuals who study management control systems is that which is concerned to design and develop the management control systems that managers will need five to ten years from now. This research entails a projection of the changes that are likely to arise in the management control process over the next ten years, the changes in technology which will be available over the next ten years for those concerned with information and control systems, and a consideration of the implication of harnessing the latter to meet the former's needs.

All such studies centre round three key elements in respect of management control:

1. The purpose of management control – and hence the criteria that a management control system should meet.
2. The management control process – including the way in which a manager might wish to use one or more management control systems to help him with that process.
3. The information that a manager needs to control effectively – and decisions about the amount of such information which can cost-effectively be carried within a management control system.

The contributions to the book have been designed to explore these elements sequentially.

PART I

In chapter 2, Machin seeks to set some of the key issues in the current debate concerning the future of management control systems in the context of the development of the study of the subject over the past two decades. He argues that as developments in information technology remove many of the constraints which were faced by management control system designers in the past it becomes a practical possibility for managers to specify the kind of information which they would choose to see carried by the system. Equally, as we learn more about the psychology of working groups it becomes increasingly important to define much more clearly the purposes for which management control systems are being used.

Machin believes that there should be public debate on the criteria which should be used to assess the effectiveness of management control systems used in organisations and therefore concludes his chapter by presenting the set of criteria developed by his research team during years of industry/university collaborative research. Eleven criteria are proposed at the end of the chapter, not in the expectation that readers will adopt them, but in the hope that readers will be provoked into developing a more personally acceptable and more clearly stated set of criteria for themselves by the time they have finished reading this book.

PART II

Part II considers the theories that might help us to understand the purpose of management control within organisations and assesses the implications of those theories for the purpose and design of management control systems.

In Chapter 3, Berry contributes to the present debate on the role of research in management control. He seeks, in particular, to distinguish between research and scholarship and in the light of that distinction proceeds to consider the relative merits of three methodologies; functionalism, verstehen and logical positivism.

In the course of the chapter Berry reviews the purposes and sources of management control research problems and argues for a developmental approach to the subject, working from the assumption that an applied social science has to develop through the tension between managerial problems and subject disciplines. Berry concludes by presenting the arguments for a contingent methodology.

In Chapter 4, Otley assesses the contribution which the related disciplines of cybernetics and general systems theory have to offer to the development of more complete theories of the management control process.

Otley argues that the concepts of cybernetics which apply so well to mechanical systems with externally defined objectives, transfer uneasily to organisations comprising human beings who to a greater or lesser extent define their own purposes. Otley sees the greatest contributions of cybernetics as the provision of a language in which concepts of control can be discussed and the demonstration of the central importance of predictive models in all control systems.

Otley regards general systems theory as having greater potential value to the management control system designer but points out that most 'soft' systems approaches, like the well-developed Checkland methodology, hold that no general theory of management control can be constructed – all one can do is to develop a method of improving real-work situations.

Otley argues, however, that the systems approach, with its concern to be holistic and *systemic*, provides a valuable countervailing force to the traditional approach to management control, based on accounting, which has approached the problems of complex organisations by an attempt to be *systematic*.

Thus although Otley argues that neither cybernetics nor general systems theory have specific theories which can be applied in their totality to the study of management control systems, they do offer an approach and a method of thinking that can assist in illuminating some of the key issues which management control theorists now face.

In Chapter 5, Berry examines control in the open social system paradigm through an exegesis of the work of Katz and Kahn, and Miller and Rice. He concludes that the functional orientation of Katz and Kahn does have powerful implications for the regulation of open social systems, principally through attention to goal directedness, integration and adaptation, and the interplay between persons and roles.

Berry regards Miller and Rice as offering a more useful framework, primarily because of their focus upon primary task and groups, and on the regulation of the boundaries of social systems. In this latter sense, control is perceivable as a property of the relatedness of persons to roles and to boundaries.

Clearly the approaches taken by Katz and Kahn, and Miller and Rice respectively, are closely related in their focus on the openness of social systems: Berry shows that they diverge mainly on the conceptual structure through which the control of open systems can best be understood.

In Chapter 6 Hopper and Berry stress that management control can only be properly understood through a broad holistic approach commensurate with organisational control. To limit it to the study of formal economic systems, thereby ignoring social factors and qualitative measures, is undesirable, for it is all interrelated. Social controls may not only be complementary to formal controls, but in some instances they may be more effective substitutes. Similarly, the approach must embrace environmental and political issues – the Anthony and Dearden approach, whilst neat, is empirically unsound and value laden. It specifically avoids the problematical issue of organisational goals, which Hopper and Berry see as central to the design of effective management control systems. They claim that since goals are derived from bargaining and are surrounded by conflict, the system designer is inevitably drawn into value issues. To believe that he can be neutral and detached is, in their view, a fallacy. Instead they argue that he should recognise the likelihood of multiple goals and see his role as helping managers tease out and articulate such differences.

Finally, and more obviously, the chapter seeks to show how knowledge in the area of organisation design is directly and inescapably related to control issues. In doing this the chapter examines the limitations of contingency theory as a basis for the design of management control systems.

In the final chapter in this part of the book (Chapter 7), Wilkinson looks closely at the relationship between the organisation within which management control systems have traditionally been developed, and the environment which largely determines the extent to which an organisation can be successful. Wilkinson argues that an effective management control system must obtain information on a systematic and regular basis from outside the organisation. Wilkinson sees management control as the process by which organisational activities are initiated, legitimised, implemented and monitored by coalitions within the organisation. The relationship between this internal control, and control by external bodies or individuals, is discussed in his chapter and he argues that internal controls must recognise and 'manage' environmental demands if the organisation is to maintain its well-being. Wilkinson describes and comments upon a methodology which he sees as a useful means of managing conflicting demands made upon an organisation by its environment.

The key elements in Wilkinson's arguments are the following:

1. The negotiated, power-dependent and therefore changeable nature of 'organisational goals'.
2. The concept of legitimacy of organisational actions.
3. The enacted environment, and the role of boundary-spanning personnel who control the flow of resources, especially information, between the organisation and its environment.
4. The Pfeffer and Salancik methodology as a means of formalising the enactment process, to create a common perception of environmental demands within the organisation, and a strategy for coping with conflicting demands.

5. The implication of the Pfeffer and Salancik methodology for the design and development of management control systems.

PART III

Part III is concerned with the 'manager' in the management control process and the influences which are brought to bear on the way in which individual managers carry out the process of management control. There is no doubt that the processes of formulating goals, planning how best to achieve those goals, working to achieve those goals, reviewing the extent to which the goals are being achieved with the resources allocated to the task, and if necessary replanning, are processes that are affected by, and have an impact on, the motivation of the individual carrying out those tasks and on those with whom he interacts.

The subject is clearly fraught with the potential for never-ending circles. Individuals and groups exhibit motivational patterns. Develop a management control system which produces better information for those concerned with the above processes, and this inevitably will affect the group. A successful study of management control is impossible without an understanding of the motivational aspects of that process and the interaction between these motivational aspects and the way in which management control is carried out.

In Chapter 8 McKenna analyses significant parts of motivation theory and uses them as a means to shed light on the motivational implications of management control. Management control is broadly conceived and this is achieved by adopting a multidimensional view. McKenna gives particular attention to supervisory control, procedural control, social control and self-control, in the belief that these dimensions capture the essence of management control.

McKenna identifies three approaches to the study of motivation, and they are placed into the following categories – personality, human needs and cognitive theory. In each category an attempt is made to discuss links between motivation theory and the different types of management control. Inevitably the behavioural implications of budgetary control occupy a prominent position in the discussion; also, the expectancy approach, in an organisational context, is acknowledged as a worthwhile approach to exploring the motivational implications of control.

In the conclusion the appropriateness of self-control in a

sympathetic organisational culture is endorsed by McKenna and recommended as a fruitful way to proceed. Reference is, however, made to the likely impact of microtechnology which may have implications for the centralisation of authority.

When goals have to be achieved and certain processes undertaken to enable those goals to be achieved, decisions have to be taken about the number of people who should be involved in the management control process relative to a given decision, and ultimately which specific people should make up that number. The word most frequently used to describe this aspect of management control is 'participation'. It is a word that has become increasingly fashionable, but unfortunately it has also become progressively less well defined. Broadly speaking, writers about participation fall into two discrete camps. The larger camp includes people who believe that participation is good in an absolute sense, and that it therefore represents a major step forward in the quality of organisational life to facilitate participation by those who have not previously been involved with the management control process. In the writings of this group, participation is seen as an alternative to confrontation between different groups within an organisation – frequently between managers and workers.

The second group of writers in the field of participation is concerned to explore the topic using a rationalistic paradigm – that is, to develop a framework within which it should be possible to work out the optimum number and membership of the participating group for any decision.

Richbell seeks to review both approaches to participation in Chapter 9. Her chapter is specifically concerned with management control over human resources in organisations where workers participate in managerial decision-making.

Under such schemes the traditional terms 'managerial' and 'non-managerial' become less appropriate as both parties become involved in the management process and hence take on managerial roles. In the participative context, management control over human resources is seen by Richbell 'as the ability of all organisational members to secure the compliance of each other with their shared decisions'.

In the first part of Chapter 9, Richbell discusses the concepts of 'participation' and 'control' and examines at a theoretical level the potential that participation holds for *increasing* management control over human resources. She considers the argument that there is a variable rather than a fixed amount of control within an organisation and that it is possible to increase the total amount of control over human resources through the use of the 'polyarchic model' where all groups have influence in the managerial decision-making process.

In the second part of Chapter 9 Richbell adopts a more critical approach. She argues that the degree of willingness of organisational members to participate, their level of ability to participate and the extent to which an organisational perspective has developed among the members may all act as major constraints on the potential of participation to increase management control over human resources.

Control in organisations has been classified into three types by Dalton – administrative control, social control and self-control.

The latter concept is clearly potentially universal. Every individual manages himself or herself and, therefore, exercises to a greater or lesser extent some measure of what might be called 'self-control'. The nature of self-control as expounded in the literature, however, is ambiguous. It has been used with a number of different meanings, associated with different 'causal' variables, and little attention has been given to the conditions under which it may be an effective means of organisational control in business enterprises.

Thomas, in Chapter 10, has sought to clarify this ambiguity and in particular to distinguish between the concepts of 'self-direction' and 'self-control'. Thomas argues that the distinction is of critical importance for any understanding of the underlying concept.

The chapters in Part III combine to present a view of the user of a management control system, and seek to understand what the user is attempting to achieve in the field of management control and why (and indeed, if) the user actually uses the management control system in the way in which the designer intended.

Those who design management control systems do so in the expectation that the information carried within a management control system will be of some use to the recipient – i.e. that the recipient will undertake some action, or have attitudes or expectations modified, as a result of the information that is received.

Given that the management control systems within an organisation are used by a large number of people, the system designer is bound to be seeking some kind of best fit between the way in which individuals control what they do in the light of information they receive, and the most effective ways of delivering the information that a manager wishes to receive.

PART IV

Part IV of the book is concerned with the information that is carried within management control systems. Three quite different kinds of information are considered: normal communicated language; accounting and financial information; and numerical information for use in cybernetic models and systems.

The three chapters in this part of the book also represent three different approaches to research in the field of management control systems. Machin's research interest has, for a number of years, been working with managers to design systems that meet the manager's needs. In a real sense, his research has been manager-led, and the responsibility for the design of the systems that his teams have developed and tested with managers has invariably lain with the managers themselves.

Professor Gee's early research was concerned to identify the information that managers actually used from the systems that they had available to them, and his chapter reflects his present research into the strengths and weaknesses of the accounting and financial information traditionally supplied to managers.

Willmer's chapter considers the progressive advances that have been made in adapting cybernetic systems and models, originally considered to be only of use in respect of programmable jobs, to help individuals and groups to understand much more clearly the relationships that exist in unprogrammed tasks.

His chapter is also based on work carried out with managers, the difference being that this work is derived from training which used cybernetic models to approach a clearer understanding of superior – subordinate relationships.

Machin and Tai in Chapter 11 describe a communication-based methodology for both research and system design in the field of management control. The methodology was developed during several years of joint industry/university research. The outcome of this work has been, on the one hand, a research methodology supported by a range of analytical techniques and, on the other, a fully operational managerial planning and control system which has proved to be simple to use, highly flexible, robust and time-effective (in the sense that the benefits that can be derived from using the system are seen by managers as outweighing significantly the time involved).

Chapter 11 has three main sections. In the first, Machin and Tai describe the methodology and proceed in the following section to provide a summary of the research results and operating experience gained during the methodology's development. In the final section, the authors use information from practical managerial testing of the system to assess the operational relevance of the eleven criteria against which to measure the effectiveness of management control systems postulated by Machin in Chapter 2.

Gee in Chapter 12 argues that the role of convention in financial control derives in part from the fact that cost and revenue allocation decisions are incapable of being proved either true or false, for the want of any market referends against which they may be compared. Since allocation decisions turn on conventionally–accepted notions of equity, measures of financial performance dependent upon allocation can always be challenged by appeals to alternative ethical standpoints.

An attractive property of cash flow measures of financial performance is their apparent lack of vulnerability to such appeals, but Gee shows that cash flow measures are not always allocation-free. In particular the question of whether corporate net cash flow is decomposable to divisions in an allocation-free manner turns out to depend upon the specifics of the tax system in operation.

Gee points out that moving from financial performance measurement to financial control entails reaching agreement upon a further set of conventions to be employed. There is, therefore, an especial need to agree which variables shall be treated as endogenous to the control system. An enterprise can go on indefinitely recognising further feedback loops between itself and its environment – some of those loops must be deliberately ignored (endogenous variables treated as exogenous) if the control problem is to be at all tractable. While business decisions are in reality uncertain, dynamic, multiattributed and interactive. Gee argues that it is necessary in practice to arrive at a convention excluding one or more of these four aspects from explicit analytical treatment. Within those aspects of a decision subjected to analysis rather than intuition, the interrelationships between variables must often be subjected to a further conventional restriction. In particular, interrelationships which are known to exist have to be ignored where information on the form of these interrelationships cannot be purchased on economically acceptable terms. Gee illustrates this final point by reference to a case study involving the ecological and financial implications of marine sand and gravel mining off the east coast of the USA.

Many of the criticisms of the application of the cybernetic approach to management control are based on an essentially dichotomic view. There is either objectivity associated with the output of an organisation or there is not: the activities involved are either routine or nonroutine. Willmer argues that the majority of management control problems do not fall neatly into any of these extremes; they are concerned with the grey area in between, and in Chapter 13 he explores this area. Willmer shows that although it may never be possible to produce a completely realistic mathematical model of complex management control problems, a number of important behavioural factors can be introduced thus enabling a meaningful framework to be produced against which the usefulness of the cybernetic approach can be assessed. The author pays particular attention to the problems associated with the superior–subordinate interface and the effects of appraisal methods on the motivation of staff and the reliability of information for control purposes.

In organisations where subordinates have scope for manipulating information flows, who controls whom? Is it the superior who formally announces his decisions to the workforce or the subordinate who understands how his superior's mind works and feeds him the information necessary to produce a particular decision?

Willmer describes research studies which show that the potential power of the cybernetic approach can be extended to cover such management situations, particularly those where the degree of routineness and the level of objectivity associated with the output are far from ideal. This potential cannot be realised automatically but is achieved only as a result of good leadership by those in command. In some quarters there appears to be a belief that the development of more sophisticated control techniques can make up for the shortcomings of the cybernetic approach. This chapter provides a timely warning to those concerned with the management of human systems who may feel tempted to put their faith in technique rather than in their judgement of people.

PART V

Chapter 14 draws together the strands that are featured in the previous four parts of the book by setting the concept of management control in the context of organisational effectiveness. In Chapter 14, Lowe and Chua argue that before we can adequately discuss the concept of a management control system and its appropriate design we need first to define the concept of organisational effectiveness. The purpose of management control, they argue, is intrinsically coupled with questions about the purpose and effective working of a human socioeconomic organisation. The concept of control is not meaningful unless we ask: 'control to what purpose?' For, depending on the purpose in question, a control system or strategy will be deemed more or less effective. Lowe and Chua argue that if we define an effective organisation as one which is adaptive, then the control system ought to be designed to ensure this degree of adaptiveness. On the other hand, if, for instance, an effective organisation is defined prescriptively as one which maximises the level of satisfaction of its most regretful participants, then a control system will only be deemed 'successful' or 'effective' if it enables the organisation to approximate this purpose.

Accordingly, Lowe and Chua proceed to review theories of organisational effectiveness in a classificatory matrix which has two dimensions: descriptive–prescriptive and holistic–parochial. The authors demonstrate the weaknesses of a descriptive and parochial theory of organisational effectiveness and propose a holistic, prescriptive theory of organisational effectiveness. An effective organisation they see as one which satisfies a feasible set of participant demands in the long run. Based on the inducement–contribution theory of March and Simon (1958), the ideas of a long-run maintenance of such a feasible set are argued to be conceptually more satisfying, and to lead to long-run macrosocietal stability: these ideas being linked to a functionalist view that organisations do not survive in the long run if they do not meet the minimal needs of participants within their environmental context.

Given this definition of organisational effectiveness, the authors offer the following definition of management control: 'structures and processes which enable an organisation to keep within the boundaries of long-run survival'. The concept of management control they argue is synonymous with the notion of holistic, organisational control and should not be narrowly defined as referring only to specific forms of controls. Management control means control of the microorganisation and its relationship to its substantive environment in such a way that it survives in the long run.

SUMMARY

Management is such an omnipresent process that it is not surprising that the search for more effective ways of controlling that process is both important and of general interest.

Management is such a complex process, however, that no single conceptual model has ever proved wholly adequate as a vehicle for research in management control or for the design of management control systems.

In the search for more effective ways of controlling the managerial process, both managers and researchers have found different models helpful in different situations, and in illuminating different elements within that complex process.

The challenge of the subject lies in the fact that each person must ultimately decide for herself or himself which model offers the greatest assistance in the pursuit of greater personal effectiveness.

2 Management Control Systems: Whence and Whither?

John L. J. Machin

Planet-wide, the increase in knowledge each year is enormous, and the pace of generation of new knowledge seems also to be increasing. One of the challenges facing the human species is how to assimilate and then harness this new knowledge in ways which are likely to lead to the more effective use of the planet's limited resources whilst maintaining and developing an environment in which it is progressively more satisfying to live. Few would claim that anyone on the planet currently has a satisfactory way of handling that problem *in practice*. Research aimed at developing better ways of managing the use of both physical and mental resources is, therefore, both intellectually challenging and critically important for the future of the species. The potential area for research is so vast, however, that the biggest problem (rather like a child facing an enormous cream bun) is deciding where to start.

This chapter seeks to sustain the argument that:

1. the traditional definitions of the area of research interest subsumed under the title of 'management control systems' are no longer appropriate to the world we live and work in, and
2. it is possible to develop and postulate new definitions of the subject area in such a way that
3. it becomes possible to postulate a set of criteria against which to judge the effectiveness of present and future management control systems.

THE PRESENT SITUATION

'Management control systems' as a specialised subject of study at university level presents, in the 1980s, a picture of uncertainty:

1. As a subject, it has no generally accepted boundary definition.
2. As a topic for research, it lacks agreement on even a rudimentary paradigm.
3. The proponents of this specialism having discovered the first two facts have had the good sense to become a great deal less confident in what they do.
4. Since in any applied research, criteria of success may possibly provide guidance in the search for a paradigm, it is unfortunate that the ultimate desired results in this area can be one or more of the following:

    (a) Raising the level of managerial effectiveness, *or*
    (b) raising the justifiable level of confidence which a manager brings to his job, *or*
    (c) raising the level of organisational effectiveness.

    Especially since 'effectiveness' at either individual or organisational level is still proving a remarkably elusive concept to define, let alone measure (Machin *et al.*, 1981).

It would be reassuring to dismiss the present disarray as a period of mere semantic disagreement capable of resolution by linguistic refinement. My own view is that our current situation is sufficiently critical to merit discussion not only amongst ourselves, but also with colleagues from other specialisms who share our goal of helping managers to become more effective, but take different paths towards the achievement of that goal.

WHAT WAS THE SUBJECT AREA OF MANAGEMENT CONTROL SYSTEMS?

It is difficult to understand the present position without setting it in the dynamic of a perspective of the development of the subject over the last 15–20 years.

Taken separately, the words 'management', 'control' and 'systems' each create problems of definition. Their juxtaposition appeared to ease the problem of boundary definition only if one assumed that each of the three words described a 'set', the last two of which were progressively smaller parts of the first.

Thus:

Management was a subset of those things which went on in an organisation.

Control was a subset of the total range of managerial activity (planning, motivating, coordinating, staffing, directing, controlling etc., the precise number of discrete subjects depending on the author).

Systems was the subset of organisational systems which included only formal, systematically developed, data-handling systems.

The combination of the three words, therefore, produced such a small subset of total organisational activity to study that a research focus was possible, namely:

Those formal, systematically developed, organisation-wide, data-handling systems which are designed to facilitate management control which 'is the process by which managers assure that resources are obtained and used effectively and efficiently in the accomplishment of the organisation's objectives'. (Anthony, 1965)

That definition of 'management control systems' was helpful to researchers. It was clear enough so that when you were researching in an employing organisation you could recognise what you were looking for and, having found it, could find where it started and finished.

The definition also has the merit that it leaves scope for academics to disagree violently whilst still perceiving themselves to be studying the same thing. In particular it does not touch on the purpose of such systems and thus gives little direction as to how better ones may be developed. Real choices have to be made of which the following are just two examples:

1. Should control be voluntary? That is, should the systems be designed to *enable* managers to control their subordinates, or should they be there to *force* them to control their subordinates?
2. How far, if at all, should top management trust their managers? That is, should systems be designed to enable/force managers to

control their subordinates and other resources?–or to enable top management to check on how well their managers are controlling their subordinates and other resources?

Such questions concerning purpose are now accepted as critical in determining the design of systems for management control but fortunately they did not get in the way of early research into 'management control systems' because in the early 1960s the only 'formal, systematically developed, organisation-wide, data-handling systems which were designed to enable managers etc. . . . ' were accounting based, were studied by qualified accountants, and therefore were virtually immune from philosophical analysis.

Mainstream research in management control systems was accounting based and at that time, probably reasonably so. The systems in use were for the most part developed during the Second World War, brushed up during the Korean War, and were obvious candidates for computerisation in the 1960s. Equally clearly, these systems are necessary for the survival and growth of large and/or complex, employing organisations, and their development was therefore a sensible and worthwhile task.

The progressive refinement of accounting-based control systems led to the recognition that whilst accounting-based control systems were necessary for the control of input costs throughout an organisation, their usefulness for controlling the effective *use* of those input costs varied widely in different parts of the organisation. In some areas it was clear that accounting-based systems were almost sufficient on their own to measure and to control input–output relationship; in others it was equally clear that accounting-based systems had nothing to offer in terms of input–output or process control.

The mainstream of management control systems needed further refinement and precision and Anthony provided it with his definitive framework in 1965 (Anthony, 1965).

His framework was definitive because although produced at the high point of accounting domination of management control systems it carries within it the seed of our present dilemma.

Anthony identified three types of cost, three types of activity, but only two types of formal accounting-based system. A summary of Anthony's conclusions is presented in Table 2.1.

The planning and control processes for committed and engineered costs have economics as their source discipline, and systems based on numbers such as statistical or accounting systems clearly have much to

TABLE 2.1   *Analysing systems in terms of the costs which they are being used to control*

Anthony's Classification	Cost	Example	Control Information	Techniques	Source Discipline
Strategic planning	Committed	Capital investment	Quantitative	Time value Risk Analysis	Economics Mathematics
Management control	Managed	Any 'managerial activity'	Qualitative	Judgement Persuasion	Social psychology
Operational control	Engineered	Direct product cost	Quantitative	Standard costs Variance analysis	Economics Physical sciences

offer as suppliers of relevant managerial information. The way forward for *accounting-based* research for these two cost categories was clear.

Valuable accounting research was undertaken into financial modelling for the strategic planners, and cost/LP modelling for logistics and engineered cost control but accountants ground slowly to a halt in researching the needs of the management control process.

Anthony's framework inevitably focused attention on the need to define the purpose and nature of systems suitable to facilitate management control, and in that 'need for a definition' lay the seeds of doubt as to the future direction of research into management control systems.

Anthony himself had specified social psychology as the source discipline of management control systems, yet surprisingly continued to hope that accounting might have something to offer. He even bound together a number of cases and a sprinkling of articles in the hope that this would establish the accountants' claim to be the social psychologists of the last quarter of the twentieth century (Anthony, Dearden, Vancil, 1965).

The reality of management gave some superficial justification for such a proposal. For example:

1. Whenever an organisation had a controllership function, it was

invariably staffed by accountants so control must be an accounting function.

2. The budget was the principal control system in most organisations and its appropriateness in areas of committed and engineered cost significantly, and understandably, overshadowed its ineffectiveness in the area of managed cost.

From the date of the publication of Anthony's framework *it was inevitable* that the mainstream of research and teaching in management control systems would swing away from accounting systems.

What was, of course, much less clear was which of the erstwhile rivulets or tributaries of non-accounting research in 'management control' or 'systems' would prove to be the most capable of supporting mainstream focus of attention and research.

There were many strands of research to choose from.

SYSTEMS

'Systems' was worth considering as a serious contender. Apart from anything else, it actually had an abstract theory which claimed to relate to any group of interacting parts – which organisations either are or strive to be – and it had enjoyed successful application in the biological sciences. It had, therefore, a rigorously defined theory and a history of useful applications.

There were, however, some semantic and conceptual problems with 'systems'.

There was no clear agreement on what was meant by the word 'system' itself. Was the attributive of the word correctly expressed as 'systematic' or 'systemic'. In other words, was a 'management control system' a formal data-handling system with a defined purpose which had been *systematically designed* by one or more designers to meet that purpose (i.e. a 'system' as the accountants had traditionally used the term), or was the 'management control system' the system of management control interactions which had *developed organically* over time to meet (or occasionally to defeat!) the needs of individuals and the organisation, i.e. 'system' as the social psychologists had traditionally used the term.

The first approach implies a system classification by purpose, and that was capable of being provided for organisational systems by a leading cyberneticist without even mentioning the magic phrase 'management control systems' (Beer, 1972), as shown in Figure 2.1.

There is no obvious set from that figure which adds up to a – let alone, the – management control system.

Even worse, the concept of formal system might also include the organisation structure as a formal system of authority and accountability which would have to be studied simultaneously if we were to understand the structure/system interface problems faced by managers.

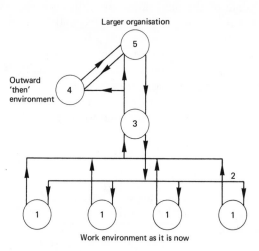

5. **GENERAL MANAGEMENT**
    setting aims
    making policy
    overall monitoring
    adjusting balance of resources

4. **DEVELOPMENT**
    looking outward and forward
    tying in subsystem 3 information (needs panic-free time)

3. **CONTROLLING**
    turning policy into plans
    monitoring performance short term
    feeding information upwards
    allocating resources between subsystems 1

2. **LIAISING**
    smoothing operations
    promoting lateral information exchange

1. **DOING**

SOURCE: Based on Stafford Beer (1972) *Brain of the Firm* (London: Allen Lane).

FIGURE 2.1   *Organisational systems as postulated by a leading cyberneticist, Stafford Beer*

The second approach, of course, calls for a system classification by nature or essence. A very useful one was readily to hand (Boulding, 1956), and is given in Figure 2.2.

Whatever quibbles one might have with the particular details of the classification he produced, Boulding's impact on thinking and research in management control systems was both important and clear-cut. Presently available, formally designed, systematically developed, purposeful management control systems were all around the thermostat level. Organically evolved reality was at levels 7 and 8. It seemed that the way forward lay either in conceptualising a level 8 system which would *lead* working groups to evolve more effectively, or reverting to level 1 to produce a conceptual framework which could *help* working groups to discover more easily for themselves how to evolve more effectively.

1. Frameworks	–	Static structure
2. Clockworks	–	Simple dynamic system with predetermined necessary motion
3. Thermostat	–	Transmission and interpretation of information
4. Cell	–	Open system, self-maintaining structure
5. Genetic–societal	–	Plant – division of labour among cells to form a cell-society with differentiated and mutually dependent parts
6. Animal	–	Behaviour is response not to a specific stimulus but to an 'image' or 'knowledge structure' between stimulus and response.
7. Human	–	6 + self-consciousness
8. Social organisations	–	Groups of 7s
9. Transcendental		

SOURCE: Based on K. E. Boulding (1956) 'General Systems Theory – The Skeleton of Science', *Management Science*, vol. 2, no. 2.

FIGURE 2.2 *Boulding's classification of the hierarchy of systems*

This thinking leads inexorably to a call for either:

1. a rigorous abstract theory of purposeful interpersonal interaction – a tough task given that sociologists themselves claim to be in a pre-paradigm stage of development; *or*
2. a truly contingent system. That is also a tough intellectual task given the overwhelming recent emphasis in research and teaching on developing purposeful, specialised, evaluatable systems.

The systems route was clearly challenging and would raise fundamental questions about the purpose and nature of the systems one was seeking to develop.

The advantages of the route were the power of systems theory and the work being done by specialists in organisation theory (Katz and Kahn, 1966, for example) which was throwing new light on managerial activity.

'System' is, however, only *one* of the three words in the title of the subject under study, so it was at least possible that there was an easier route mapped out by specialists in one or other of the remaining two words.

CONTROL

'Control' offered an even wider range of possibilities. Shorn of the words 'management' and 'systems', control seems to be capable of covering almost anything.

Societally, it appears (in *1066 and All That* terminology) to be a 'good thing'. Situations or people which are out of control are seen as 'bad things' and that encompasses inflation, population, epidemics, children and tightrope walkers.

Given the rich diversity of the English language, it is quite staggering that the word 'control' has not long since been discarded in favour of a plethora of words offering greater precision. Yet it remains – indeed if anything its use increases and the area it subsumes widens. It is embarrassing to have to admit that academics in the field of management control systems have even contributed to that unfortunate state of affairs.

There is, however, another side to the coin and it may in fact be much the more important side. It is important to recognise that any situation which proves durable in the face of precise and justified intellectual criticism must have a very firm basis derived from satisfying some strong needs in society. Of course, those needs may be felt by the few strong people in a community or they may be felt strongly by the majority of people in a community. 'Control' has survived or, more accurately, flourished, as a diffuse concept for so long that maybe it is supported by both sets of needs and is thus inviolate for all time!

The question we are led to ask, therefore, is not, 'How can we define better the quintessential characteristics of control?' but, 'Why has it been in apparently everyone's interests for the past three or four decades to use the word control in so diffuse a manner that misunderstanding in discussion of the subject is the rule rather than the exception?' There has to be a powerful rationale hiding somewhere in amongst a welter of ostensibly irrational behaviour. No doubt each management control systems specialist has his own pet answer because without one, research in the field would be pointless.

There certainly seems to be no currently accepted answer or even a coordinated search for one. Any quick recap of management control theory shows usually both the staggering breadth of material involved and the bias of the person doing the recapping. It would no doubt be as surprising to Giglioni and Bedeian that I see Dalton and Tannenbaum as central to what is happening currently in management control systems, as it is staggering to me that Giglioni and Bedeian in their review of management control theory (Giglioni and Bedeian, 1974) specifically excluded Tannenbaum from their consideration of control and did not even mention Dalton.

The spread of topics covered by management control can be presented as four spectra, as illustrated in Figure 2.3. The spectra can be amplified as follows:

A. The *managerial output* which has to be planned and controlled may range from 'concrete' items such as units of product to 'abstract' output such as improved teamwork or more effective coordination or job satisfaction.
B. The *information* we use to measure the successful generation of planned output will range from objective, frequently numerically-based data to subjective, usually if not invariably linguistically-based data.
C. The *philosophy* underlying the control process may range from that manifested when a manager orders or directs his subordinates to carry out certain tasks to that which is manifest when a manager invites his subordinates to seek advice and assistance from him

whenever they feel it would assist them to achieve their previously agreed objectives.

D. The *management control system* may be called on to operate in any mode ranging from feeding control information back to the manager who directed action to be undertaken in order to facilitate retrospective performance appraisal, to feeding changed views about the future to the subordinate so that he may decide whether advice and assistance are necessary to support the achievement of future performance objectives.

The word control is found in the literature in respect of all kinds of managerial output, using all kinds of information, with manifest philosophies of control spread across the entire spectrum and with systems which feed performance reports to the boss before the subordinate and vice versa.

To the question, 'Why, in a language so capable of precision as English, do we have one word covering such an immense range?' the author offers the answer that it is in fact necessary to have a fuzzy concept to represent fuzzy managerial reality.

The conclusion reached by the author from research into the diversity represented in the spectra in Figure 2.3 is that diversity is the reality, i.e. that managers in different organisations or in different parts of the same organisation, and the same manager at different times of the day or at different points in his or her career, find it positively helpful to be able to switch their position from one stance to another without being immediately or clearly seen to be doing so.

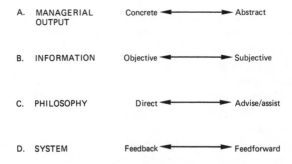

FIGURE 2.3   *Spectra of the elements in management control*

Two of the key workers in the field of control in organisations, Tannenbaum and Dalton, offer, when their work is related, a way forward in tackling this problem of diversity and the consequential choice between contingent acceptance or rigorous analysis.

Tannenbaum's control cycle (Tannenbaum, 1968) takes the simplest of interpersonal situations and views it essentially, for discussion purposes, as a closed system (see Figure 2.4).

This cycle can be broken down into a number of elements:

(a) Intention of A.
(b) Choice by A of appropriate influence necessary to lead B to carry out the desired activity.
(c) Communication by A.
(d) Transmission of communication.
(e) Reception by B of communication.
(f) Interpretation by B of communication.
(g) Decision by B on what action if any to take.
(h) Action by B.
(i) Informing A of B's action (itself obviously a multistep communication and interpretation activity).
(j) Comparison by A between his intention and B's action.

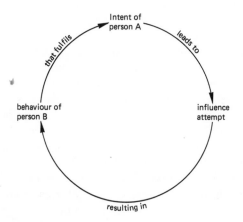

SOURCE: A. S. Tannenbaum (1968) *Control in Organisations* (New York: McGraw-Hill).

FIGURE 2.4 *Tannenbaum's control cycle*

If, in step (j), A discovers that B has done something quite different from A's original intention, he has a large number of variables to check to see what 'went wrong'.

Of course, Tannenbaum's cycle is a very simplified closed-system description of interpersonal control but, like all simple models, it serves to concentrate the mind on deciding which constraints should first be released.

One way of releasing constraints would be to recognise that in most organisations there will be a number of individuals trying to influence B at any point in time so there is a complex interactive network made up of Tannenbaum cycles affecting B – either protecting him or weighing him down.

Another way of releasing constraints would be to recognise the different types of control influence which can be, and almost certainly are, affecting B in an open-system view of B as a manager in an organisation.

Dalton has classified control influences into three categories (Dalton and Lawrence, 1971) (see Table 2.2).

Dalton's classification highlights the fact that organisational control influences (manifest in management control systems by the formal, systematically developed, organisation-wide data-handling systems described earlier), are just one of three influences on managerial decision-making and activity; Hofstede's research indicates that the influence may not be great (Hofstede, 1968).

If 'management control systems' is the study of how managers control the use of resources, it must be the case that informal group norms and informal means of influencing others form a central part of such a study (Nelson and Machin, 1976).

This in turn requires a methodology which captures situational and informal data as it is used in level 8 social interaction in working groups. Such data is communicated during the course of level 8 social interaction and the informal systems which facilitate informal group influences are communication systems. Dalton's second category, therefore, points to the importance of the communication systems as being vital for control to be exercised and informal communication of messages in language becomes a critical part of any concept of systems of control.

If 'control' in organisations has something to do with influencing human beings then a study of control in organisations after Dalton must include all the influences which affect a manager and that includes self-expectations, and must therefore include the concept of self-control.

TABLE 2.2 'Dalton's' three types of control in organisation

Controls administered by	Direction for controls deriving from	Behavioural and performance measures	Signal for corrective action	Reinforcements or rewards for compliance	Sanctions or punishments for non-compliance
Organisation	Organisational plans, strategies, responses to competitive demands	Budgets, standard costs, sales targets	Variance	Management commendation Monetary incentives, promotions	Request for explanation Dismissal
Informal group	Mutual commitments, group ideals	Group norms	Deviance	Peer-approval, membership, leadership	Kidding Ostracism, hostility
Individual	Individual goals, aspirations	Self-expectations, intermediate targets	Perceive impending failure, missed targets	Satisfaction of 'being in control' Elation	Sense of disappointment Feeling of failure

SOURCE: G. W. Dalton and P. R. Lawrence (1971) *Motivation and Control in Organizations* (Homewood, Ill.: Irwin).

Self-control is a very daunting concept to a management control systems specialist, because self-control affects everything which a manager does. As a result, control becomes not a subset of management, but the sum of the influences, helps or hindrances that affect the way in which each manager performs the whole of his job of managing – and management we now recognise is a very complex activity.

MANAGEMENT

Field research in management has recently been leading to the recognition by academics of what managers had known for quite a while – that managing is a complex activity and that it is getting progressively more complex. The variables involved seem to be getting larger in number and specialisation seems to be increasing without a commensurate increase in our understanding of that other specialisation – integration.

Human interaction based on real interpersonal understanding seems to be becoming harder with increasing job mobility. In such a situation it becomes even more difficult when things go wrong to identify which of the items in Tannenbaum's cycle was not working as well as it should – or at all!

Equally, it is becoming clear that management as an activity is not restricted solely to 'what managers do'. Indeed it is something of an American/English quirk to distinguish 'managers' from other people. Reverting to Anthony's definition, the process 'by which resources are obtained and used effectively and efficiently' is clearly influenced to a greater or lesser extent by all workers in an organisation, not just by those workers we call managers. Ensuring that those who have the most to contribute beneficially to the process are given the opportunity to do so becomes a critical element in the management of an organisation, and this is discussed fully by Richbell (see Chapter 9 by Richbell).

The need is for a better understanding of how integration, coordination, cooperation or balance can be achieved in an active manner. In particular, there needs to be some understanding of where to look for an academic rationale for approaching integration as a topic of study.

Is it an individual activity as Lawrence and Lorsch saw it (Lawrence and Lorsch, 1967a)?

Is it something to do with structure as Texas Instruments saw it (Helms, 1975)?

Is it the real subject of management control systems as Lowe and McInnes saw it (Lowe and McInnes, 1971)?

MANAGEMENT CONTROL SYSTEMS IN THE 1980s

Eighteen years after the publication of Anthony's framework, management control systems looks very different indeed. The author suggests that the subject has evolved into: 'The study of those formal and informal systems which help an individual to control what he does with himself and other resources.'

KEY DECISIONS FOR THE FUTURE

There is universal acceptance that the Holy Grail for management control systems researchers is 'effectiveness'. There is some disagreement about whether individual effectiveness will be consistent with group effectiveness and there is fundamental disagreement as to what constitutes either a theoretical definition of effectiveness or a practically useful way of measuring it. 'Effectiveness' is something like 'truth' or 'beauty' – managers can recognise it easily enough but they cannot define it!

It is the very elusiveness of the concept of 'effectiveness' which, coupled with the fuzziness of the concept of control, makes management control systems such a compulsively interesting subject to study.

The way forward in research and teaching in the subject, however, is dependent on the answers we give to a number of key questions concerning the purpose, boundaries, and methodologies of work in the newly defined field.

Purpose

Is the purpose to develop new systems which will force, lead or drag managers to be more effective? That is, systems which will normatively measure how far managers are from the level of effectiveness which they should achieve?

OR

Is the purpose to develop new systems which will help a manager to be as effective as he wishes to be? – that is, systems which will have the capacity to facilitate total effectiveness, but which will still 'work' for managers who have no intention of raising their level of effectiveness and seek only an easier way of achieving it.

This is a choice between different levels in Boulding's hierarchy.

Types of control influence

Given the acknowledged range of influences affecting a manager, should a new system support only organisational control influences or also support informal group norms? Some of the latter have been known to be antagonistic to organisational goals – should these be supported?

Is it even possible to conceive of organisational information systems supporting informal influences? Would not such an approach be doomed to failure unless the informal part were voluntary and/or individually controlled?

This is a choice between supporting only organisationally approved influences or all influences.

Variety reduction or contingent complexity?

Given the acknowledged diversity of management, should management control systems, as now defined, deal only with specific variables or accept contingent reality?

Here the choice is between a system based on the analyst's traditional approach of variety reduction, and developed to handle only certain predetermined variables, or a system whose precise content would be determined by each manager using the system, to meet his own contingently relevant complexity.

What, if any, philosophy of control should systems embody?

Given the acknowledged diffuseness of the word control, should management control systems designers choose a particular 'approved' managerial house-style for their system (as the MBO people did), or, learning from the fate of systems which are dependent on a uniform acceptance of a given control philosophy, should systems be designed to accommodate diffuseness?

This is a choice between a stated view of what an optimum control style should be or an acceptance of diffuseness of managerial style which will differ from person to person and from day to day.

The system/structure interface

Given:

(a) the fact that organisations' structures change frequently within a given form, and that new forms such as matrix and fluid structures are in current use, and
(b) the fact that structure is only a formal system of authority and accountability,

which is the key variable in the structure/system interface? Anthony had no doubts, 'Structure is a given – systems are therefore designed to meet the needs of a given structure' (Anthony, 1965). But structure is just a formal organisational influence attempt, so it could be treated as part of the new concept of management control systems.

Here we have a choice between:

1. Structure-dependent systems.
2. Structure-linked systems.
3. Systems independent of structure.

These choices are critical for the future of research, system design and development, and teaching in the field of management control systems.

The implications for research methodology

Each of the choices posed above presents a challenge to researchers in terms of both the purpose and the methodology of research. In the aggregate they highlight the need for, and present the opportunity to design, completely new research methodologies. The practical arguments for a major step function change in research methodology seem equally strong. Previous methodologies have led us to the point where integration born of effective operation of Tannenbaum's control cycle (Figure 2.4) in organisations is acknowledged to be inadequate (notably in respect of lateral and diagonal interaction). Until recently (see Chapter 11 by Machin and Tai) we have lacked even the most rudimentary methodology for monitoring each of the ten steps (a–j) which collectively make up that cycle, so as to be able to ascertain the cause of ineffective operation of the control process.

The increasing power of information-handling technology and the decreasing cost of information storage and retrieval provide all the practical support which researchers will need at precisely the time that theoretical considerations demand that new methodologies be found. In moving into this new and uncharted area it becomes imperative that researchers and managers jointly determine the criteria against which new research methodologies and new management control systems will be both designed and evaluated. The following set of criteria are presented only to spur others into replacing them with a better set.

A set of criteria to guide future research and system design

It is the author's belief that many of the fundamental choices which have to be made follow almost inevitably from the reasoning included earlier in this chapter.

Tannenbaum's control cycle is conceptually independent of:

1. the hierarchical relationship of B to A,
2. the managerial styles of A or B,
3. the nature of A's intention – i.e. it may be to influence B to produce anything from a concrete item to an abstract outcome.

To follow Tannenbaum means designing a system which is not dependent for its successful operation on:

1. any particular organisation structure,
2. any particular philosophy of managerial interaction,
3. any particular type of managerial output.

To follow Lowe and McInnes (1971) in their concept of resolution levels, it is necessary so to design a system that it treats organisational interactions with the environment in exactly the same way as it treats an individual manager's interactions with his environment.

General systems theory indicates that any contingent system must accept the situationally-derived, complex, omnidirectional pattern of influences affecting a manager in connection with his job (Katz and Kahn, 1966). (It is worth pointing out that whilst the previous sentence poses no conceptual difficulty the practical implementation of the ideas embodied in it would have been impossible until the availability of large computers and the chip, which have made it possible to design systems which can document both the contents and direction of every interpersonal interaction in a managerial group.)

Dalton's classification can only lead to an acceptance that any system which purports to facilitate the achievement of organisational and managerial effectiveness must be capable of supporting both formal organisational influences derived from authority, responsibility and accountability, and the informal group influences derived from much more complex combinations of ostensibly the same variables.

Control theory – whether of the mechanistic, closed-loop, feedback variety or the more relevant open-looped, feed-forward variety – makes the clear demand that any management control system worthy of the name must, as a minimum, enable a manager to ascertain first, what his goals are, and secondly, whether or not he is achieving them.

Dalton's concept of self-control systems poses a real challenge to a tradition based almost exclusively on managerial and research experience of *purposeful* systems. The conflict of choice is apparent. If a management control system is to facilitate self-control then its purpose will be dependent on the motivational needs of each manager and we may reasonably assume that occasionally managers may wish to use the system to reduce both organisational effectiveness and the demands made on themselves. To people reared on a tradition of purposeful systems based on beliefs such as:

1. Management control systems are there to achieve goal congruence, OR
2. Management control systems are there to prevent individuals from wasting organisational resources,

it is hard to contemplate a 'purposeless' system whose purpose would be defined by the user. Yet Dalton's classification of control influences demands a system which can help a manager to achieve whatever he decides he will try to achieve.

In this dilemma we can turn to Boulding's hierarchy. Level 8 in the hierarchy is descriptive of self-deciding societal systems, most if not all of which are virtually purposeless in other than closed system terms.

Clearly, to service the needs of level 8 systems nothing will do between 8 and 1, so a level 1 framework, or inert contingent system, it has to be. These choices, once made, produce a set of criteria which can be postulated in a slightly fuller form. They are listed in Figure 2.5.

1. The system must permit clear links to be developed from planned organisational purpose to operational activity.
2. The system must be able to assist managers both when planning purpose and when controlling its achievement.
3. The system must be designed to help a manager deal with the actual complexity of his job.
4. The system must not be dependent for its successful operation on any particular organisational structure and, therefore, must be capable of being used successfully in matrix or even fluid structure.
5. The system must be 'open' in the sense that it will accept omnidirectional communication patterns.
6. The system must not be dependent for its successful operation on the nature of the output generated by a manager, and, therefore, must be capable of being used successfully by managers whose organisational output may range from the concrete to the abstract.
7. The system must not be dependent for its successful operation on a particular philosophy of managerial interaction, and, therefore, must be capable of being used successfully by managers whose approach may range from the completely dictatorial to completely self-effacing, group participation.
8. The system must enable a manager who so wishes to ascertain exactly what output is expected of him and by whom.
9. The system must enable a manager to obtain information on the extent to which he is generating the output which is expected of him.
10. The system must enable a manager who so wishes to explore his actual responsibility, his actual authority, and his actual accountability within the organisation.
11. The system must be designed to enable each manager to develop the contents of the system to meet his own particular needs.

FIGURE 2.5   *Key design criteria for effective management control systems*

CONCLUSION

The criteria documented in Figure 2.5 offer both an analytical framework for research into the effectiveness of management control systems currently in use in given organisations, and a specification for the design of new and more effective management control systems. They also, of course, reflect and make public the values of the author! This is particularly appropriate at the start of a book concerned to explore new perspectives in management control. In the past, the purposes of management control systems and the value systems of those who designed them were at worst hidden, and at best implicit, in the systems which were produced.

It is vital that those values are subject to public debate at a time when it is clearly in everyone's interest to develop more effective systems for helping us 'to control ourselves and other resources'.

Part II

3 Management Control and Methodology

Anthony J. Berry

SUMMARY

The debate on research in accounting and management control is lively. This chapter sets out to distinguish between research and scholarship and then considers three methodologies: functionalism, verstehen and logical positivism. This leads on to consideration of the purposes and sources of research problems. The conclusion is an argument for a contingent methodology.

RESEARCH AND SCHOLARSHIP

In the United Kingdom, and I suspect elsewhere, the word research is used with something approaching abandon. Here I wish to distinguish between research as the development of explanation of phenomena and scholarship as an exegetical task (commenting upon texts) or a hermeneutic task (interpreting or explaining texts). There is a myth that American accounting academics have a tradition of research while the British have a tradition of scholarship. Within the tradition of scholarship there is much concern with correctness, as evidenced by the current debate upon accounting measurement of value in inflation, this correctness being derived by logical deduction from premises (texts) together with work to clarify those premises. In accounting and in management control there is a problem of distinguishing what is research and what is scholarship, as evidenced by the methodologies in use.

The debate on research in accounting in the United Kingdom has been somewhat more vigorous than the activity of research. For example Burchell *et al.* (1980) quote more than 120 sources, with perhaps ten or so being reports of empirical research. Of course, many of these sources are related to empirical data, but such a limitation is indicative both of the difficulties of research in accounting and of the traditions of scholarship in the subject.

Tricker (1979) arugued that accounting developed from changing (practical) needs, that the pressure for changes in understanding was great and that accounting in a society was a function of the ideology, or political system in which it operates. Tricker then argued for a process of research in accounting based upon a two-way process between researcher and practitioner, addressing problems rather than applying current theories. This problem-centred approach has been put forward by McCosh *et al.* (1978), Otley (1978b), Otley and Berry (1980). The hope underlying this approach is that not only will relevant and useful research be undertaken, but that theoretical development will go hand in hand with practical problem-solving.

Eilon (1975) classified management researchers by the nature of their interaction with the phenomena which they study. He suggested that researchers tend to pick approaches to research with which they were comfortable; his remote researchers, chroniclers, classifiers, puzzle-solvers, iconoclasts, would not interact with their phenomena; his empiricists, dialectitians and action researchers most certainly would so interact. Thus Eilon conceives of a strategy of research which would be contingent upon the personality of the researcher. Mason and Mitroff (1973) also argued for research in management information systems to be contingent but in their view the personality of the manager, rather than the researcher, was to be a contingent variable.

These contingent approaches are arguments about the nature of the research process, not the nature of the theory or knowledge with which the research problems are to be addressed. This distinction is important, for Waterhouse and Tiesson (1978) in a paper entitled 'A Contingency Framework for Management Accounting Systems Research' argue that the theoretical framework of research in management accounting should be the contingency theory of organisation and do not argue for a contingent methodology.

The existence of the debate on research in management accounting and control is evidence for dissatisfaction with the current state of understanding, and suggests moreover that the current state of theory is inadequate to help us understand the phenomena we encounter. This would in Kuhn's (1970) language be the ferment accompanying a breakdown in the paradigm and the struggle for a new paradigm or paradigms. Thus problem-centred control research programmes can be undertaken in the hope that a new set of ideas, disconnected from the previously accepted dogma, will now emerge (Tricker, 1979; Wells, 1976).

The process of developing knowledge depends upon the methodologies used. Methodology is not just about data collection and the rules for evidence; in its larger conception it is about the nature of explanation and the means by which explanations are produced. Of course, a theory which explains some phenomena may also be used for prediction. For example Edwards and Bell (1961) contend that the purpose of accounting data is to (be used to) explain past economic events, while Caspari (1976) suggests that a main purpose of accounting data is to predict future economic events. Both views mistake the measures of variables (accounting data) for the theories (statements of relationships between variables) which might be adequate explanations and might yield useful predictions. Methods of identification and measurement of variables are important features of methodology but this chapter is not principally concerned with these issues or issues of statistical inference. The methodologies through which explanations are sought in the social sciences are functionalism, verstehen and logical positivism. This chapter now discusses each of these in relation to management control.

THREE METHODOLOGIES

Functionalism rests upon a few assumptions:

1. a system of interrelated parts exists
2. this system has certain basic needs which must be met (or it dies)
3. to maintain equilibrium, the parts of a system must be meeting these needs
4. parts can be functional or dysfunctional in relation to the system
5. system needs can be met by a variety of alternatives
6. only recurring patterns are appropriate to analysis.

The objective of this kind of explanation is to demonstrate or show the contribution to the parts of the system for the whole. There are two strands to this, one dealing with organisations or groups, namely structural functionalism and the second dealing with individuals, namely psychological functionalism.

The management control literature, Anthony (1965), is mainly within this tradition. That is explanations of the form; control procedures (pieces of information) are needed in order that the system survives. The social system and environment paradigm is usually in the form of a functional approach. The work of Beer (1972) in control is in this structural functional tradition; for example in *The Brain of the Firm*, Beer borrows a structural model of a brain and transposes it onto a social organisation with five necessary and sufficient distinctive subsystems. Again, Jaques (1976) in his *General Theory of Bureaucracy* argues that bureaucracy is a universal form because it meets the dependence needs of most people.

There is a strong relationship between the cybernetic model of Beer, the Anthony classification and the model of Parsons. Beer has:

System 5　Strategic choice
　　　4　Adaptation, future planning
　　　3　Managerial or coordination
　　　1　Operational units (2 is a minor antioscillation or stability device)

Anthony has:

Strategic Control[1]
Managerial Control
Operational Control

while Parsons works with:

Goal directedness
Integration
Adaptation
Pattern maintenance (includes relationship of persons)

While it is observable that Parsons at least introduces the issues of persons and values it is also clear that much management control debate is not about whether functionalism is appropriate but how well functional theories can be constructed (e.g. Lowe and Tinker, 1977). Even within this tradition the limitations of Anthony's framework are clear enough (see Lowe and Puxty (1979) for an analysis). However, management control can be seen in the Parsons framework as:

instrumental controls to *attain goals* (while avoiding the goal formation process). This is akin to the non-examination of the process of rule-making spoken of by Hopwood (1978) and Boussard (1979) for in this framework rules are necessary functions

integration controls to pull things together (while generally ignoring the social context of task integration mainly because there is no accounting measure of the social or human context)

adaptive controls to enable survival to take place: that is the planning procedures through which adaptation is required to take place

pattern maintenance which in management control is usually manifested as the imposition of constructs of responsibility and authority (e.g. rules, discretion limits) in a social hierarchy as against the issue of a logical hierarchy of tasks – a focus which Herbst (1976) points out is a confusion of the logical nature of hierarchies of tasks with social hierarchies.

Thus functionalism as a methodology in management control has a theme of social system technology and asks how it can be made to work 'better' for the survival of the system. Its adherents are led to examine the technology (what Boussard calls the 'hard' content of accounting), the kinds of rules and procedures it contains and tend to lay aside the question of understanding the actors in the process, or indeed varieties of meanings in the technological procedures. The purposes of accounting and control are rarely challenged. The argument of Lowe and Tinker (1977) for a methodological basis for management accounting is observably an argument for a functionalist orientation: 'The management control problem is explicated in terms of maintaining a relationship between the enterprises structure and its environment.'

The critical problems of a functionalist orientation in social science have been written about at great length and not always with charity. Principally they relate to problems of evidence: what are the rules of evidence that permit statements of the form that a management control procedure is necessary for the survival of an organisation which themselves are not tautologies: i.e. that the organisation is necessary for the survival of a management control procedure? Secondly there is a universalistic streak to this tradition, its language is all encompassing. Thus it tends to appeal to those whose concepts of social order are similarly universal, for who can complain when all is ordered to achieve the system's purposes?

Some of these arguments have been with us for centuries (see Paul to the Corinthians) and have been worked upon in the political and philosophical traditions. 'Does survival mean the greatest good of the greatest number?' is the question that effectively puts paid to functionalism as a necessary and sufficient framework. It is similar, is it not, to the question 'why do accountants do what they do?'

The second methodological strand is called (in England) verstehen, which rather encompasses all those who would not be described as functionalists or logical positivists. Examples of this tradition in accounting and control are Bower (1972) and Carter's (1971) work on capital investment, Otley (1978a) on operational budgeting and Burchell *et al.* (1980) on accounting in society. Clearly much of what is interpretation of social role is using this methodology. It has parallels in clinical medicine. Action research lies in this methodological domain.

There are, in this tradition, no clear rules for inference. The task is not only to observe and describe phenomena but to explain them in a plausible and aesthetically pleasing way. Thus great dependency is laid upon: (i) accuracy and honesty of observation; (ii) sensitivity and perception of the observer; (iii) imaginative interpretations of observations. This method is close to what Plato called *episteme*, which embodies awareness of the known, of the knower and of knowing. Inevitably such approaches are criticised as being either individual or eclectic and lacking in subject-centred rigour. Yet there are questions which can be addressed in no other way. For example, how I know about a person must be through this methodology. But is that, asks the sceptic, intersubjectively testable – to which I might be forced to reply sometimes not, but that does not mean that I do not know, nor does it mean that my knowledge is wrong.

If, for example, you are told something of your experience of accounting or control procedures, which you then *know* would diminish your knowledge if you were to accept it, then you can be free to reject it, for it is your feeling, your insight that you are right in this instance. Obviously such insight may not travel too well – consider the interpretations of the role of accounting in your own organisation, or the promotion of one accountant to a more senior position.

Of course there are methodological approaches associated with neither the functionalist nor with the positivist tradition which are not readily subserved under the verstehen rubric. The ethnomethodology approach is to present as clear a picture as possible of the social reality of the persons in a group or in a society. This approach is an attempt to answer one central criticism of the verstehen approach which is that as no observation can be theory free, for all observers are the prisoners of some theory whether explicitly or implicitly expressed.

The researcher in management control is thus caught up in a well-known dilemma: should he be merely a tourist – taking snapshots of management control through a well-controlled lens; should he engage with the phenomena in a way which would risk the initial theoretical positions through debate, dialectic or intuitive thought; or should he 'go native' in pursuit of the inner meanings to the accountants of what they do. This latter is the risk of the anthropologist, the second is the risk of the verstehen methodology, the former is the risk of the functionalist and, I think, the logical positivist, to which tradition I want to turn.

The positivist tradition in social science is based upon the premise that social phenomena are not basically different from physical phenomena and therefore social scientists can use the scientific method of knowledge attained through hypothesis testing. Statement of the form – in conditions set C, if X then Y – are established and through empirical examination of the state C, values of X and Y are measured in order to establish the range of validity of the statement. In management control we find ourselves dealing mainly with weak forms of this method: for example tests of association are used where we seek to test whether:

variable values change in conjunction with each other;
time priority, does the sequence of events-A always follow;
non-spuriousness, is there is a possible relationship between the
    variables (profit measures and stock prices);
rationale, is there is a connecting theory.

In the verstehen tradition we tend not to construct experiments as physical scientists would understand them, a fact which does not prevent us from considering the ethical problems. The principal ethical problem we face is what experiments are we entitled to conduct, what phenomena are we entitled to observe (e.g. Milgram's (1963) experiments on authority and obedience). In management control and accounting we tend not to design experimental control methods in 'real' organisations and monitor the results, we tend to use a method of comparative analysis.

A further question of hypothesis testing relates to statistical inference and is the problem of controlling the type-II error (i.e. the probability of believing your hypothesis to be correct when it is false). In general it is almost impossible to control the type-II errors, yet lacking such control could lead to desired positive results of experiments.

The general criteria for choice of a methodology rests upon validity and reliability. By validity I mean that it is true that the methodology does lead to research observations, descriptions and explanations of phenomena that the researchers intended to address. By reliability I mean that what was done is replicable by other researchers. Now it is not possible to replicate social phenomena exactly, so we have to take a weaker form of that criteria which is based upon examining what was done and making a judgement about its replicability.

Positivists also argue the case for predictability (including the accuracy of prediction) as an essential element in their traditions. From this perspective they argue that functionalism is incapable of prediction, is vague in definition and use of concepts, is unable to explain changes and is basically tautological in nature. Some of these criticisms are certainly appropriate to the Anthony classification of management control. Further, positivists can argue that verstehen is incurably subjective, and given the public and intersubjective testability criterion, then verstehen is irrelevant to the scientific study of social phenomena.

In turn the positivist methodology tends to overemphasise experimental technique. This approach is inherently inapplicable to social phenomena and the positivists become addicted to measurement and quantification as ends in themselves. It is, according to this criticism, what Plato described as techne, the lessons of experience, of trial and error, of clever skills refined through diligent practice.

For management control theorists, problems in using this methodology lie in access to phenomena, varieties of theoretical positions, the vast sampling frame needed for the array of variables and a lack of trained researchers.

The methodologies discussed here are all attempts to generate explanations of phenomena. The question therefore arises of how can we decide whether to use one methodology in preference to another.

If we regard management control as a defined[2] set of theoretical propositions in relation to a field of phenomena we would have established a starting point. Problems arise when we have not defined management control nor have we bounded the phenomena of interest. Figure 3.1 illustrates this problem.

If we seek to test the applicability of the theories of management control, which we believe adequately explain the field of phenomena (i.e. bounded) to a new set of phenomena, then we could use the positivist methodology of hypotheses formation and testing and if the phenomena are in accord with the theory we will have incrementally extended the applicable range of the theory. That is, we will have chosen path 1 in Figure 3.1. Possibly, however, the experimental results may be such as to throw some doubt upon the theory, the researcher may doubt the range of variables in his theory and seek to admit new variables. (In management control, for example, it is asserted that theories of control in relation to profit maximisation can be extended to non-profit-making enterprises.) Thus path 1 in Figure 3.1 extends not just the domain of phenomena but also the nature of the definition of the theory. Positivism is about theory building.

In contrast, path 2 is a venture which moves into the task of bringing that which is undefined into the domain of theoretical definition – it is the explicit task of extending the definition of the subject, and perhaps, at the same time, extending the domain of phenomena. It is a research problem to which positivism is unsuited, the appropriate methodology being verstehen. The evidence of Tricker, Otley and others quoted earlier suggests that this methodology is applicable to the development of the subject of management control from its present state (an engagement with phenomena was demanded).

However, to describe the possibilities in such terms is to recognise that the research task is to establish defined theories (bodies of knowledge) which have been tested. The commendable rigour of the positivist methodology may be regarded as a goal of research endeavour, through which validity and reliability might be attained.

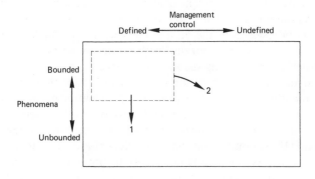

FIGURE 3.1

From the discussion it might appear that the methodological problem is solved by the use of a developmental process. However, this leaves the functionalist methodology rather in limbo. Yet it is clear enough that we can only test focal theories, that is statements which have empirically observable variables. The background theories to which focal theories are related are not themselves tested. Functionalist theories of control are background theories from which testable theories may be derived (and perhaps logically deduced). Thus there is a role for the functionalist methodology in relation to questions of theoretical definition from which which researchable questions such as how does an organisation adapt its behaviour might be derived. The reverse link, between a focal theory, an observed relationship between variables (e.g. accounting information and decisions) and a background theory is more intractable, as the process of inducting or inferring a connection between focal and background theory is not readily described.

Secondly the question of how research projects in management control arise has not been addressed. The connection between the search for knowledge, action in research and the motivation to participate and perhaps to finance this activity is by no means simple.

KNOWLEDGE, PROBLEMS AND MOTIVATION

In any study of a social technology there is an inevitable and perhaps unconscious linking of knowledge with action. That is, there is a tendency to believe that research must be immediately useful to the subjects of the research, rather than generally useful as a contribution to knowledge. In management control, and I suspect in accounting generally, there is a tendency to blur the admittedly difficult distinction between research as the development of new understanding and research as the solving of puzzles[3] with extant knowledge.

In order to clarify this distinction a process is suggested which would involve first, the generation of new understandings; secondly, the examination of these in relation to a problem or problems to see whether they are useful to practitioners and/or to other theorists; and thirdly, the solving of puzzles[4] with the new understandings. Hopwood (1978) pointed out that practitioners are more interested in the latter category – which is not research, but may be scholarship. But while it is not research, the process of puzzle-solving itself may be both the subject of research and the opportunity to undertake research. The only danger here is that research could be trapped by a narrow social utility criterion which diminishes the longer-term task of theory-building.

This classification of understanding and application has within it the questions raised by Hopwood (1978) Watts and Zimmermann (1979) and others of the sources of research problems and the availability of resources to attack them. Research problems are usually generated from a perceived inadequacy in a present explanation (Popper's problem shift is similar to Lindblom's disjointed incrementalisation) or the flash of insight which generates new understandings or new possibilities for understanding. But we must still consider the motivation to undertake research and the manner in which research problems are chosen. It is possible to use this current exercise as an example of motivation. In one sense I write this paper in the pursuit of personal things; the knowledge and experience I gain, the possibilities of insight, and the satisfaction for organising some ideas. This is uniquely mine. But I am presenting this in a collection of papers where my intent is both to stimulate, to influence thought away from much muddle and metaphysic and towards doing some research. This then is the professional or social role of the academic as an independent searcher. But then again I am an agent of action and change and my intent may well be political, to push ideas back into my own colleagues and associates after they have been partly sanitised through publication. Thus the motivations are personal, professional, social and political. Motivation may be connected to a sense of the power which knowledge brings. Boussard (1979) picks up a neat splitting in the role of researchers when he postulates a difference between 'strategical researcher' whose task is 'relevant contribution' and the 'operational' researcher who produces 'nice things called papers'. (One looks for the managerial researcher who could complete Anthony's functional triad!)

Once the issue of motivation is raised then it is clear that it is not only nuclear physicists who find themselves in an ethical dilemma about the use of their understandings. Management control researchers, too, face this dilemma. Are the results of our research, which we all know to be partial in relation to problems, limited in application and limiting in relation to possible actions, to be given general release to practitioners? From a reading of the papers in the Stockholm workshop, much social accounting research activity is about manufacturing the weapons of war with professional accounting bodies and government, with power as the prize. For example

Boussard quotes Klaosen and Schreuder: 'The basic point of departure for any examination or construction of accounting research methodology would necessarily be a clear positioning of the accounting function in [the] wider social framework.' To me and to Burchell *et al.* (1980) the understanding of 'the position' would seem to be the research problem: here it is the opening salvo. We, too, need a campaign for the peaceful uses of management accounting and control theories.

The relative lack of research in accounting and management control related to explanation of phenomena may not be the responsibility of the academic community and is not simply a question of motivation. Perhaps it is an inevitable fact that management control academics are trapped in a mode of work which is either scholarship or application – not by choice – but because there are such limited possibilities of gaining access to undertake research. When access to data is possible it is clear that the costs in terms of time are very considerable. For example Bower's study (1972) of capital investment took more than three man years. I tend to disagree with Boussard when he dismisses the supply and demand argument of Watts and Zimmerman; but rewards in academic communities are such that empirical research output is small in relation to the alternative uses of time.

The scope or range of the research problems chosen by either academics for research or others for solution are inevitably bounded. That is they are stated in ways which limit the field of study. This process of bounding and the process of definition would itself be an important area for research. What would be interesting is how the bounding took place – whether implicit in theory, through ideas in good currency, through pressure of a competitive academic world (that's my problem – get off), through a political process of either openness or protectiveness, or through the availability of resources to tackle any but the most perceivedly central issue.

TOWARDS A CONTINGENT METHODOLOGY

The search for knowledge, the tackling of problems and the motivation to do either are issues which apply to researchers in all of the methodological traditions. However, the argument in this paper is that methodology may be regarded as contingent upon the nature of the research problem to be addressed.

This is not an argument for methodological anarchy (Feyerabend,

1975) or even for methodological pluralism. The choices which researchers make are not simply matters of personal preference. The thesis of contingency does imply the death of an imaginary positivist hegemony and denies that there is one unique and universally applicable methodology. (Unless one is prepared to argue that a contingent methodology is such a universal – to which I would answer that it explicitly argues for a methodology relevant to the nature of problems, phenomena and explanation.) It would thus be quite possible to construct explanations of phenomena from different theoretical perspectives which are then not readily translatable from one theory to another, that is incommensurable theories or different paradigms as the basis of theoretical definition.

The argument of Kuhn was that progress is made through shifts in paradigms and that these paradigms or world views both consciously and unconsciously affect the nature of explanations which are accepted. It has been implied in this chapter that management control is in Kuhn's sense pre-paradigmatic and I have shown that it currently has a strong functionalist orientation. However, it is clear that Kuhn had no rules to distinguish the last holder of the old paradigm from the first holder of the next one, and that research has always taken a place within several paradigms, a poly-paradigmatic state observed by Wells (1976).

In management control research I would suggest that we might proceed by recognising that the functionalist orientation has closed down curiosity (few research problems) and hobbled development (little theoretical development).

Only through the generation of insight and understanding of phenomena will we ever bring ourselves to the position of being able to formulate a research programme which might be subjected to the criterion of prediction. Clearly this means a methodology of verstehen to respond to the challenge of developing 'intuitive insight with enriching novelty' and a 'reliance upon a disciplined method with controllable and reliable results' (Gouldner, 1967).

Of course we as academics work in a micropolitical context within which our own values are revealed both to others and to ourselves. To assert the independent role of the academic researcher is also to assert the rediscovery of the integrity of the academic role, within which we are reunited with knowledge.

CONCLUSION

In order to make progress in research in management control we must distinguish what is research from what is puzzle-solving, from what is scholarship and from what is application: we must distinguish, too, from the kinds of methodologies available to us in order to focus upon the generation of insight and understanding. To work from a premise of short-run social utility will not be in the best long-run interests of the development of research in management accounting and control. It is my belief that the longer-run benefits of this approach would outweigh any short-term costs, for this is a programme for engagement with phenomena and with theory.

NOTES

1. Boussard unconsciously takes this model on when he writes of the strategical accountant (potent) and the operational accountant (impotent).
2. I wish to acknowledge the valuable comments made upon an earlier draft of this paper by Andrew McCosh. The responsibility for this section is, of course, my own.
3. I am indebted to Dr John Bourgoyne for this distinction.
4. The distinction between puzzles and problems is that the former may be solved with extant knowledge while the later may not. Of course, in such a distinction some degree of subjectivity is inevitable.

4 Concepts of Control: the Contribution of Cybernetics and Systems Theory to Management Control

David T. Otley

Quis custodiet ipsos custodes (Juvenal)

INTRODUCTION

The purpose of this chapter is to examine and evaluate the contributions made by the disciplines of cybernetics and general systems theory to the study of management control. It seeks to do this by drawing out the concepts of control developed in each of the disciplines and considering their applicability in the context of organisational control systems. However, because of the wide variety of uses of the term 'control' mentioned elsewhere (Chapter 2, p.30) it will be prudent to begin with some preliminary definitions to make clear the area of application being considered.

The term 'management control system' conveys quite different meanings to different people. This is perhaps only to be expected when one reflects upon the ambiguity inhenent in the concept of management, the wide range of connotations of the word control (Rathe, 1960, provides 57 varieties) and the pervasiveness of systems ideas in the modern world. As might be foreseen, dictionaries provide little assistance in the midst of such confusion; two recent dictionaries of management, one British and the other from the US, do not even list the term 'management control' as one requiring definition (French and Saward, 1977; Rosenberg, 1978). It is therefore necessary to spell out the boundaries of the subject area as seen by the author of this chapter.

First, the function of management in an organisation can be normatively viewed as being concerned with 'initiating appropriate actions for the benefit of an organisation' (Rosenberg, 1978). This is distinct from the descriptive view of the role of managers as individuals as developed by, for example, Mintzberg (1973) and also distinct from the activities such individuals might engage in whilst pursuing their own, rather than organisational, interests either individually or as a group. That is, management is regarded here as a systemic characteristic displayed by organisations in seeking to attain certain ends. However, this view should in no way be taken as a device to avoid the issue that both 'organisation' and 'organisational ends' are highly problematic concepts. Indeed it may be that a major reason for the failure of management science to make more substantial progress in the past two decades has been its avoidance of these very issues. Secondly, control is viewed in the wide sense of both selecting ends to be attained and attempting to ensure that they are attained. In this sense the exercise of control is central to the function of management as they are each aspects of the same concept: the direction and coordination of organisational activity in the selection and achievement of some goal. Management control is thus concerned with discovering courses of action that will contribute to the general welfare of an organisation (however defined) and with ensuring that the implementation of these actions produces the desired effects. Finally the term system is used primarily to convey the systemic nature of the organisation that is being managed, its internal relationships and its interaction with its wider environment, rather than to suggest any systematic properties that a formal control system might possess (Fig. 2.5., p.42). The study of management control systems in the context of economic organisations is thus concerned with the ways in which diverse activities may be coordinated into coherent strategies and patterns of organisational behaviour, and with ways of monitoring and regulating actual behaviour so that it contributes to some overall desired pattern.

The area of study mapped out by this preliminary definition is thus very wide, encompassing most aspects of organisational functioning. It may also become problematic to the extent that it emphasises a view of human organisations as designed artefacts for attaining certain purposes in contrast to a view which emphasises them as naturally occurring phenomena. Real organisations exhibit characteristics of both views and this dual aspect of their nature must be always borne in mind, as the subsequent discussion will show. Our definition is also in sharp contrast with the classic definition used in the management accounting literature which distinguishes management control from strategic planning on the one hand and from operational control on the other, and concentrates upon the development of formal systems for the control of economic organisations by managers (Anthony, 1965). Such a distinction appears to permit the fundamental issues involved in the setting of organisational objectives and the process of strategic adaptation to environmental contingencies to be avoided; it also avoids the need to become entangled with the complexities of technological differences at the operational level. In this way management control becomes largely synonymous with management accounting. Such an approach is criticised by Lowe and Puxty (1979); suffice it to state at this point that a much broader view of the concept of management control is being considered here. However it is important to note that the concern expressed by Hofstede (1978) at 'the poverty of management control philosophy' was directed at the tradition consolidated and developed by Anthony. Indeed, if management control must rely upon accounting technique then Hofstede's criticism is amply justified.

From the perspective of the wider definition of management control it would appear that the related disciplines of cybernetics and general systems theory should have much to offer. Cybernetics has been defined as the 'science of communication and control' (Weiner, 1948) in general, and should be expected to have insights to contribute to the particular area of management control. General systems theory (GST) takes an holistic point of view as its fundamental stance and should therefore be relevant to the concern of management control with the *overall* well-being of the organisation. Further, it is appropriate to consider the joint contribution of cybernetics and GST as they have developed in such a parallel and closely-linked manner that it is difficult to define a meaningful boundary between them.

The main thrust of this chapter is therefore to evaluate the contribution that can be made by cybernetics and GST to the study of management control in organisations. It is in no sense meant to give a survey of the whole of these source disciplines, which are, in any case, now so extensive and rambling as to make such a task of Herculean proportions. Neither is attention given to the substantive contribution of social systems theory (which is dealt with elsewhere by Berry (p.88), although some discussion of its philosophical antecendents is inevitably included here. The aim is to help provide access to a set of concepts that it is hoped will give richer insights into the practice of management control and to help alleviate the undeserved poverty of management control philosophy.

THE CONTRIBUTION OF CYBERNETICS

The term 'cybernetics' was coined by Norbert Weiner and was intended to denote an area of study which covered 'the entire field of control and communication theory, whether in the machine or the animal' (Weiner,. 1948, p. 11). Essentially born during the Second World War (although its roots go back into the Industrial Revolution), it provided a framework within which individuals who are attacking common problems in different disciplines could relate. It rapidly became concerned with the coordination, regulation and control of complex systems for, as Ashby (1956, pp. 4–6) pointed out

> the virtue of cybernetics is that it offers a method for the scientific treatment of the system in which complexity is outstanding and too important to be ignored ... Cybernetics offers the hope of providing effective methods for the study, and control, of systems that are intrinsically extremely complex.

The ideas of cybernetics seem to have been seized upon by two major groups of scientists. First, there were those concerned with machines and automation (control engineering) together with those interested in computers and communication (communication theory, but also artificial intelligence etc.). This led to the development of mathematical theories of communication and control. Secondly, there were the biologists who found in cybernetics an organising framework within which they could begin to understand the ways in which complex living systems operated and interacted. Indeed, cybernetics might be thought to be solely concerned with biological phenomena if one confines oneself to certain of its literature. For example, it is defined by Pask (1961, p. 11) as being concerned with 'how systems regulate themselves, reproduce themselves, evolve and learn. Its high spot is the question of how they organise themselves'. In this way cybernetics is applied to specific phenomena and is seen as relating solely to them. Thus Wisdom (1956, p. 112) argues that

> The basic hypothesis of cybernetics is that the chief mechanism of
> the central nervous system is one of negative feedback. The field of
> study is not however restricted to feedback of the negative kind.
> Secondly, cybernetics makes the hypothesis that the negative
> feedback mechanism explains 'purposive' and 'adaptive' behaviour.

However, despite such restricted approaches, there has been a
continued effort to ensure that cybernetics keeps the main elements of
its initial role as a general science of regulation and control. As
Parsegian (1972, p. vii) has pointed out

> it has come to represent a quite general search for relationships
> among phenomena. Some people distinguish the term cybernetics
> from what is called General Systems Theory, but all too often the
> distinctions seem to be more superficial than real.

In what follows no attempt will be made to limit the scope of what is
referred to as cybernetics although issues relating primarily to GST
will be considered in the next section; the aim will be to draw out these
concepts which will be useful in understanding the process of management control in organisations.

It would appear that there is a *prima facie* case for assuming that
cybernetic ideas will be of considerable value in the area of management control. After all, organisations are systems of very great
complexity and the task of management may be viewed as that of
regulating their activities so that they adapt and evolve in relation to a
changing environment. The point of view taken is similar to that
expressed by Amey (1979, p. 84) who, referring to his summary of
ideas on control drawn from other disciplines, states:

> Inclusion of the present chapter was prompted by the strongly held
> belief that, as accountants, we understand very little as yet about
> the *nature* of control. A number of other disciplines, ranging from
> biology to engineering, share an interest in control problems, and a
> growing body of knowledge on the principles of control has been
> emerging in cybernetics, systems theory and control theory. This
> may have relevance to the problems of financial and economic
> control of business enterprise, enabling us to analyse their
> behaviour more effectively. Certainly it is too great a body of
> knowledge to be ignored.

The cybernetic concept of control

Cybernetics is intentionally non-specific about the nature of the process being controlled; in this way it is hoped to derive general principles of control that may be applied to many different kinds of situation. The process is thus treated as a black box, the internal workings of which need not concern the analyst. The basic control activity is that of reducing differences that may occur between actual process outputs and those which are considered desirable. That is, the fundamental concern of cybernetics is with negative feedback controls. Although this may appear at first sight to be a limited point of view, part of the contribution of the cybernetic approach lies in its contention that this mechanism of negative feedback is able to explain apparently purposive and adaptive behaviour.

This basic control process by error reduction can be elaborated somewhat following Tocher (1970). From his work a basic model of a cybernetic control process can be derived having four necessary conditions that must be satisfied before control can be said to exist. These are:

1. the existence of an objective or standard which is desired
2. the measurement of process outputs along the dimension specified by this objective
3. the ability to predict the effect of potential control actions
4. the ability to act in a way that will reduce deviations from the objective.

These conditions are schematically represented in Figure 4.1, taken from Otley and Berry (1980).

The contribution of this particular scheme over and above similar models (often presented in the opening of management accounting texts in terms of a detector, a comparator and an effector) is that it emphasises the central role of the predictive model. Although it might be argued that such a model of the process is not *essential* for control, for random actions could be taken initialiy but those having other than the desired effect could be rejected on subsequent occasions, such a process is akin to constructing a predictive model. Further, it is unlikely that such a random trial and error process would be effective in the control of complex, human organisations, due to the considerable time-lags inherent in assessing the effects of a given action. Thus the construction of predictive models for control is likely to be a central concern of the control system designer.

The central position of the predictive model is reinforced when anticipatory or feedforward control is considered in addition to reactive or feedback control. Whereas feedback control awaits the occurrence of an error and then takes action to counteract it, feedforward control anticipates the future occurrence of an error and takes action so as to prevent its actual occurrence. Thus control is more effective in that the process behaviour remains as desired at all times. In the context of the business enterprise, feedforward controls are essentially the operation of planning systems. The more complex the system, the more reliance is likely to be placed on anticipatory controls in comparison to reactive controls. Ashby (1956) notes that systems designers would do well to bear in mind what has been found so advantageous in biological systems and to consider whether it might not be better to control, not by error, but by what gives rise to the error. Amey (1979) picks up this point to suggest giving more emphasis to planning and forecasting, and to anticipatory control in business enterprises.

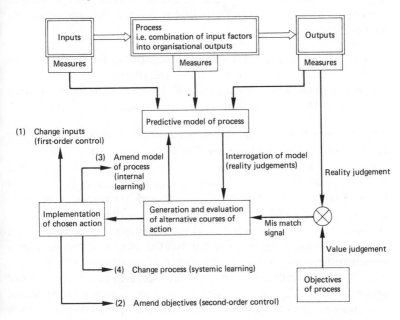

SOURCE: D. T. Otley and A. J. Berry, 'Control Organisation and Accounting', *Accounting, Organisations and Society*, vol. 5, no. 2 (1980).

FIGURE 4.1 *Outline scheme of necessary conditions for a controlled process*

Unfortunately these concepts of control do not apply in any straightforward manner to the analysis of organisational control. In particular, the nature of organisational goals is arguably very different from that of individual goals and the locus of predictive models of organisational behaviour ill-defined. Nevertheless the contribution of cybernetics may well lie most importantly in the idea that error avoidance can explain much apparently goal-seeking behaviour. This idea is put forward most strongly by Morgan (1979) when he states that:

> Organisms in nature do not orient themselves towards the achievement of given purposes or ends; they do not orient themselves towards the goal of survival. Rather they adopt modes of behaviour and organisational forms which help them to avoid certain undesirable states.

Such an approach certainly seems applicable in explaining many aspects of the behaviour of economic organisations, but it must be recognised that feedback information is often highly imperfect. As Vickers (1967) states:

> in the management of human organisations, feedback is often absent, ambiguous or uninformative and [the cybernetic concept of control] points to the complementary process of mental simulation which enables management to function in such conditions.

This process of mental simulation is essentially that of attempting to predict the possible outcomes of alternative courses of action. If one takes the idea of the dominance of error-avoidance seriously, then managerial decisions will be interpreted as being primarily motivated by the desire to avoid some possible undesired consequences; in short, a satisficing theory of decision-making whereby the selected course of action is that which has the lowest likelihood of negative consequences.

In this context it should be noted that the cybernetic control model presented here allows for the possibility of adaptation and learning. Indeed this is one of the most important features of a viable control system operating in an open system. The control action implemented can take one or more of four forms, as indicated by Otley and Berry (1980). It can involve:

1. Adjustment of the process inputs so as to stabilise the process output at a desired level.

2. Amendment of the process objectives to be attainable in the light of previous experience (an activity noted both in human learning behaviour and in budgetary control systems).
3. Reformulation of the predictive model to incorporate what has been learnt from the errors detected (most formally achieved in adaptive control models).
4. Change of the whole activity being engaged in (as when a company pulls out of a whole line of business).

Both (2) and (3) are learning processes; the former involving a change in expectations, the latter requiring modification of the predictive model.[1] However it should be noted that if the practice of feedforward control based on error-avoidance is as widespread as suggested earlier, the conditions for learning may not be satisfied. For if courses of action are selected primarily to avoid predicted undesirable states, inappropriate predictive models can persist in use indefinitely. That is, managers' beliefs that some actions are to be avoided because they are expected to lead to undesired outcomes will not be modified because the true outcome will never be experienced. Thus the operation of a feedforward error-avoiding control system, whilst it may result in the maintenance of a given (not unsatisfactory) state of affairs, also provides the conditions in which the discovery of better courses of action is unlikely to be pursued.

It may be protested at this point that, valid as the preceding ideas may be, they do not form part of the subject-matter of cybernetics, which is concerned with control by reaction to errors in closed systems. Amey (1979), for example, contrasts cybernetic controls which operate in a closed system with non-cybernetic controls which take into account the open nature of the system being controlled. However it should be noted that the distinction between open and closed systems is often imprecisely defined and, in any case, depends upon how the system is itself defined (an issue that will be pursued in a subsequent section). A closed system is essentially one which has no relevant environment (Ackoff, 1971); it will thus inexorably tend to move towards a state of increasing disorder. By contrast, an open system, by being a net importer from its environment, can maintain its distinctive characteristics and increase its internal order and complexity. It is thus evident that an organisation (a social system) must be treated as an open system in the same way as a living organism (a biological system), although care must be taken not to pursue the biological analogy too far. The cybernetic concepts which apply to closed systems (e.g. requisite variety, entropy increase) do not necessarily apply in open systems. However, two points require clarification. First, there is a role for negative feedback controls within organisations. Indeed, von Bertalanffy (1968) would argue that as complexity increases, so the importance of such close-loop controls will increase, although this claim is difficult to evaluate (Amey, 1979, p. 118). Secondly, cybernetics is not restricted to the study of closed systems, as the definitions given earlier clearly indicate. However the wider issues raised in the study of open systems will be discussed in the context of GST, but before leaving the cybernetic literature we must consider the writer who has made the greatest use of cybernetics in the study of management, Stafford Beer.

The contribution of Stafford Beer

Stafford Beer has been the leading exponent of the application of cybernetics to management and has written a series of books on the topic (Beer, 1959, 1966, 1972, 1975). In these he has stressed the holistic nature of cybernetics and the power of 'black box' approaches. This has led him to make extensive use of organic analogies which are justified only in a reductionist manner. That is, by arguing that all control models are recursive in nature and by noting that the individual human being will form one level of analysis he concludes that because the human being is controlled by his nervous system, this is an appropriate model for other levels of analysis. The model thus derived is then applied in a normative manner.

To Beer cybernetics is concerned with 'exceedingly complex, and probabilistic systems of homeostatic character' (1959, p. 23). The holistic nature of cybernetic systems is such that he argues that 'it is characteristic of a cybernetic system that one can hardly discuss it with any meaning at all except as a whole organism'. Although he briefly questions the early use of biological models of industrial behaviour, he argues that the definition of what is included in a 'system' is arbitrary (or, at least, selected by the analyst). This is true, but it is equally true that any model of a real-world system is imperfect, and will produce results conditioned by its imperfections.

Three main approaches are identified by Beer. First, the issue of control of a self-regulating system is dealt with by the concept of feedback. The most economical control process is argued to be where the very act of going out of control automatically instigates a compensating control action (e.g. the Watt's governor). Secondly, the fact that organisational systems are not deterministic is dealt with by assuming they are probabilistic and amenable to statistical approaches, the most developed of which is information theory (although it is notable in that it quantifies the value of information quite independently of the values of the user). Finally the extreme complexity of systems is dealt with by the concept of the black box.

There is no doubt that many devices constructed on cybernetic principles show a capacity for adaptation and learning, at least of Bateson's (1973) first type. However they usually involve highly repetitive tasks and limited changes in their operating environments; within these constraints they work incredibly well, so that simple mechanical devices display behaviour usually considered the prerogative of sentient beings. It is therefore likely that the first main impact of the cybernetic methodology will be on repetitive tasks, i.e. what Anthony would describe as operational control. To the extent that management control depends upon the appreciation of unique characteristics of a situation and upon value judgements, it has less to offer.

However Beer would not doubt disagree with this conclusion and his book *Brain of the Firm* represents an attempt to apply a cybernetic model to the process of management control. The model chosen is based on the mechanisms observed in the operation of the human nervous system. It is regarded as appropriate for the design of management control systems since the object of an MCS is seen as to preserve the continued viability of the enterprise; the object of the central nervous system is to preserve the viability of the organism. From this neuro-physiological model, he identifies five levels of control, labelled Systems 1 to 5. Systems 1 to 3 are concerned with the regulation of internal stability, System 4 with the maintenance of dynamic equilibrium with the external world and System 5 with the self-conscious determination of goals. The interactions between these systems are modelled directly from the neuro-physiological analogy and are then interpreted in terms of managerial situations.

The presentation of Beer's work is essentially intuitive rather than carefully argued. There is much stimulating material contained within it, but it is difficult to assess how much derives from the models used. More seriously, most of the examples used depend upon the collection and analysis of time-series of data, whereas much information of use to organisations may be of a rudimentary and ephemeral nature. In essence, the operation of a cybernetic control system is dependent upon monitoring actual results and then reacting, despite a disclaimer that although 'most organisations are directed with the driver's eyes fixed on the rear view mirror' the construction of appropriate Systems 4 and 5 will avoid this defect.

Systems 4 and 5 are thus concerned with anticipatory control, based upon predictive models constructed from and validated by past experience, appropriately recorded and identified. Although the database approach is rejected as unmanageable, it is not clear how the required information is to be collected, filtered and stored. Indeed his concept of an organisational control centre (based on a cross between a Second World War War Room and Mission Control at NASA), using graphic displays generated by hybrid digital-analogue computers is absolutely dependent upon the construction of appropriate predictive models. As presented, it is feasible only if computerised methods of model construction can be devised. The nearest model so far available of this type is perhaps the Box-Jenkins adaptive forecasting model which can be used to select an appropriate formal model for a given time-series of data. Even so, the methodology still requires a considerable amount of human judgement in interpreting results and is in no sense a fully automated procedure, although current advances in computer hardware, and much more importantly, computer software may begin to make such systems a possibility for the future.

Conclusions

The standard concepts of the cybernetic literature do not have such a straightforward application to the issue of organisational control as some presentations of them seem to imply. However they do provide a language in which the central issues of the design of management control systems may be expressed. Their particular contribution is to suggest that managerial decision-making behaviour can be divided into categories on two major dimensions, namely:

1. the extent to which actions are selected on the basis of goal achievement as distinct from constraint avoidance.
2. the relative importance of feedback mechanisms of error-reduction to feedforward mechanisms of error-avoidance.

The former dimension may assist in the resolution of some of the problems associated with the concept of organisational goals and the latter stresses the importance of predictive models in management control systems. However, as organisations are open rather than closed systems, the cybernetic concentration of the analysis of closed systems does not produce many applicable findings. Although cybernetics has included open systems in the remit, much of the work undertaken has been under the umbrella title of systems theory, and it is to this that we now turn.

THE SYSTEMS APPROACH

The idea of a general theory of systems

The central concept of systems thinking is that of a 'system' itself. That is, the systems approach stresses the point of view that seeks to explain behaviour by means of studying the interrelationship of parts rather than by the nature of the parts themselves. It is thus essentially holistic in nature, in contrast to the reductionist approach of much scientific activity. This point of view is well put by Checkland (1972) when he writes:

> The systems movement (and any other term would imply a structure or unity of outlook that does not exist) . . . represents an attempt to be holistic, and to find out the consequences of being holistic, in any area of endeavour. The only unifying element is the notion 'system', and this is the movement's paradigm, in Kuhn's sense . . . The systems movement believes that the concept 'system' can provide a source of explanations of many different kinds of observed phenomena – which are beyond the reach of reductionist science.

This approach to systems analysis stresses the importance of *emergent* properties, that is to say, properties which are characteristic of the level of complexity being studied and which do not have meaning at lower levels; such properties are possessed by the system but not by its parts. An example from a physical system would be the concept of temperature which is a property of an assembly of molecules, but has no meaning in relation to a single molecule. However it is not always clear in what sense the holism advocated by systems thinkers is intended, although it is often contrasted with the alleged reductionism of much scientific method. Phillips (1977) produces a useful classification that throws some light on this comparison. He distinguishes between Holism 3 which states that it is necessary to have terms referring to wholes and their properties and Holism 2 which states that a whole, even after it is studied, cannot be explained in terms of its parts. Holism 3 would be quite acceptable to supporters of the analytic method and of reductionism whereas Holism 2 would be opposed by them. It is not always clear whether supporters of systems theory are advocating Holism 3 as a matter of expedience or Holism 2 as a matter of principle, although the latter seems more general. Further, Phillips put forward a definition of Holism 1, or organicism, which has five theses opposed *in toto* by those who support the analytic method, although individual organic theses may be accepted by them. These five theses are:

1) The analytic approach, as typified by the physico-chemical sciences, proves inadequate when applied to certain cases – for example, to a biological organism, to society, or even to reality as a whole.
2) The whole is more than the sum of its parts.
3) The whole determines the nature of its parts.
4) The parts cannot be understood in isolation from the whole.
5) The parts are dynamically inter-related or interdependent.

However it is not necessary to accept Holism 1 or even Holism 2 to be convinced that systems thinking may represent a valuable approach. It is sufficient to believe, as a matter of expediency, that the behaviour of many systems can be usefully explained in terms of the organisation and interrelationship of their parts even if it subsequently proves possible to explain that behaviour purely in terms of the properties of the parts themselves.[2] The conclusion that the approach has the potential to be valuable in the study of management control systems seems inescapable, for such systems are highly complex and interconnected, involved with the coordination of human activities and concerned with the overall activities of the organisation. It is therefore of great interest to explore whether the methods of systems thinking do in fact prove to be of benefit to the study of management control.

The gathering together of a body of knowledge concerning the behaviour of systems in general, has proceeded under the title of general systems theory (GST) and was associated with the founding in the mid-fifties of what is now the Society for General Systems Research by L. Bertalanffy, K. E. Boulding, R. W. Gerard and A. Rapoport. The aims of GST were to be (Bertalanffy, 1968):

1. To investigate the isomorphy of concepts, laws and models in various fields, and to help in useful transfers from one field to another.
2. To encourage the development of adequate theoretical models in areas which lack them.
3. To eliminate the duplication of theoretical effort in different fields.
4. To promote the unity of science through improving the communication between specialists.

Little progress has been made in fulfilling these aims during the subsequent 25 years, for the great generality of GST has also meant that it has little content, although 'systems movements' have developed in many disciplines. Systems ideas have become influential by becoming part of the conceptual language of a discipline, for example in organisation theory where a whole movement (socio-technical systems) has developed and the categorisation of organisations as 'open systems' is widely used. In the area of management accounting theory it is also notable that many of the theoretical articles on management accounting published in the last five years draw upon interdisciplinary sources and use cybernetics or systems theory as an integrating device.

Systems thinking is then primarily a tool for dealing with high levels of complexity, particularly with reference to systems which display adaptive and apparently goal-seeking behaviour. Lilienfeld (1978), in analysing the rise of systems thinking, states the case most strongly:

General Systems Theory represents a new world hypothesis; Stephen Pepper, who had, in 1942, described four 'equally adequate' world hypotheses – mechanism, formism, organism and contextualism – has recently added a fifth world hypothesis that he now regards as likely to be even more adequate than the others: this is selectivism based on the 'root metaphor' of a purposive, self-regulating system.

That this approach to complexity may be of value in the study of management control can perhaps be best illustrated by a definition of accounting put forward by Weick (1979a): 'Accounting is the attempt to wrest coherence and meaning out of more reality than we ordinarily deal with.' Although borrowed from a definition of art, it is a graphic portrayal of the central problem faced by accounting, and by management control more generally. Indeed, the approach to management control *via* accounting, as exemplified by Anthony (1965), can be seen as an attempt to deal with the control of a complex, interconnected human activity system by a *systematic* approach. The problems faced by such an approach, summarised in Weick's definition, can perhaps be best appreciated when one adopts a *systemic* viewpoint. Thus, accounting controls are the result of a great deal of effort being applied to organisational control by being systematic; it remains to be seen what effects will result from a similar amount of effort being applied to being systemic.

Finally it should be recognised that GST is only one part of a more general systems movement. Checkland (1979a) provides a useful map when he distinguishes the main strands in the systems movement as shown in Figure 4.2.

The distinction between 'hard' and 'soft' systems is that the former tend to be physical systems having relatively clearly defined objectives and decision-processes and having quantitative measures of performance; the latter tend to be systems including human beings, where objectives are vague and ambiguous, decision-processes that are ill-defined and possibly irrational, and, at best, only qualitative measures of performance exist. From the distinction, it appears likely that it will be the 'soft' systems approaches, characterised by the Checkland school at Lancaster, that will have most to offer the study of management control systems.

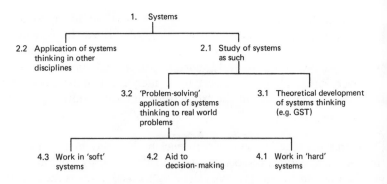

SOURCE: P. B. Checkland (1979) 'The Shape of the Systems Movement', *Journal of Applied Systems Analysis*, vol. 6.

FIGURE 4.2

Some problems with systems theory

Before proceeding to identify the potential contributions of systems methodology to the study of management control systems, it is necessary to consider some criticisms of and objectives to systems theory that have been put forward. These fall into two related parts: the criticism that systems theory carries implicit within it an authoritarian and conservative ideology; and the criticism that, in its application to human organisations, systems theory is but a variety of sociological functionalism and thus subject to all the criticisms of that position.

Systems theory as ideology

The most comprehensive critique of systems theory as ideology has been put forward by Lilienfeld (1978). In this he sets out some limitations of systems thinking, namely the arbitrary choice of system elements, the imputation of purposes of systems rather than to men, and the arbitrary nature of systems boundaries. This latter problem is also commented upon by Phillips (1977): 'in isolating a system for study the theorist is necessarily severing some inter-relationships – the very thing that his own creed tells him should not be done'. Further, social systems are seen as essentially cooperative; Lilienfeld argues that the systems analyst works within a 'framework of co-operative people who co-operate with the ends of a system'. Thus systems theory is seen as 'the latest attempt to create a world myth based on the prestige of science'; it is essentially an ideology, designed to preserve the *status quo*. Moreover, it has an authoritarian potential which 'seems striking to all but the systems theorists'.

This is a comprehensive critique, although the argument is not well sustained at all points. In his review Naughton (1979b) suggests that systems theory is not the coherent body of thought that Lilienfeld assumes but rather a 'mélange of insights, theorems, tautologies and hunches'. Nevertheless the basic criticisms are still important and have not always received recognition by practitioners. However Checkland (1979b) counters by arguing that the criticisms are more relevant to those practitioners of systems engineering and systems analysis who deal in 'hard' systems; the 'soft' systems methodology deflects such criticism by using 'systems ideas only in a *process of inquiry*, an exploration of the meanings which men attribute to what they observe'. Thus Checkland concludes that 'soft systems thinking, though he does not realise it, is the kind of social science of which Lilienfeld approves'.

However, it is important to note that the criticism has been escaped only by moving from a view of systems theory as technique to systems theory as methodology. It is arguable that all scientific method involves the use of metaphor (Morgan, 1979); what perhaps needs to be avoided is the implicit and uncritical use of organismic metaphors when dealing with social systems. Such metaphors, although widely used by systems theorists are not central to the systems methodology, and it must be assessed separately from them. Thus the central problem inherent in the application of systems thinking to human organisations lies in the imputation of objectives to the system.

'Soft' systems methodology copes with this central issue in a quite subjective manner. First, there is a stage of analysis, deliberately undertaken in non-systemic terms; here the analyst familiarises himself with the rich complexity of the situation being studied (Checkland, 1972). Secondly a root definition of the basic nature of the system or systems thought to be relevant to the problem situation is constructed. This stage is fundamental to the success of the methodology and Checkland comments:

> There will of course never be a demonstrably 'correct' root definition, only a range of possibilities, some glib and shallow, some full of insight. What is needed is a penetrating definition, derived from the richness of the analysis, which is revealing to those involved in the day-to-day workings of the systems concerned.

The third stage of the methodology is the formulation of a conceptual model of the systems being studied by constructing the minumum necessary system that can achieve the root definition and validating this model by comparing with the data gathered in the analysis stage. The crucial step in this methodology is thus the construction of a root definition, and it is this step which appears to be the most subjective.

Nevertheless, certain safeguards are built into the methodology. First, it is recognised that multiple root definitions are possible and that effort should be devoted to exposing as many of these as possible. Smyth and Checkland (1976) note that the methodology 'tries to analyse problem situations in a way that enables different *weltanschauungen* (world-images), which may be conflicting or incompatible, to be exposed and made the subject of concerned debate', and they develop a checklist designed to ensure that important aspects of a root definition are included in specific applications. Secondly, a further test of the adequacy of a root definition that is recommended is that it should be acceptable and revealing to those involved in the problem situation, although little guidance is given concerning how this might be achieved. Both safeguards are designed to facilitate what Vickers (1965) would term the process of *appreciation*, that is, the development of a rich and insightful way of viewing a real-world situation; such an appreciative judgement requires both factual or reality judgements and value judgements, and any assessment of its validity is itself an appreciative judgement.

Despite such safeguards it is inescapable that the application of the 'soft' systems methodology is dependent upon the subjective judgement of the analyst (unlike the 'hard' systems approach where objectives are taken as being externally defined). Whether this is considered to be a weakness or a strength depends upon your point of view; however it signifies a substantial shift from the methodologies of the physical and biological sciences which have traditionally been assumed to take an objective view of observable real-world phenomena. The model of scientific activity used by this type of systems approach is distinct from that used in the natural sciences.

Systems theory as sociological functionalism

Another, but related, criticism of the systems approach applied to human activity systems, is that it is in the same philosophical tradition as sociological structural functionalism. Despite the strong attacks that have been made on the functionalist position in the sociological literature, it must always be remembered that theories and methodologies must be assessed in relation to the problems they attempt to tackle. As Pratt (1978) succinctly observes:

'Functional analysis' applies to some things and not to others; and the question arises: what then is the difference between the two sorts of things? The answer, so it seems plausible to suggest, has something to do with *purposes*, or *goals*, or *'ends''* .... But the *goal* here need not be a pre-conceived purpose – it need not be an aim actually entertained by a mind.

We must therefore establish whether the systems approach is functionalist in character and, if so, what implications that has.

The 'hard' systems movement seems to be inescapably bound up with a functionalist point of view. System parts are assessed in terms of their contribution to the whole; goals are imposed upon the system, mechanisms are postulated to indicate how a part of a system fulfils its function. But is such an approach also part of the 'soft' systems approach? Prévost (1976) would argue that it is, claiming that the 'root definition' of a system is equivalent to its 'function'. Naughton (1979a) challenges this analysis by suggesting that Prévost has fundamentally misinterpreted the methodology as *an analytic perspective* rather than as *an applied, synthesising tool*. However, although 'soft' systems methodology may not be correctly categorised as sociological functionalism, in the strict sense, it is admitted that it has strong functionalist overtones. Burrell and Morgan's (1979) description of functional theories in sociology bears a strong resemblance to the description of systems methodology:

> [Theories located in the functionalist paradigm] are committed to a view of the social world which regards society as ontologically prior to man, and seek to place man and his activities within that wider social context.... Theorists located within the context of the functionalist paradigm tend to assume the standpoint of the observer and attempt to relate what *they* observe to what *they* regard as important elements in a wider social context.

However, the Checkland methodology also has marked similarities with the verstehen tradition of thought. As Berry (p.50) observes, in this school great dependency is laid upon the accuracy and honesty of observation, the sensitivity and perception of the observer and on imaginative interpretations of observations.

The importance of classifying a systems methodology as functionalism lies in establishing whether criticisms of functionalism can also be applied to the systems approach. For that purpose it is sufficient to observe that enough similarities exist for it to be worthwhile to subject the methodology to such a test. The main planks of the critique of the functionalist approach to sociology rest upon the postulate that 'society itself somehow directs its own internal organisation' (Pratt, 1978), or, failing that, an evolutionary explanation is possible. In explaining societal behaviour the former postulate seems unlikely and the latter fails by having no analogue of death for societies to explain the survival of those best suited to their circumstances. However in explaining organisational behaviour, neither objection has the same force. Human organisations demonstrably direct their own internal organisation; further they may be observed to cease to exist. Thus the critique of functionalism has less force when applied to organisations within society. Such organisations occupy a point between the extremes of: (i) designed artefacts having a clearly defined purpose; (ii) naturally occuring phenomena having no designer. This difference in emphasis is similar to that found between approaches to organisation theory which stress the formal organisation (i.e. that which is designed) and those which stress the informal organisation (i.e. that which occurs). The 'soft' systems approach may therefore be viewed as particularly appropriate for the study of human organisations, for it avoids the imputation of predefined purposes yet keeps the concept of goal-oriented behaviour.

However, in not rejecting the functionalist approach, it is important to recognise that it is sometimes advanced as being more limited than it need be. For example, Burrell and Morgan (1979) point out that organisation theorists have often mistakenly equated open systems theory with the use of an organismic analogy. There are also wider perspectives available that have been much less fully explored by organisation theorists. These involve either taking a more subjective stance and moving to an interpretive position, or being more concerned with radical change than with regulation. From the perspective of the study of control systems, the former appears to be more easily acceptable, and it may be that the 'soft' systems methodology represents a contribution in this area.[3] Thus although criticisms can be made of the methodology, none of these are damning, and represent considerations to be taken into account in its application, rather than reasons for its rejection.

The contribution of systems thinking

It is probably fair to conclude that the contribution of systems thinking to the study of management control systems (MCS) has yet to be made, although there are a number of pieces of work available that indicate some of its potential. It should also be noted that the contribution that might be made can be of different types. They may represent:

1. the adoption of a systems point of view in MCS analysis (e.g. Vickers, 1965).
2. the use of a systems approach or methodology in handling real-world MCS problems (e.g. Checkland, 1972).

3. the application of concepts developed in cybernetics or GST in the study of MCS and in the construction of a theory of MCS (e.g. Beer, 1974; Amey, 1979).
4. the use of systems ideas applied in other disciplines related to the study of MCS (i.e. the open systems and sociotechnical systems movement in organisation theory).

Each of these approaches will therefore be briefly considered and evaluated.

The systems point of view

Such a use of systems ideas in the study of MCS may involve little more than the adoption of an organisational level of analysis, and the conscious attempt to be holistic rather than reductionist in approach. The most insightful piece of work of this nature, so it seems to me, is that by Vickers (1965, 1967) who, as a practising administrator, has attempted to codify his experience into more general terms. In so doing, he explicitly takes a systems point of view and makes liberal use of cybernetic concepts. However his contribution is of most value because of the concepts that he himself introduces to the analysis; the idea of judgements – reality, value and instrumental – the concept of appreciation involving both reality and value judgements, and the overriding concept of regulation. Both sets of concepts are combined into an insightful analysis of the nature of the senior managerial work. In particular, Vickers argues for a systemic point of view which explains organisational behaviour in terms of ongoing relationships and processes rather than by the imputation of objectives.

However, it is also notable that Vicker's work has received very little attention from students of management or organisation theory. Part of the reason for this may be that it does not fit neatly into the theoretical schema used in these disciplines. For example, Naughton (1979a) comments that his work 'remains epistomologically problematic' and that 'the relationships between Vickers' views of social processes and contemporary psychological and sociological theory remain unclarified'. Nevertheless it would seem that work of this nature, based on long observation of participation in the management process, and illuminated, but not dominated, by systems concepts, is essential in the construction of sound theories of management and management control. It is noteworthy that the 'soft' systems approach has utilised some of Vickers's work.

Systems methodology

This approach treats systems theory as a methodology to be applied in handling real-world problems, rather than as a theoretical structure that will result in a general theory of the area being studied. In the study of MCS it has been argued that the so-called 'soft' systems approach is more likely to be applicable than the 'hard' systems approach. This former approach is perhaps best exemplified by the Checkland methodology discussed in some detail earlier. But although this approach may provide a means by which real-world problems may be dealt with, it does not provide any theoretical basis for the study of management control; indeed it discounts the possibility of such general theories, arguing that each problem situation is unique and must be treated on its own merits.

Such a contention raises the issue of how a methodology is to be evaluated, for different methodologies will produce different recommendations for action. Indeed it is likely that different analysts, attempting to implement the Checkland methodology, will produce different conceptual models and different recommendations for action. As a methodology is a means to an end, the appropriateness of a particular methodology can be assessed, given sufficient time, by the contributions that it makes to that end. But whereas the contribution a methodology has made to the theoretical development of a discipline can be assessed (albeit with difficulty), the contribution made by a methodology designed to handle supposedly unique situations cannot be assessed. This is an important issue, and one which does not appear to have been discussed by those involved with the methodology, save for a mention that confidence in a methodology can be built only by using it to solve problems.[4]

The application of systems concepts

Systems ideas have been in currency long enough for there to be textbooks detailing their application to specific disciplines. Indeed, the inclusion in a title of the appendage 'a systems approach' seems to have become a publishers' device for sales promotion. Nevertheless there is still a considerable gulf between the general systems concepts available and their application to the study of management control. For example, the introductory text by Schoderbek *et al.* (1975), which presents the basic concepts of systems theory and their application to management systems in a particularly lucid manner, immediately gets into difficulty when it attempts to apply the concepts to any particular topic. Admittedly, this is partly because of a 'hard' systems orientation, but nevertheless the conclusions seem disappointingly diffuse and vague after the initial excitement offered by the original concepts.

One of the more recent attempts to utilise cybernetic and systems concepts in the study of MCS is Amey's (1979) analysis of budget planning and control systems. In this, he spends a considerable amount of time in a wide-ranging review of ideas of control (which is well worth reading as an introduction to the subject), but the application of these concepts to budgetary systems produces little of interest. This is again partly due to a tendency to emphasise 'hard' systems concepts; as one reviewer (McCosh, 1980) put it:

> It has a lot to do with cybernetic mathematics, and with mathematical statements of control theory, but these are quite different topics [to budgetary planning and control systems], which do not have any behavioural, organisational, forensic, strategic or political elements.

There thus seems to be considerable difficulty in applying general systems concepts to the specific area of MCS in a way that is either practically useful or which contributes to the theoretical development of the subject. One of the major reasons for this difficulty is the orientation of much systems thinking to 'hard' systems, rather than to the analysis of human activity systems.

Systems ideas in other disciplines

Finally, it is worthwhile to consider whether there have been any fruitful applications of systems ideas in other disciplines related to MCS, particularly in the social sciences. The obvious candidate for consideration here is the use of open systems ideas in organisation theory, although it should be noted that much that goes under the title of social systems theory are systems theories in name only (Burrell and Morgan, 1979). We will therefore limit consideration to open systems approaches which include the socio-technical systems movement (Trist and Bamforth, 1951; Miller and Rice, 1967), the open systems approach of Katz and Kahn (1966), and the contingency theories initiated by Lawrence and Lorsch (1967b), and are perhaps best summarised in Thompson (1967).

It is notable that all the open systems theories considered here adopt, explicitly or implicitly, an organismic analogy, utilising concepts such as survival, functional attributes related to this end such as differentiation and integration, and purposive rationality. Although many writers such as Katz and Kahn attempt to focus on organisational processes rather than structure, it is apparent that attempts to operationalise these theories rapidly move back to a traditional structural functionalist orientation. Typical subsystems identified include the strategic control subsystem, the operational subsystem, the human subsystem and the managerial subsystem within which choices have to be made. The most recent manifestation of this tradition, the contingency approach to the study of organisations, has been the leading paradigm in organisational theory during the 1970s (Child, 1977). This approach argues that in an effective organisation there will be a match between its internal structure and processes and the characteristics of its environment, and much empirical work has been conducted to explore such relationships, although the methods used have often not been as closely connected with the underlying theories as would have been desirable. Such work has also neglected other important organisational issues such as the distribution of power within organisations, as Burrell and Morgan (1979) point out:

> An organismic systems model stresses the functional unity of system parts, and views the organisation as being geared to the achievement of end states shared by the system as a whole. Functional imperatives and unity of purpose tend to dominate the analysis. Although the contingency model implicitly identifies power as a variable, it does not address it in any specific fashion. To do so in a meaningful sense involves a shift in perspective away from the bonds of social systems theory.

It would thus be useful to consider open systems approaches which do not involve use of an organismic analogy, but none seem to exist, although Pondy and Mitroff (1979) attempt to develop an approach beyond that of current open systems theory.

The work on contingency theories of organisation was applied to the study of management control systems in the last five years by way of contingency theories of management accounting. These sought to identify the circumstances under which specific features of a management accounting and control system were appropriate. To date much of this work has been solely of a theoretical nature, and the empirical work that has been conducted (e.g. Bruns and Waterhouse, 1975; Hayes, 1977), suffers from methodological problems. In particular, little consideration has been given to a criterion of organisational effectiveness that permits appropriate choices to be made. (Otley, 1980, gives a fuller critique.)

Thus, although work in related areas is being carried out in the systems tradition, there are few results that give significant insight into the design and operation of management control systems. There is however a danger of management control theorists taking on board results from other disciplines that are less satisfactory than some presentations of them would suggest.

CONCLUSIONS

The application of systems thinking and cybernetics to the study of management control systems raises more questions than it answers. Yet the very fact that these approaches raise questions may be valuable in itself for a field of study that appears to be pre-paradigmic in its development. The discipline that has played the greatest role in the development of management control has been that of accounting, pioneered by Anthony; and it has been argued that accounting is a systematic approach *par exellence*. It would therefore seem that the systemic approach of systems thinkers can provide a valuable counter-vailing force in developing a theory of management control.

Yet it must be admitted that much systems thinking and cybernetics is frankly inappropriate to the design of human activity systems, as it stems from the study of physical or 'hard' systems. Here goals can be taken as given and systems parts engineered to fit into some overall design. This is not so in social systems, and it is disturbing to note the emphasis that has been laid on biological analogies in studying human organisations. The only systems approach that has specifically faced the methodological and conceptual problems in the study of organisa-tions – the 'soft' systems approach – has deliberately eschewed the development of general theories in favour of the construction of a methodology with which to deal with supposedly unique cases. Despite the practical experience that has been used in developing this methodology, it is by no means obvious how it can be assessed, verified or tested.

It is thus the potential of the systems movement for contributing to management control theory that is being put forward, rather than any great achievement to date. To fulfil this potential will require the extension of 'soft' systems approaches into the development of theories of management control – albeit partial theories, and preferably theories based on close observation of actual organisations. In so doing, it is vital that so-called 'principles' of systems control are not transferred inappropriately from other types of system to management control systems. Lloyd Amey (1979) puts it quite clearly:

> Furthermore, principles formulated for certain kinds of systems (e.g. physical, chemical, biological) are freely extended by many writers to other kinds of system (social systems, for example) without making the modifications or re-interpretations which are inevitably necessary.

Anderton (1978) makes a similar point with regard to the development of methodological approaches, but which also applies to theory construction:

> The second level [of the professional development of systems activity] aims at a meta-theory: its topic is *the transfers* [*of concepts*] *themselves, their validity, the scope and limit of the general models they employ.* My reading of these pieces of work, for example, suggests two critical distinctions which recur. One is between living and non-living systems. The second is between these systems which contain a model of their situation, and those which do not .... The four systems which result from this 2 × 2 typology may perhaps have fundamentally different logics which it is important to understand when making transfers.

A social system evidently contains living components, each of which contains a model of its own behaviour, although it may be argued that such a system of sentient subsystems is itself essentially different from its constituent parts. Further, in the study of organisational control, the system environment is itself complex, as noted by Buckley (1968): 'The environment of the enterprise is largely composed of other equally groping, loose-limit, more or less flexible, illusion-ridden, adaptive organisations.' Whilst findings about other types of system may suggest directions of study for organisational control systems, their validity in the new situation must be most carefully assessed and evaluated.

If management is an activity which involves the attempt to control situations involving greater amounts of complexity and uncertainty than we have techniques adequately to cope with, then the systems approach offers a method of studying management control which has the potential to begin to deal with some of the underlying problems. For example, it may indicate areas in which the wrong questions are being asked and in which inappropriate concepts are being adopted. It is in no sense a complete theory, but it is the nearest to the beginning of a method of developing a theory that we currently possess, and it deserves serious consideration for that reason alone.

NOTES

1. There is a close parallel between these four types of control actions and the types of learning identified by Bateson (1973). Adjustment of process inputs is a kind of zero learning; it can be made a completely programmed response to a stimulus as in a thermostat. Amendment of process objectives may also represent zero learning or perhaps more often a type of Learning I (revision of choice from a given set of alternatives) an example being the amendment of individual levels of aspiration following success or failure. Reformulation of the predictive model is also a type of Learning I in that it involves making a new choice from a previously identified set of alternatives. Finally what we have called systemic learning, involving a change in the whole process, has similarities with Learning II which involves a revision of the set of alternatives from which the choice is made.

2. Checkland (1981) has recently stated this point of view in relation to his soft systems methodology by claiming that 'systems is an epistemology (making a statement of the kind: "A certain type of knowledge may be expressed in systems language") before it is an ontology (which would make a statement of the kind: "The world *is* systemic"); and in the case of work whose concern is social reality it may never be possible to make ontological statements in systems terms.'

3. In the first attempt to identify the social theory that is inherent in soft systems methodology, Checkland (1981) uses Burrell and Morgan's (1979) typology and places it on the subjective side of the objectivity dimension whilst spanning both regulation and radical change. It is thus seen as occupying ground also covered by phenomenological sociology, hermeneutics and critical theory. The prime value seen as being incorporated by this type of systems approach is that 'continuous, never-ending learning is a good thing'.

4. Again the recent book by Checkland (1981) has addressed the issue of what kind of theory of social systems can be developed. He argues that 'social reality is the ever-changing outcome of the social process in which human beings, the product of their genetic inheritance and previous experiences, continually negotiate and re-negotiate with others their perceptions and interpretations of the world outside themselves'. It is therefore inappropriate to expect to derive laws of the kind developed in the natural sciences

and that 'no once-and-for-all substantive account of social reality is possible because there *is* no social reality to set alongside what appear to be the well-tested physical realities of the universe . . . hence the importance of methodology rather than findings, of process rather than content.'

5 Open Social Systems and Management Control

Anthony J. Berry

INTRODUCTION

A theory of organisations, known commonly as open social systems theory, is widely used as an organising framework. The elements of the basic theory are quite simple. Organisation and environment are separated by the idea of boundary, and one key focus of attention is transactions across the boundaries, whether these are exports such as goods, services, funds or human satisfactions or imports such as technology, funds, skills, goods and human resources and needs. The second focus is upon the processes through which inputs are transformed into outputs.

The elements of this model may be applied to any domain of activity. The key decision of the theoretician lies in locating the boundaries of the domain or activity, such that the transactions across the boundaries so deployed and the transformations are of interest. Typically organisation theorists adopt the legal definition of an organisation, or a unique processing element (e.g. a production plant or department) as a focus for examination.

There has been a slightly regrettable tradition of locating ideas of complexity within and at the boundaries of a system while locating uncertainty as a characteristic of the environment creating a somewhat false sense of quasi-stability in the transformation processes. In a similar manner internal order is presumed to be of necessity a matter of goal congruence through planning – or the alignment of subsystem behaviour in relation to the loss function of the corporate entity (Bower, 1970).

The theory of open social systems is explicitly adopted by Katz and Kahn in the second edition of *The Social Psychology of Organisations*

(1978). The next part of this chapter takes their exposition as a point of departure for tracing ideas of control in the open social systems theory.

KATZ AND KAHN

'In some respects open-system theory is not a theory at all': that is, it cannot be used for prediction. 'Open-system theory is rather a framework, a meta-theory.' For these authors it is an organising frame of reference from which, in some unspecified way, we might deduce or maybe conjecture a basis for hypothesis generation.

'Open-system theory is an approach and a conceptual language for understanding and describing many kinds and levels of phenomena.' The open-system approach and the major concepts of open-system theory are applicable to any dynamic recurring process, any cyclical pattern of events that occurs in some larger context.

Before discussing some more detailed issues of control in relation to this theory we note two broader issues: first, the closed nature of open systems models; and secondly, the methodological context of the theory.

Open systems theorists build closed models to account for the organisation–environment linkage. This closedness implies that control may be exercised either by the environment upon the organisation or vice versa. Often this idea of control is expressed by a recognition of the organisation's dependence upon an environment for its survival. This in turn leads to an idea of control as exchanges at the boundaries, a theme that will appear later in the discussion.

Open social system theory is structural functional in approach. In this sense control as an idea is embedded in the concepts of processes through which goals might be achieved and the system maintained and developed. Katz and Kahn present a view of 'functioning' of an open system and write, 'To locate a system, to specify its functions and to understand them therefore, requires that this cyclical energic process be identified and traced. An open system is located by its boundaries for the selective reception of inputs . . .', but clearly 'system' here is not what is observable – it is what is observed and described.

Katz and Kahn choose not to address the problem of assumed universal applicability of open system theory and state

Our view is that theoretical progress can best be made by attempting instead to adapt the open system model to each genotypic category of phenomena (which rather assumes an appropriate classification) to which it (the theory) is to be applied (rather as if it were a microscope for observation) adding specification to the meta theoretical framework in order to maximise its explanatory power for the population category under study ... We have attempted such a theory for human organisations.

THE THEORY APPLIED TO HUMAN ORGANISATIONS

'Human organisations lack structure in the anatomical sense, land and buildings are trappings; its members come and go. Yet it has structure; membership is not accidental and the behaviour of members is not random.' 'Social organisations as contrived systems are sets of patterned behavioural events'; surely what is meant by the authors is that we can contrive an explanation of patterned behavioural events through the organising principles of open systems theory. There is in most of the open systems theory a general and enduring confusion between the phenomena which are observed (our accounting system) and the theoretical structures which we use to observe, describe and attempt to explain them (the open systems theory). Katz and Kahn point to one unique element in open systems: 'the approach reminds us that organisational inputs are neither constant nor guaranteed. A human organisation endures only so long as people are induced to provide those inputs, including membership and role performance.'

Katz and Kahn take up the problem of conceptualising inputs into the system; they suggest two – *Production* inputs to the accomplishment of work and *Maintenance* which are the energic and informational contributions necessary to hold the people in the system and persuade them to carry out their activities as members of the systems. These authors then take an approach from role and role theory to explain how patterns of behaviour persist; 'the organisation is a structure of roles', though these may change. But clearly this is as yet inadequate as a basis for explanation, so the concept of authority is introduced to explain the patterns of persisting behaviour – 'The formulation of rules and sanctions of rewards and punishments constitute the authority structure of an organisation.' It follows that such authority is accepted because it is legitimate; however they note, 'increasingly in contemporary organisations the values emhasise an ethic [of authority] from below deriving its tone from special competence or divine revelation. Legitimacy ... thus takes on the pragmatic meaning of observing traffic rules rather than obeying a moral imperative.'

In this latter sense authority as legitimate is undermined as the explanation of persisting phenomena. We are rather pushed back to an inducement–contributions ethic, a trading culture, which is a move from the holistic concept of the system to an atomised explanation for persisting behaviour. This shift does connect with the idea, expressed earlier, of control as exchanges at the boundaries. Where there is no settled value, or theoretical injunction, to regulate behaviour, then the idea of a trading culture is needed in order to pass the question of criteria for exchange back to the actors in the system.

SUBSYSTEMS

Functional subsystems may be specified in relation to the maintenance of the structure (socialising of new members, rule enforcement) and obtaining environmental support; adapting to environmental change (R and D planning) coordinating and controlling activities, managerial–conflict resolution, presumably based upon power. It is not clear how these subsystems are related to either the system or to each other. It seems that each is rather arbitrary.

'The dynamics of the organisation as a whole emphasise survival, growth and maximisation', state Katz and Kahn, which seems more of an assertion of hope than an empirical assessment of an organisation.

The switch, quite often made by Katz and Kahn, from the simple construct of open social systems theory to an operationalisation of the dynamics of organisation is confusing. What they seem to do is to attempt to hold together incommensurable theories (open-social system and psychodynamic theory) by a process of projective imagination, which enables them to avoid specifying their ideological standpoint.

'*Models of authority*' discussed by Katz and Kahn are based upon the typology of Etzioni (1961):

Coercive : the issue here is power and compliance with those wielding power

Instrumental : responsiveness of individuals to actual incentives, in exchange for which contributions

		may be given
Normative	:	authority here is held by individuals which
		produces internalised motivation.

These three types of authority are presumably present in any organisation, but with more apparent emphasis on any one of them.

PROCESS IN SYSTEMS

Processes which are recognised are:

Energy transformation, at direct level (physical)
   and at a symbolic level – meaning information, communication

and 'The authority structure is nothing more than the pattern of such legitimised and influential communicative acts' and such acts are acts of leadership in that it depends (i.e. influence via authority) upon authority of expertise and personal affiliation or affinity.

RULES AND REGULATIONS

The outcome of leadership acts is policy which is defined by Katz and Kahn as 'an abstraction or generalisation about organisational structure. A proposed policy describes some acts of transactions . . .' 'Policy' is clearly a statement of desired action rather than an interpretative analysis and holding of internal and external uncertainty. Katz and Kahn's view of policy is essentially that of a set of administrative guideliness.

Inevitably in this structural–functional perspective conflict is seen as dysfunctional; 'a category of behaviour in which two or more parties attempt to block, damage or incapacitate each other'. Conflict is not seen as a property of the exchange processes at differentiated parts of the organisation–environment linkage, or as a property of the structure role–relationship or as a stimulus to reconciling the consequences of the terms of exchanges.

The last point raised by Katz and Kahn relates to organisational effectiveness, which is put in a maximising frame of reference, which given the implicit reification of the organisation is inevitable but not necessary.

COMMENTARY

This brief review of the Katz and Kahn exposition of open system theory (perhaps through my special filters of prejudice and awareness) is of interest to us because the issue of management control is more implicit than explicit. Let us see then if we can tease out some of the ideas about control in their approach. Given a structural functional orientation then control or regulation of the system is embedded in the structure in the nexus of roles and the behaviour of role incumbents. Through structure and role in relation to tasks, inputs are transformed into outputs which are exchanged to energise the system. It is legitimised authority which holds the members in role. The thrust here is to explain persisting behaviour in terms of its function in maintenance and goal achievement – that is good (functional) controls get correct (functional) outputs. These controls need not be the same for each organisation, e.g. the typology of authority implies control through power and coercion, control through exchange or control through shared norms.

A second strand of control is that of policy, which here is administrative guidelines, rules, etc. to guide behaviour in relation to objectives.

A third strand of control is maintenance of the structure of role behaviour in accordance with policy (law and order is the theme here).

A fourth strand of control is adapting to environmental change (with change and uncertainty lying outside rather than inside).

A fifth strand of control is coordinating and controlling in relation to established programmes of tasks.

A sixth strand of control is managerial conflict resolution – usually by superordinate authority.

A seventh strand of control is that of ensuring the flow of information necessary to hold to programmes and also to hold people in roles.

The common theme is that 'management control' as a construct in the theory of open social systems is necessary for the functioning of the system as construed by the theory. Whether the actors in the phenomena would agree is quite another matter, even at the level of traffic rules.

The problem of thinking about managing an 'open system' requires some attention to the discretion of persons. Essentially Etzioni's typology is used to reintroduce choice by individual actors in an otherwise unpeopled set of roles. Typically management theorists do not focus upon either the agencies of repression (coercive organisations) or with the institutions such as monasteries (normative organisations) but mostly with organisations which produce outputs some of which are distributed through external markets by price or by administrative allocation.

The difficulty here is that the rapid introduction of economic concepts such as value, cost, benefit, revenue and the like, mask a process of simplification (not variety reduction – it is more variety-ignoring). And further, this process of simplification translated into accounting measures would lead to a substantial fragmentation of the general problem of organisational control. This tradition has had a tendency to avoid the problem of authority and to concentrate upon the linkage of one element of the environment – financial markets. From these strands it is clear that a lot of behavioural research would focus upon the role incumbent's effect upon role-specified financial information and tasks as a kind of pathology or dysfunction.

Control in Katz and Kahn's exposition of open system theory is handled at two distinct levels. First, by shifting to a closed model to explain environment effects but then embodying control in exchanges. Secondly by the creation of constraints of role systems with an explicit authority structure to explain the regulation and persisting patterns of behaviour.

The central thrust is structural functional with controls being recognised as that which contributes to the functions (externally and internally legitimised). What these controls might actually be is not made clear. Equally the definitions of function in terms of controls is possible.

In contrast to the approach of Katz and Kahn, the Tavistock school eschew the problem of theoretical incommensurability and address open social systems from the standpoint of the concepts sentience, task, authority and the idea of boundary regulation (Miller and Rice, 1967). Control herein is the regulation of the system to achieve its primary task, by which is meant that task which serves to sustain the organisation. Miller and Rice approach the question of authority through an examination of the authority given and taken between persons in role. In this sense authority is an empirical and an experiential phenomenon to be examined in relation to the maintenance of boundaries appropriate to task and sentience. In this tradition, Menzies (1970) observed that the structures of roles are not simply a matter of task performance but emerge from the sentience also.

This latter idea, the emergence of control as a phenomenon to be studied through open social systems theory, is similar to the idea of control as an emergent phenomena. Homans quotes Mary Parker Follett (1956): 'As every living process is subject to its own authority, that is, the authority evolved by or in the process itself, so social control is generated by the process itself.'

Thus we arrive at the central issue in control related to open social systems theory. Is control a property of the system or is it imposed upon the system by either environment or by a function called management? The way in which this question is approached critically affects the approach which scholars would take to the phenomena of control and regulation in organisations. Katz and Kahn appear to me to take the second strand approach, in common with many more traditional management theorists and almost all management accounting and finance theorists. This second approach leads to questions of the form: How is it that these controls don't work in the required way? Miller and Rice take the first approach, an approach which directs attention to the research question: How is this organisation regulated? It is true that such a question needs to be operationalised. It is the task of future work to discover how the concepts of financial or management control can be related to this approach to regulation.

6 Organisational Design and Management Control

Trevor M. Hopper and Anthony J. Berry

Traditionally the management control literature concentrates its attention on formal systems and takes the view that their creation follows the design of organisations. The view of this chapter, however, is that management control is an interactive and often over-lapping process with that of organisation design, which frequently involves the manipulation of social processes. Whilst this approach may be unexceptional from the perspective of organisation theory, this chapter proceeds to a discussion of how management control procedures and organisation design may be related. This is done by tracing the development of organisation design theories and showing how each advance had implications for management control. The final section of this chapter critically examines contingency theory and questions its treatment of effectiveness and its depiction of decision-making within organisations.

INTRODUCTION

Organisation theory is concerned with explaining and describing phenomena of, and related to, organisations. Scholars currently approach this study from a number of viewpoints, depending on the phenomena they seek to explain and the degree to which they are able to isolate such phenomena for explanation. Lupton (1966) identifies three distinct but overlapping approaches to the study of internal problems of organisation – first, the factors which shape the structure of organisations and the roles within them (Gouldner, 1955; Weber, 1947); secondly the problems of the individual human satisfaction and the quest for efficiency (human relations school); thirdly, the attempt to establish general principles for designing formal organisations (Fayol, 1949; Urwick, 1947). Following from experiences with these three older approaches, other scholars have established separate approaches; the study of decision-making, conflict and goal formation (Cyert and March, 1963), the influence of technology (Woodward, 1965), and the influence of the general character of the environment (Chandler, 1962; Lawrence and Lorsch, 1967b; Rice, 1963; Burns and Stalker, 1961).

The relationship between organisation theory and the design of organisations is problematic for there is no overarching theory of organisations which specifies all the requisite variables and their inter-relationships. Hence the organisational designer, like other designers, must draw from his background of knowledge and experience and fuse disparate elements through insight and creativity. It is arguable that all organisation theory is relevant to the design of organisations, not as a process of naive prescription, but as part of a dialectic between design, analysis and a synthesis of experience. Lupton (1966) details the steps that might be followed, adding here, as elsewhere a cautionary note in respect to structural and psychological universalism. The task is to establish the 'best' organisation to achieve the varied goals of participants. Thus organisation design is an instrumental activity, though not necessarily the instrument of one group in the organisation. Consequently organisation design is defined in a modified version of Khandwalla (1977) as being concerned with how the elements of organisation structure, processes and its environment can be interrelated in order to achieve effectively and efficiently the objectives of the designers.

Management control has been defined in a number of ways. For many it is still the design of formal feedback systems. Anthony (1965), by defining it as: 'the process by which managers assure that resources are obtained and used effectively and efficiently in the accomplishment of the organisation's goals', broadened its meaning considerably. By locating management control in a hierarchy between strategic and operational control, Anthony was able to put aside the problems of goals and implementation. A broader typology of management control, perhaps more appropriately termed organisation control, would include Anthony's strategic management and operational controls. A full description of organisational control procedures must include an analysis of those procedures which act to maintain organisational viability through goal achievement, those concerned with the integration and coordination of differentiated parts, and those which promote adaptation to both internal and external change (Otley and Berry, 1980). If this approach to control is compared with that previously given for organisation design then it is difficult to distinguish the subject-matter of each, as organisation design is about processes of organisational control. This identity is not uncommon, for control has been the central theme of recent texts on organisation theory (Salaman, 1979; Clegg and Dunkerley, 1980).

A major difficulty in reconciling much of the management control literature to organisational design literature is that the former has been based on economic and accounting paradigms with their stress upon profitability, profit, contribution and cost centres; together with short-term financial planning, reporting and performance evaluation. These are also essentially normative constructs. Organisation design tends to be based upon ideas of social systems, social psychology and a considerable experimental and empirical tradition with control viewed as an emergent phenomenon (Homans, 1951).[1]

A point of commonality between management control and organisation design is that systems theory has been utilised extensively in both areas, possibly due to its attention to variety, interdependence and levels of analysis.

It is possible, for convenience of explanation, to distinguish between the horizontal and vertical dimensions of control systems. The horizontal dimension of systems is taken as the throughput, i.e. the process whereby inputs are transformed into outputs. The vertical dimension is the control system regulating the throughput and its relationship to the environment and includes as its elements, objectives, standards, a discriminator, feedback, sensor and decision-maker.

With respect to the horizontal dimension, management control literature has concentrated largely on output controls. This chapter will argue *inter alia* that alternative strategies of control can exist and that input, behaviour and environmental controls can be complementary to, or substitutes for output controls, and that in some instances control by outputs may be impossible, superfluous or possibly dysfunctional. Until we know more about organisational control generally, then design prescriptions for a single type of control will be difficult, as Otley (1980) notes with respect to management accounting.

The contemporary analysis of the vertical dimension of management control systems has been similarly partial, with an overconcentration on formal feedback mechanisms which assume that goals are given and are non-problematical. The latter part of this chapter attempts to indicate that this is often not the case.

Stated formal goals may only be an outdated description of the goals of the dominant coalition or represent managerial attempts to legitimise or rationalise their actions. Often informal and politically amended goals are more useful in understanding decisions and actions than are formal goals. Thus if one seeks to design control systems which serve the goals of participants in organisations then it may be necessary to include the planning and goal-formation processes within the design remit. Such an inclusion would entail the study of social and political processes.

Control procedures are designed with attention to the use of data so provided in decision-making. However, much information used in decisions is derived not from formal procedures but from social inter-action (similar to the idea of emergent control). Given rapid change and uncertainty this is inevitable. In this sense the task of the systems designer would include an examination of how the informal processes generate and evaluate information and constrain behaviour and how these might be facilitated. Finally, as will be examined, rewards may be so integral to control that they need to be treated as an additional vertical element of control rather than as an external means of reinforcement.

These issues are addressed by initially tracing the development of organisation theories and their relevance to conceptions of control and latterly to illustrate how contemporary concerns in the literature may assist further development of control theory and the design of management control procedures.

EVOLUTION OF THEORIES OF CONTROL

Detailed study of organisation structures and formal planning and feedback mechanisms is essentially a twentieth-century phenomenon. Prior to this control tended to be perceived as being achieved by owner entrepreneurs exercising personal centralised authority, reinforced by close personal supervision (Pollard, 1965). Such processes were a black box with respect to formal knowledge, being seen as a consequence of the unique attributes and intuitive flair of each proprie-tor. Figure 6.1 traces these relationships whereby control (meaning greater economic efficiency) is achieved by centralised and persona-lised supervision of the transformation process.

Personal attributes of   Centralised authority
the proprietor   →   and close personal   →   Efficiency
                          supervision

FIGURE 6.1   *Entrepreneurial control*

As Ouchi (1977) indicates, under certain circumstances, particularly small and simple firms, such a form of control may be effective. For example, formal management accounting systems tend not to be widely in evidence in many small companies (Duck, 1971). However, the absence of a formal system may not indicate an absence of control. The centralised decision-maker copes with the planning and control processes personally without any need of formal procedures.

THE BUREAUCRATISATION OF CONTROL

In contrast, the management literature which evolved from the turn of the century, often described as Classical, emphasised the achievement of efficiency through professional managers creating formal structures of control.

Senior Management   →   Formal Structure   →   Efficiency

FIGURE 6.2   *Bureaucratic control*

This process, illustrated in Figure 6.2, was an attempt to control through bureaucracy in order to cope with the larger and more complex organisations which grew up with technological economies of scale (Littler, 1978). There were perhaps two complementary schools of thought; one emphasising direct supervision, e.g. Fayol (1949), Urwick (1947); the other prescribing standardisation of work, e.g. Taylor (1947) and Weber, (1947): thus, 'for about half of this century organisation structure meant a set of official standardised work relationships built around a tight system of formal authority' (Mintzberg, 1979, p. 10).

Some of the Classical prescriptions regarding organisation structure are detailed in Table 6.1. Whilst such writers often do not employ identical dimensions and measures for structure, the table is probably representative of their efforts and owes much to similar derivations by the Aston Group (Pugh and Hickson, 1976).

TABLE 6.1   *Elements of organisation structure*

Element	Description	Classical prescription
1. Role specialisation	Horizontal and vertical division of labour	Horizontal – extensive Vertical – commended to a degree
2. Role formalisation	Specification of tasks by formal rules and written documents	Recommended
3. Role standardisation	Predetermining activities	Recommended
4. Organisational shape	Spans of control No. of hierarchical levels (same as vertical division of labour)	Narrow (at managerial levels) Ambiguous
5. Grouping	How roles are assigned to departments, departments to divisions, e.g. by product, geographical areas	Functional grouping
6. Centralisation	Extent to which decision-making is concentrated at the apex of the organisation	Centralisation

The implicit models of control in Table 6.1 and Figure 6.1 are similar in that both prescribe centralised authority and communication. The differences lie in how this centralised control is exercised. If there is extensive specialisation of labour, as advocated by the Classicists, then personal centralised control becomes difficult due to its demands upon the decision-maker. Instead centralised control might be retained in three ways: programming behaviour formally, delegating responsibility for behavioural control, control by output regulation. Such forms of control require considerable preplanning, often undertaken by staff specialists acting as agents for senior management. The role standardisation and formalisation referred to in Table 6.1 may occur in two ways. Sometimes expected behaviour may be specified in advance by documentation (hereafter referred to as impersonal behaviour control). More often perhaps, such documentation will not detail means, but ends (output controls). The latter enables higher management to control by formal feedback mechanisms based upon a management by exception principle. It is in this area of output controls that conventional management control has made its greatest contribution, e.g. quality controls, budgets.[2]

Two broad sets of research have severely criticised such conceptions of control. First, there are those who have tested whether the prescribed elements of organisation structure are a unitary concept related to efficiency. These are discussed in the section on contingencies. Secondly, researchers working at the social psychological level have found that the mechanistic approach incorporated an inadequate theory of motivation and neglected important facets of interpersonal behaviour, especially regarding groups and leadership. This second strand of criticism is developed in the following section.

CONTROL AND SOCIAL PROCESSES

The Classicists' prescription of control by hierarchical formal controls reinforced by individual economic rewards was based on an individualistic and materialistic conception of motivation, that has been considerably undermined by social psychologists. As McKenna (Chapter 8) explains, individual goals are more complex and varied, but can be a source of personal identification and satisfaction, as well as being an aid to managerial decision-making and education. Further, authoritarian leadership styles may be ineffective under certain situations (Vroom and Yetton, 1973). In short, it has repeatedly been shown that much of the behaviour within organisations is shaped by emerging social standards and interaction rather than by the formal control system. Consequently an understanding of the nature of control within organisations must embrace an analysis of such social standards and interactions.

The process of attempting to influence the mode of social controls is included within the study of organisation design. For example, Galbraith (1977) designates 'the integration of the individual into the organisation' as one of his three main design areas. This is taken to consist of selection, training and designing the reward system. Galbraith concentrates on the reward system and poses a question of matching the reward system with the type of task and desired behaviour. His reward systems can be grouped into three main categories; (i) extrinsic material – rule compliance, system rewards, group wage rewards, individual economic rewards; (ii) intrinsic rewards – task involvement, goal identification; (iii) extrinsic social

rewards – leadership, group acceptance. Classes of resulting behaviour are given as 'join and remain', 'dependable role behaviour',
'effort above the minimum', 'spontaneous behaviour', 'co-operative
behaviour'. From these two dimensions a matrix is produced showing
how each class of reward reinforces or blocks each behaviour pattern.
Crudely put, the choice of reward system should be dependent upon
which sets of behaviour are deemed necessary. Thus it can be seen that
rewards are an integral element of control of personal behaviour and
that they are not restricted to the design of payment systems, but
extend to job design, the style of supervision, and the ability to
participate.

If control is being sought by means of the reward system, then
individuals may only respond as sought if the reward system is
sufficiently aligned with their goals. Consequently inappropriate
individuals may be filtered out by the selection system. Silverman and
Jones (1973) illustrate such a control mechanism in action. Alternatively, or additionally, 'acceptable' norms and values amongst
personnel may be inculcated through socialisation processes and
induction courses. For example, Edstrom and Galbraith (1977) show
how multinationals may use job rotation of key executives as a means
of propagating the organisational culture. The attempts to control
human inputs into the organisation are increasingly being recognised
as complementary to, or substitutes for, formal controls over
behaviour and outputs. These are referred to under various guises,
e.g. Perrow (1979) as 'unobtrusive controls'; Kast and Rosenzweig
(1974) as 'indirect controls' and Ouchi (1977) as control by 'ritual'.
These processes of control do not directly programme behaviour or
decisions but instead secure appropriate premises and values for
actions. However, it is increasingly being recognised as an important
possibility of control which must be considered within the design
process.

CONTINGENT THEORIES, STRUCTURES AND CONTROL STRATEGIES

When the Classicists' prescriptions regarding structure (described in
Table 6.1) were subjected to empirical testing they were not found to
be intercorrelated, nor were they related to efficiency (e.g. Blau and
Schoenherr, 1971; Pugh and Hickson, 1976; Hall, 1963; Woodward,
1965). However, researchers claimed their data indicated typologies of

structure which were associated to contingent factors, of which size, technology and the environment were the most notable.[3] This led to claims that structure was dependent upon such contingencies.

Of the three meanings associated with technology: operations, materials and knowledge; operations technology has probably not proved to be as closely associated with structure as once believed (Donaldson, 1976); materials technology has been subjected to little empirical testing; and knowledge technology has perhaps yielded the most consistent results. Knowledge technology, often referred to as task uncertainty, is frequently measured by the nature of decision-making involved in a task in relation to the number of exceptions and the nature of the search (Perrow, 1967; Lynch, 1974). When re-searched at the unit level, results have tended to be consistent and significant (Gerwin, 1979). Van de Ven and Delbecq (1976), for example, found that as task uncertainty of units increased, then internal coordination by programming and hierarchical means was substituted by horizontal communication channels and group meetings, which suggests that formal controls may be of limited use in uncertain situations, and that social or informal means may be a necessary supplement or substitute for them.

Research on the environment, despite pioneering work by Gouldner (1955) and Selznick (1949) on societal impacts upon organisations, has tended to concentrate on its technological and economic spheres, especially their complexity, rates of change, threat, diversity and unpredictability. Such measures are often related to decision-making and labelled environmental uncertainty, which has clear similarities and overlaps with those of task uncertainty. The suggestion of research to date, e.g. Lawrence and Lorsch (1967b), Duncan (1972), is that dynamic environments tend to lead to adaptation (with less formal controls) and complex and diverse environments lead to a matching complexity (with more differentiated and decentralised structures). The response to hostility is often a temporary centralisa-tion. However, given the little research to date and its methodological problems any such generalisations must be tentative (Downey and Slocum, 1975).

Child (1973) and Blau and Schoenherr (1971), both strong advocates of size as a major determinant of structure, found a strong association between greater size and increased differentiation with respect to roles, departments and the vertical hierarchy. They suggest that senior management attempt to cope with increased differentiation by decentralisation and greater role formalisation. If, as is claimed, greater size is associated with increased standardisation, then this may permit wider spans of control. However, such propositions are not universally accepted, e.g. Hall (1977).

To summarise, the contingency theorists are essentially stating that the appropriate organisational form is a product of the variety confronting the organisation. As is shown in Figure 6.3 the design problem then becomes one of choosing the correct structure, reinforced by an appropriate reward system and mode of leadership.

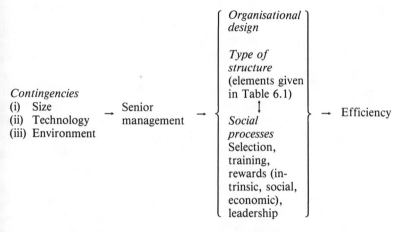

FIGURE 6.3 *Contingency approaches to control*

A major problem with such prescriptions is that they have lacked a sufficient theoretical basis. Correlations have often been taken to imply causality. Further, if social processes are taken to be part of the design problem, then design of social processes needs to be related to structure and other contingent variables. Galbraith (1977) provides such a theoretical basis, as his text incorporates a contingency analysis of organisation design which encompasses structural and social psychological factors underpinned by the decision theory of the Carnegie School. The design problem is depicted as a search for coherence or a fit between three areas: (i) strategy, the choice of domain and objectives and goals; (ii) the organising mode; (iii) the integration of individuals. The first area will be discussed later under environmental management. The last two areas correspond to what we have called structure and process respectively. Galbraith sees these as the two principal means of coordinating activities, which, in turn, is seen as one of the two major tasks of management (the other being choice of domain). The form of coordination used is described as being dependent upon the degree of uncertainty confronting senior management. Uncertainty is defined by Galbraith as 'the difference between the amount of information required to perform a task and the amount of information possessed by the organisation'. (This definition seems to be a definition of ignorance. Uncertainty must be a question of what it is possible to know.)[4] The amount of information required is a product of: (i) the level of performance sought; (ii) the amount of division of labour within the organisation, which is closely related to its size; (iii) the diversity of goals associated with output categories, which is a consequence of its environment. The greater the uncertainty the more information must be processed, which creates a situation of overload upon management who must resolve this by reducing the number of exceptions referred to them. The initial response will be to move from personalised and centralised control to a form of control exercised through a hierarchy of authority (vertical specialisation of labour, Table 6.1). Subsequent responses will be instituting rules and procedures (role formalisation); planning and goal-setting which utilises staff specialists in functional departments, and incorporates a degree of centralisation and output control. Exceptions may also be further reduced by narrowing spans of control. When these possibilities are exhausted it is claimed that management is confronted by two sets of alternatives to reduce uncertainty. First, the information needing to be processed might be reduced by environmental management, creating slack, or re-combining units from a functional grouping to a task-oriented mode. The second alternative seeks to increase the organisation's capacity to process information by either improving the vertical information system, or by creating lateral relationships, e.g. greater horizontal interaction, liaison roles, task forces, matrix organisation.

Child (1977, p. 232) and Mintzberg (1979) give similar depictions of how and why controls may vary, based on syntheses of recent research. Table 6.2 summarises Mintzberg's major points.

The contingency factors of size, environment and technology are the same as Galbraith's. Mintzberg also includes the power needs of managers (discussed later), the age of the organisation, and fashion (not discussed in this chapter). He illustrates five major types of coordinating (control) mechanisms, along with their major design considerations. It is assumed that the contingency factors are listed according to greater uncertainty. The five coordinating mechanisms

TABLE 6.2 *Mintzberg's five configurations of structure*

Name	Prime coordinating mechanism	Main design parameters	Contingency factors
1. Simple structure	Direct supervision	Centralisation; organic structure	Young; non-sophisticated technical system; simple, dynamic environment; possible extreme hostility or strong power needs of top manager; not fashionable; small
2. Machine bureaucracy	Standardisation of work processes	Behaviour formalisation; vertical and horizontal job specialisation; usually functional grouping; large operating unit size; vertical centralisation and limited horizontal decentralisation; action planning	Old; large; regulating, non-automated technical system; simple, stable environment; external control; not fashionable
3. Professional bureaucracy	Standardisation of skills	Training; horizontal job specialisation; vertical and horizontal decentralisation	Complex, stable environment; non-sophisticated technical system; fashionable
4. Divisionalised form	Standardisation of outputs	Market grouping; performance control system; limited vertical decentralisation	Diversified markets (particularly products and services); old; large; power needs of middle managers; fashionable
5. Adhocracy	Mutual adjustment	Liaison devices; organic structure; selective decentralisation; horizontal job specialisation; training;	Complex, dynamic, (sometimes disparate) environment; young (especially operating Adhocracy);

TABLE 6.2   *Continued*

Name	Prime coordinating mechanism	Main design parameters	Contingency factors
		functional and marketing grouping concurrently	sophisticated and often automated technical system (in the Administrative Adhocracy); fashionable

SOURCE: Table developed by the culture four points raised in H. Mintzberg (1979) *The Structuring of Organisations* (Englewood Cliffs, N.J.: Prentice-Hall).

outlined bear considerable resemblance to the methods of coping with uncertainty described by Galbraith. Both show how management initially shifts from behaviour control (transformations) by personal means to impersonal methods, reinforced by hierarchical supervision, to short-run output control with centralised coordination, to longer-run output control with decentralised coordination. The effect of increasing output control is to grant greater discretion to managers over means, but hierarchical control is maintained by setting and evaluating ends, thus achieving what Pfeffer (1978) refers to as the paradox of decentralised centralisation. Finally, as envisaged in Mintzberg's adhocracy and Galbraith's descriptions of the lateral structure with essentially intrinsic and social reward systems, the uncertainty may be so great that output goals cannot be set, as they need frequent mutual adjustment. The suggestion is that a major form of control will be over inputs, especially training and selection. This latter case will be returned to when organisations without established goals are discussed.

The implications of the above are considerable for those seeking to design control systems. First, if we view control from the aspect of senior management, it would appear that the design problem can be redrawn as a question of choosing an appropriate strategy of control. This is illustrated in Figure 6.4.

Secondly, the work of Galbraith follows our earlier analysis that design of organisations and management control is a compendium of interdependent variables which include the type of information system, structural arrangements, training and selection, and rewards.

Thus design for one set of variables will affect the other variables. For example, in adhocracies the organic structures with their lateral and information and decision-making processes can be exceedingly stressful and necessitate having members with considerable commitment and technical and social skills. Hence to reduce personal role ambiguity, reward systems must stress intrinsic and social rewards rather than immediate output.

Thirdly, the work illustrates the significance of lateral and informal information flows, particularly in respect of uncertainty. This suggests that formal hierarchical systems of a recursive nature will not always be appropriate.

CONTINGENCY MANAGEMENT

Choices are made in organisations regarding the domain in which they operate (Chandler, 1962; Thompson, 1967). Meyer (1975) traces how public accounting departments developed new domains according to their beliefs about their role and what their relevant clientele were: some restricted their role to stewardship accounting whilst others extended their domain into computing and management. Meyer's

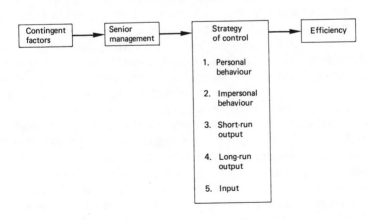

FIGURE 6.4 *Strategies of control*

research is an indication of how deliberate choices were made about the tasks performed, the customers served, and the technology employed. Thus the environment is itself selected by an organisation to its advantage as indeed prescriptive texts in strategic management suggest. For example, Argenti (1974) states that strategic choices should be partly based on the analysis of company strengths and weaknesses. The implication is that internal factors influence the relevant environment. Also, the size of organisations is chosen; for example, proprietors have spurned company growth as they do not wish to alter their personalised mode of control. In a similar vein, Salaman (1979) argues that the choice of technology is not an imperative of efficiency but rather an aspect of control chosen to reinforce the decision-makers' assumptions about the nature of authority in an organisation, the degree of participation and discretion which is desirable, and the quality of work experiences sought.

Once chosen, contingent variables are capable of being influenced by the organisation. Indeed management of contingencies may be part of a strategy of control rather than merely being a precursor to it (Pfeffer, 1978), and environmental management is one of several means of reducing uncertainty. Thus rather than make internal changes to cope with uncertainty, the organisation may seek to change its external relationships. Environmental management is a process of balancing the organisation's desire for autonomy and flexibility against the wish to reduce uncertainty by including other organisations in its decision-making process. Galbraith (1977) breaks down strategies of environmental management into two groups. First, independent strategies (the maintenance of self-control in a situation of interdependence), have three major possible responses; (i) competitive – maintain independence and compete with others for resources; (ii) public relations – maintain independence but attempt to establish and maintain favourable image; (iii) contractual – enter contractual commitments with others as a strategy of negotiation. The second group, cooperative strategies (coordinated actions by two or more organisations to resolve joint problems), is given four subgroups; (i) implicit cooperation – no explicit communication or coordination but established patterned and predictable behaviours, e.g. price leadership; (ii) contracting – entering formal negotiations and agreements with others, e.g. cartels; (iii) coopting – absorbing others into the leadership or policy-making structure to avert their threat; (iv) coalition – coalescing and acting jointly with respect to some issues, e.g. joint ventures.

Much of the above is conjectural, given the dearth of specific organisational studies on the topic; however, industrial economics and corporate strategy cases can provide a rich source of examples and ideas. However, its relevance to an argument is that the environment is part of the organisation design problem, and can lead to a significant impact on management control.

ARE CONTROL STRATEGIES DETERMINED?

The process of the choice of control strategy indicated in Figure 6.4 remains unsatisfactory in several respects:

1. Contingencies may not be given but chosen, and are not then determined for all time.
2. Decision-makers may yet have considerable scope for choice between strategies of control.
3. The approach assumes power to be non-problematical and that decision-making is rational and ordered.
4. Evaluative criteria for design prescriptions are often absent. Implicitly, or when explicit, they tend to be biased towards shareholders and managerial needs.
5. The evaluative criteria can be major inputs into the process of design as well as being outputs.

The above deficiencies may stem from a tendency to seek simple causal chains which so readily lend themselves to prescription. However, variables may often be interdependent and a constant sequence of changes between variables may often not be discernible. In looking for causal chains the researcher may be employing a false conception of the problem, asking the wrong questions and seeking an impossible answer. Weick (1979a, p. 86) expresses such points well:

Most managers get into trouble because they fail to think in circles. Managerial problems persist because managers believe that there are such things as unilateral causation, independent and dependent variables, origins, and terminations. Examples are everywhere: leadership style affects productivity, parents socialise children ... those assertions are wrong because each of them demonstrably also operates in the opposite direction ... causation is circular, not linear. And the same thing holds true for most organisational events. Suppose you thumb through books to find the answer to a question you have. Your first temptation might be to say that the question caused focused searching. But that's not the way it works. Searching is circular. You start with a question, you stumble on some apparently relevant item, which in turn affects subsequent searching, which in turn redirects your question etc.

If you become obsessed with interdependence and causal loops, then lots of issues take on a new look.

It might not be too useful to become obsessed by anything, but Weick has a good point for he invites us to consider the simultaneous interaction of the elements of our emerging design problem (see Figure 6.5).

The immediately apparent change is that the design problem – what is the appropriate control strategy – is itself not a linear process, as any change in the control strategy will affect the distribution of power (who are the dominant group), the nature of variables recognised and the manner of handling uncertainty, and the processes of decision-making.

The following sections detail the derivation of the model and its implications for the study of management control.

DOMINANT GROUPS, DECISION-MAKERS AND THEIR CRITERIA

Galbraith constantly refers to 'the organisation' making decisions without ever clearly delineating its membership. As most potential members are regarded as part of the design problem needing to be integrated into the organisation, then the presumption is that they lie outside. Implicitly when Galbraith writes of the organisation he is

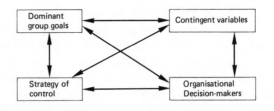

FIGURE 6.5 *Control and causality*

referring to senior management, as the dominant group. This would be clearer were his criteria for prescribing designs explicit, but unfortunately like so many design writers, they tend to be unstated. However, with some risk of oversimplifying Galbraith's subtle and searching text, the design problem is presented as social engineering indulged in by those at the apex of the organisation and dictated by criteria of economic efficiency.

This assumption may not accurately describe (i) who makes the decisions, (ii) by what criteria, and (iii) by what process.

Economic efficiency criteria are usually utilised on the assumption that they are dictated to decision-makers by the necessity of organisational survival in competitive capital markets. However, as is illustrated in Figure 6.5 by the substitution of dominant group goals for criteria of efficiency, the operating managerial criteria may be wider. In some instances this may be due to the existence of slack, which may be common given the high concentration in many industries, the possibility of separation of ownership and control, and the fact that many public bodies operate outside immediately competitive markets. Also, equifinality in design strategies may be possible, which gives scope for other criteria to be employed. Whilst Nicholls (1969) argues that prevailing managerial ideologies are consistent with efficiency criteria, Child (1973) suggests otherwise, claiming that one weakness of current contingency theory is that it failed to recognise that political and ideological factors may be significant in shaping managerial decisions.

Child's arguments gain some credence when empirical studies of the decision-making process are examined. For example, Cyert and March (1963) and March and Simon (1958) substitute the hierarchical step-like rational model with one whereby decisions are a consequence of negotiated consensus between conflicting parties: organisational goals being a product of pluralistic compromises which may alter as power balances change. Consequently in Figure 6.5 organisation decision-makers are connected to dominant group goals, in order to indicate that decision criteria may be generated internally, rather than being an externally imposed constraint.

Cohen *et al.* (1972) in their garbage-can depiction of decision-making and Weick (1979a) in his theory of retrospective action suggest that even the aforementioned model of quasi-rationality may be wrong in assuming that the decision-making process is always overlaid by goals, albeit goals which are politically determined. Goals may be just one set of inputs to a process and may be unclear or constantly changing. Such a likelihood is perhaps greatest where decision-makers experience considerable uncertainty (Hayes *et al.*, 1979) and the presence of uncertainty may itself affect dominant group goals.

One response to great uncertainty may be to avoid output goals. Here, because of the constant change it is probably impossible to control by specifying transformations or even long-run outputs. Instead the control system emphasises mutual adjustment between units and levels of the hierarchy and is essentially social, lateral and, if effective, speedy. It is the contention of the writers that in such instances hierarchical control is not merely reduced to a coordinating role, but may continue through an attempt to regulate inputs, either people or cash. Given the complexity and change associated with transformations and outputs, senior managers may minimise direct intervention on such matters but instead attempt to control the premises of decision-making by careful selection, induction and training of personnel. Also some financial control may be attempted by limiting cash inputs, for example, cash limits in the public sector may be a response to the difficulties in securing agreed outputs.

Whatever the process of decision-making, i.e. rational, quasi-rational or garbage-can, the question of how certain decision-makers achieve a degree of dominance needs addressing along with its relevance to design. Jackson and Morgan (1978) quote Jacobson (1972) as attributing the power of groups within organisations to three sources; personal, institutional and situational. The latter two sources are directly pertinent to this analysis. Institutional power stems from an individual's position within the structure, his formal title, his control over rewards and sanctions, his geographical position within the organisation, and his associated access to valuable information or persons. Several of these elements are part of the strategy of control outlined, hence it might be argued that key decision-makers and their behaviour are in part determined by the strategy of control, hence the reverse arrow between strategies of control and organisational decision-makers in Figure 6.5. The major source of situational power is the person's or unit's ability to cope with uncertainty, given that it is not easily substitutable and that it is central to the organisation (Hickson *et al.*, 1971). Whilst uncertainty is related to the contingent variables it may also be a product of the internal strategy of control, e.g. the absence of role definition and formalisation may increase uncertainty (Burns and Stalker, 1961). Thus it might be argued that organisational decision-makers are so because of uncertainty. However, it has been previously noted that decision-makers can influence these institutional and situational factors. If so, then design procedures represent not only important sources of power, but are also important means of maintaining and reinforcing power. Hence the subsequent form of controls may owe much to the power needs of dominant coalitions rather than simply being a consequence of rational choice against efficiency criteria. Pettigrew (1973) vividly describes an instance of an individual using his position of 'gate-keeper' for information to obtain his influence over decisions. Whilst it may be in an organisation's interests to reduce uncertainty in a sector by redesigning it, dominant units may resist such moves if it might undermine their sources of power.

Also, if decision-makers have discretion over strategies of control, then the resultant strategies may owe much to their dominant orientations as well as their power needs. For example, Channon (1973) and Allen (1979) both found that corporate strategies adopted by companies were significantly associated with senior management values, independent of other variables. Rumelt (1974) indicates that managerial fashions may be significant in design and that divisionalisation may have become common because it had become an accepted norm. On a more general plane, contingency theory would have difficulty in explaining the emergence of Robert Owen's New Lanark Mills and why his ideas were not widely imitated, despite their relative efficiency. Correlations between contingencies and design features are often modest and not always consistent between studies. Thus there is a degree of evidence to show that managers can and do exercise design choices according to their preferences and values. Hence in Figure 6.5 lines have been drawn from dominant group goals to contingent variables and strategies of control to indicate that they may be chosen rather than being imperative.

CONTROL, DESIGN AND IDEOLOGY

Thus the design task of the management control specialist is established in relation to the dominant group goals. This implies that all other groups and individuals are constraints – contingent variables which need to be considered. Such an approach may well fit an instrumental or coercive organisation but not a normative one (Etzioni, 1961).

However, this is an ideological position which cares nought for an alternative conception of control as the regulation existing in a social structure, whereby system breakdowns are avoided by maintaining an acceptable flow of inducements to and contributions from each organisational subsystem and its substantive environment. In this latter sense equality, kindness and human concern may well dominate considerations of efficiency or even instrumentally observed human satisfactions. Power itself may be the objective of a control strategy.

Control strategies may have to be developed in relation to multiple goals of equally powerful groups – all of which have separately the power to destroy the organisation but which need to cooperate to sustain it.

What has become clear is that the act of design in itself is a value-laden problematic process as surely affected by the contingent variables as affecting them. To this problem of design we turn in the last section.

DESIGN AND MANAGEMENT CONTROLS

The design and implementation of management control or organisational control procedures can not be done in the abstract. Design is about bringing something into being, in this case procedures for regulation of an organisation.

We could propose control strategies as normative statements derived from theoretical preconceptions. Traditional management control has done this and left us with a legacy of inappropriate universalism. Taking the broader view of organisational control we have an insufficiently specifiable theory to permit confident prescription. The thrust of the argument here is to suggest that such an approach is not fruitful.

A second approach to design would be via instrumental kits, which would be basic materials. Lots of 'extras' could be offered – but fundamentally the key problems of what to do are passed on to the user. The main advantage of this approach would be that the principal decisions are made by managers and practitioners.

A third approach would be through action research. This would be in the nature of a joint exploration of theory and insights, problems and constraints between academics and managers and organisational participants. This approach, common enough in the literature of management development, would permit the issues of organisational complexity and uncertainty to be addressed, with the benefits of joint discovery, in an ambience where multiple goal approaches would need to emerge.

CONCLUSION

Organisation design has been examined as an instrumental activity concerned with creating and maintaining organisational viability. The design criteria have been seen as emerging from the interaction of dominant group goals and internal and external constraints. Management control has been manifested not as the specific normative implications of financial markets, but as the design of control procedures developed through an interactive process with organisational design and dependent upon the same variables.

Thus the principal conclusion of this paper is that organisation design and management control are similar in that both are approached as an emergent phenomenon. A consequence of this is that the path to improved knowledge of management control may be through action research programmes which themselves would be subject to the considerations identified for control and design. (Revans, 1980).

NOTES

1. The identity between organisational control and management control requires some attention to the idea of a state of control. The idea that controls do not necessarily lead to control (Drucker) is familiar enough. However, to speak of such control is to require control procedures to lead in the direction of some desirable end. Some familiar ends may be economic efficiency and technical efficiency. However, control may also be a matter of effect. In formal language control may be said to exist where

$$P (S \rightarrow Ds) \mid_{CA} > P (S - Ds)$$

that is the probability that the state variable S approaches its desired value Ds is greater if control action is taken. But of course these are matters of preference for the state variable S might also be a greater degree of determination or the capacity to adapt to changes.
2. Budgets, though, are often used as devices to regulate the use of inputs.
3. Each of the three contingent factors isolated for examination is fraught with conceptual and methodological difficulties (Hickson *et al.*, 1969; Kimberley, 1976; Downey and Slocum, 1975). A critical examination of these is beyond the scope of this chapter.
4. The conceptualisation of uncertainty in the contingency literature is problematical. Galbraith's definition is illustrative of this. The writers' later usage of the term refers to the relative ability of decision-makers to map significant relationships in the organisation and its environment and to assign probabilities to them. This is taken as a perceptual process related to, but not exclusively determined by, the actual characteristics of the organisation and its environment.

7 Organisational Control: a Resource Dependence Approach

Charles Wilkinson

INTRODUCTION

The aim of this chapter is to present some ideas concerning the inter-actions between an organisation and the environment in which it operates and to demonstrate the implications of these ideas for the design of management control systems. The importance of environmental contingenices for organisations and their management control systems is widely acknowledged (see, for example, Bruns and Waterhouse, 1975; Hayes, 1977; Waterhouse and Tiessen, 1978), and this literature points towards an analytical framework which includes the whole range of control mechanisms within the organisation rather than management accounting controls in isolation (Otley, 1981). Much attention has been focused on structural considerations, such as how best to organise in order to cope with the effects of complexity and unpredictability in the environment (for example, Lawrence and Lorsch, 1967b; Gordon and Miller, 1976; Amigoni, 1978), though rather less has been written about the mechanics of that coping process (but see Weick, 1969; Pfeffer and Salancik, 1978).

This chapter deals with the interactions between a part of the 'internal' control system, namely the goal formation process, and with 'external' control, i.e. the demands made upon the organisation by powerful sectors of its environment. (Goal formation is considered to be a part of the control process, in which differing personal or subgroup outcome preferences are negotiated and traded in order to secure agreement on immediate and short-term future actions, rather than a 'pre-control' activity.) These two aspects of control have

118

important implications for the concept of organisational effectiveness, and, since the desire for effective performance provides the rationale behind any control system (see Chapter 14 by Lowe and Chua), so the interaction of internal goals and external demands needs to be well understood by those who design and operate management control systems. A methodology for developing such understanding has been proposed by Pfeffer and Salancik (1978). This is described and commented on at the end of this chapter.

THE GOAL FORMATION PROCESS

Organisational control systems, like any other type of control system, require explicit objectives (Otley and Berry, 1980) if current performance is to be evaluated. For an organisational control system, the relevant objectives are desired standards of organisational performance, but as the term 'desired' implies, and as Vickers (1965) has pointed out, these objectives are based on 'value judgements' by those who set the standards. The process of setting these standards is usually referred to as the goal formation process, though the use of the word 'goal' is problematic, since it could imply some single permanent objective for the organisation. Indeed, there is a long tradition of that usage of the word (e.g. Blau and Scott, 1962), but the meaning of 'goal' as used in this chapter is appreciably wider.

This more enlightened usage, which stems from the rise of the 'open systems' movement, does not imply that goals are well defined or permanent, but suggests that they are multifaceted, possibly conflicting, and subject to change within an organisation. As Thompson and McEwan (1958) perceptively observed, 'Purpose becomes a thing to be decided rather than an obvious matter.' This insight gave rise to considerable interest in the processes through which issues of purpose are decided. Thompson (1967) remained at the forefront of the discussion and, building upon earlier work by Perrow (1961b), expounded the 'dominant coalition' model of goal determination.

This model focuses on the interaction of individuals and groups within the organisation. People have their own needs which they expect the organisation to satisfy, and these needs will differ between individuals and between groups (Fox, 1966). These differences can stem from conflict between functional roles, as in the oft-quoted 'argument' between sales and production functions, with their preferences respectively for production flexibility with its (higher) level of customer satisfaction on the one hand, and for long-run production with its (more) efficient use of resources on the other. Differences can also stem from personal preferences, such as for more, or less, autonomy or self-determination at work, or for a desired pattern of contributions and inducements (March and Simon, 1958).

Whatever the reason for these differences, they are differences in preference concerning the distribution or use of 'supra-survival wealth' (Machin and Wilson, 1979). This is that level of (organisational) achievement over and above the minimum which is necessary for the survival of the organisation; survival being the common objective which binds the organisation participants together (Thompson, 1967), ensuring the continuance of their contribution/inducement relationship. Where there is significant interdependence between groups, the ability of any group to control its own pattern of contribution (and inducements) will depend on its ability to influence others within the organisation. The ability to exert this influence is directly related to others' dependence upon the group, since this determines a group's power relative to the rest of the organisation.

Part of this power resides in a group's (or individual's) ability to control or manage the availability of scarce or unpredictable resources on which the organisation is dependent. When dependence on a particular resource is high, then the organisation is similarly dependent on those who control access to it. The more critical the resource to the success or survival of the organisation, then the greater the power of those who can ensure its constant availability (Hickson *et al.*, 1971). The term 'resources' may also include 'abstract' as well as material resources, such as knowledge, ideas and access to information or important external groups. These 'critical dependencies' allow those who manage them to utilise their power to satisfy personal or group requirements within the organisation (Thompson, 1967). In other words, a group's influence over the distribution or use of supra-survival wealth is directly related to its ability to ensure the generation of adequate survival (or essential) output.

In organisations in complex environments with more than one strategically critical resource, it is likely that this source of power will be available to a number of resource controllers, each of whom will attempt to pursue his own objectives simultaneously. Thompson argues that in order to bring some stability to the process (which is itself a legitimate objective) those who control the critical dependencies will form a 'dominant coalition' which collectively decides issues of organisational activity, and commits resources to those activities. Though coalition members are unlikely to hold agreed long-term objectives for the organisation, as the notion of a coalition implies, they will find agreement on current actions which will satisfy, for the time being at least, their diversity of goal preferences.

Membership fo the coalition is a basis for exchange, through which some ambitions can be satisfied in return for conceding others in favour of competing aims. Such arrangements are not permanent however; something conceded now may be achieved later when conditions are more favourable, when the distribution of power changes within the coalition.

In order to review and possibly revise their positions, members will engage in bargaining processes periodically. Continuous bargaining activity would detract from the stability which the coalition seeks to maintain (as was the effect in the political 'Lib-Lab pact' in the UK in 1978–9). Some bargaining processes are structured as regular organisational activities, such as budget setting, or revising the corporate five-year plan, but others may be irregular, triggered by changing perceptions of relative power within the coalition.

In summary, the results of this intra-coalition bargaining are a set of commitments for the immediate future, carrying the general agreement of the members of the dominant coalition. It is these plans for future action which are referred to under the term 'organisational goals' for the purposes of this chapter. This is not meant to imply that members of the dominant coalition are the only participants who hold goals for the organisation, but since they are the ones most able to make resource commitments on the organisation's behalf, they are the most relevant from the planning point of view. Nor is it intended that the goals of the dominant coalition should be regarded as being in any sense the 'right' ones for the organisation, or that the goals of non-dominant members should be ignored by their more powerful colleagues. The model is simply a description of the goal formation process which accords with the author's observations of the planning process in a number of business organisations.

ENVIRONMENTAL DEMANDS

Before discussing the interactions between an organisation and its environment, it is necessary to be clear of the distinction between them, or more specifically, of the locus of the boundary which

separates one from the other. As there is no generally accepted definition of an organisation boundary, perhaps we would be wise to follow
those systems theorists who maintain that (system) boundaries should
be drawn for analytical convenience (Checkland, 1979a). From a
control perspective, an organisation boundary can usefully be considered to be 'where the discretion of the organisation to control an
activity is less than the discretion of another organisation or individual
to control that activity' (Pfeffer and Salancik, 1978).

Up to this point, the main actors considered in the goal formation
process have been those within the organisation who control the
organisation's critical dependencies, but complete control of these
dependencies does not rest entirely with the organisation's members.
As Thompson (1967) points out:

> ... an organisation is dependent on some element of its task
> environment (1) in proportion to the organisation's need for re-
> sources or performances which that element can provide and (2) in
> inverse proportion to the ability of other elements to provide the
> same resources or performance.

There is one important 'resource' for which control rests largely
outside the organisation, which is 'legitimacy'. Parsons (1956) identified the importance of the legitimacy concept for our understanding
of organisations, though he did not call it a resource. Nevertheless, it
can be regarded as an abstract resource in the sense that without it, the
organisation cannot flourish. Legitimacy is society's assessment of the
usefulness of the organisation and its output, though as Parsons
reminds us, different interest groups within society will apply different
criteria when making their assessment, naturally dependent upon their
own preferences and values.

The importance of this resource was underlined by Lowe and
McInnes (1971), with their observation that 'an enterprise exists by
means of its environment' and 'its success depends upon the degree to
which it satisfies those [environmental] needs'. By their actions,
organisations will influence society's perception of their usefulness,
but they cannot demand legitimate status. By the very nature of the
concept, legitimacy can only be given by the wider society of which the
organisation is part.

Dubin (1976) considered the question of organisational effectiveness from the perspective of the wider society within which the organisation exists and with which it conducts exchange relationships. He

concluded that this perspective is 'worlds apart' and impossible to reconcile with the organisation's internal view of its effectiveness.

The author of this chapter recognises that the perspectives are different, but believes that within the organisation, some reconciliation does, and indeed must, occur since many organisations do appear to enjoy a legitimate status and survive for many years. It is therefore important to understand how external demands or needs are incorporated into the 'goals' of an organisation, and thereafter into its management control system.

Jacobs (1974) identified five areas in which organisations interact with their environments and are to some extent dependent upon external actors to satisfy their exchange requirements. These areas are: input acquisition; output disposal; capital acquisition; acquisition of production factors; and the acquisition of a labour force. The strength of the dependency in each case depends upon the level of substitutability of, or willingness to do without, a particular resource, and the number of alternative suppliers of the resource. To the extent that an organisation is dependent upon a single resource supplier, that supplier has power over, or the potential ability to control, the organisation. In Jacob's own words: 'Where an organisation finds exchange it must make with its environment problematic . . . it must bend to the wishes of those who control these exchanges.' This argument is obviously similar to the earlier discussion on the power which accrues to those who control the critical dependencies within the organisation. In both cases, the concept of power stems from the work of Emerson (1962).

An organisation's dependence on an element of its environment for a valuable resource is a necessary condition for a power relationship, but this is separate from the actual processes of that relationship. The question of how powerful environmental sectors use their advantage to exert control over the organisation and how the organisation in turn responds to environmental demands still requires much attention. Clearly, there is no external 'dominant coalition' which can negotiate together and commit the organisation's resources independently. Rather, their demands must become known to the organisation via the members who manage the dependency relationships. This process is called 'enactment' (Weick, 1969).

Enactment is not simply the process of reacting to the environment, but includes the process of attributing meaning to events in the environment and planning accordingly. (By implication, organisations are not aware of any absolute meaning of environmental events.)

Environmental demands are not necessarily presented directly to the organisation, but those members occupying roles involving interaction between organisation and resource source interpret events in the form of demands, which will to some degree determine their behaviour.

Organisational roles which involve contact with the environment have been called 'boundary spanning' roles, since their occupants operate at the organisation boundary. The importance of these roles has been recognised in the work of Aldrich (1971), Adams (1976), and Leifer and Huber (1977). They are important because these roles control the flow of information and resources between the organisation and other members of the 'organisation-set' (Evan, 1966).

If one is to adopt a resource dependence model of the organisation–environment relationship (Aldrich and Pfeffer, 1976) as the basis of goal formation, it becomes essential that the transfer of information and resources should be considered together if that relationship is to be both completely understood (Aldrich and Mindlin, 1978) and effectively controlled, especially when uncertainty about the environment, and dependence on the environment, are both high.

One of the prime functions of boundary-spanning roles is to manage a part of the environment, but it should not be assumed that they are active only at the periphery of the organisation. Many senior managers leading functional groups in such areas as sales, procurement, personnel, finance and research and development are boundary –spanners, but by virtue of their position in the organisation, they have a general responsibility for the welfare of the whole of the organisation, as well as for their particular part of the environment. Employees in far less prominent positions can also fulfil boundary functions; for example, a counter clerk in a bank, or an employee who purchases his company's product, is also in a position to provide feedback from the environment on the organisation's performance, and could be utilised in this capacity.

Such widespread participation in environment management is apparently rare (Richbell, Chapter 9) however, and enactment of a particular sector of the environment is generally done by those more senior members, often members of the dominant coalition, whose attention is focused on that sector. The price of failure to interpret correctly, or of ignoring, environmental demands is likely to be the withdrawal or restriction of critical resources, so it is in the interest of the members of the dominant coalition to identify those demands accurately. Otherwise, the inability to manage the dependency successfully will weaken the members' power base within the organisation.

Unfortunately, just as member's own interests are likely to conflict, so are the interests of different environmental sectors. Indeed it has already been noted that environmental conflicts are a partial cause of internal difference. For example, the interests of capital suppliers and labour force are much cited as being in opposition. Once again, the onus is with the dominant coalition to negotiate a plan (i.e. commit resources) in a manner which is, for the time being, acceptable to all concerned. In this way, the environment's goals for the organisation as perceived by its members are incorporated into the goal formation process. Since these are perceptions, however, rather than the 'real' environmental demands, the ability of the organisation to satisfy those demands, and hence to be effective, will depend upon the accuracy of that perception.

Richbell (in Chapter 9) has addressed the subject of worker participation in management as a means of increasing organisational control, but observes that 'Control over uncertainty surrounding external factors such as technology, the market, the economy cannot be secured solely through an increase in compliance between the labour force and management.' Whilst recognising the precision of Richbell's analysis of the constraints inherent in participative approaches, this author believes that at lower hierarchical levels, particularly where boundary-spanning employees are involved, participation can reduce the uncertainty associated with externalities to a considerable extent. Those employees whose jobs involve frequent contact with customers, suppliers and other organisations accumulate a rich and detailed appreciation of the attitudes, habits and values of these important groups. If this data can be incorporated into the enactment and decision-making processes, then the corporate appreciation of the environment can be greatly enhanced, increasing the potential for control over organisational outcomes. A beneficial secondary effect of wider involvement of low-level employees in such a process could be the development of the 'organisational perspective' which is necessary for successful participation (Richbell, in Chapter 9).

One formalised methodology which has been used to study the relationships between an organisation and the various components of its environment is the expectations approach (Machin and Tai in Chapter 11). Though the methodology was developed as an aid to control within organisations, it has on occasions been used to focus attention on relationships which cross organisational boundaries. This suggests a promising avenue which could lead towards one form of lower-level participation in management which is highly functional and yet is capable of avoiding the more ideological barriers to participation, since the approach is independent of the values and attitudes of the participants for its successful operation. Whilst there are limits to how far extra-organisational actors may care to participate formally in the expectations approach methodology, their expectations can be canvassed informally, as in the case of the retail outlet cited by Machin and Tai (in Chapter 11) and fed into the internal decision-making process via the boundary-spanning role occupants.

The subject of worker participation in management and the expectations approach are both discussed elsewhere in this volume, by Richbell, and Machin and Tai respectively. The reader is recommended to contrast these ideas with the methodology for identifying and managing environmental demands which is described and discussed in the next section of this chapter.

THE MANAGEMENT OF CONFLICTING DEMANDS

To help organisations to manage their environment more successfully, Pfeffer and Salancik (1978) have proposed a methodology which is dependent for its appeal on its inherent assumptions about the meaning of organisational control, organisational effectiveness and management control systems.

An *organisational control system* (see Figure 7.1) can be regarded as a set of activities whose purpose is to ensure that the organisation performs effectively. An important component of such a system is the *management control system* which includes both purposefully designed activities such as management accounting systems and informal means of control such as the acceptance and maintenance of particular attitudes and values amongst organisational members. The other components of the organisational control system which Pfeffer and Salancik have called external controls have their origins outside the organisation, and include statutory regulations, the activities of customers and suppliers, and the prevailing values of the society in which the organisation exists.

Organisational effectiveness can be viewed as the measure of goal fulfilment, and since organisations are subject to a variety of goal preferences, so the criteria of effectiveness need to be flexible enough to take account of a diversity of goal preferences (Steers, 1975). Since the term goal as used here includes not only the official and unofficial goals of the organisation's members, but also goals held for the organisation by the constituents of its environment, this approach aligns closely with what Lowe and Chua (Chapter 14) classify as the prescriptive organisational approach to organisational effectiveness. The consequence of adopting such an approach is that the ability of the management control system to cope with a diversity of goals, which include those of dominant and non-dominant members and environmental demands, becomes a matter of great importance.

The exact nature of the management control system which is appropriate to any particular organisation is thought to be contingent upon certain organisational and environmental variables, although satisfactory evidence to support this hypothesis is as yet rather sparse

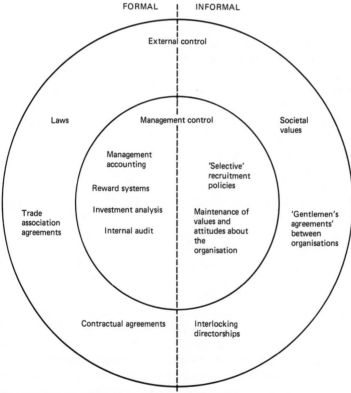

Note: The examples of different types of controls are illustrative and by no means exhaustive.

FIGURE 7.1 *Organisational control and management control*

(Pennings, 1975; Otley, 1979). Traditionally, management control systems have tended to concentrate on matters of internal effectiveness, assessing performance against plans which carry the commitment of organisation members. As has been argued already, these will partially be the result of indirect influence from strategically important environmental sectors, as a consequence of members wishing to preserve their own positions of influence in the organisation. The aim here is not to suggest that environmental demands will automatically be either excluded or included in the organisation's goals however. The weakness in the traditional management control process is that the interests of the environment are likely to be satisfied only to the extent that they are accurately perceived by organisation members who are able to make resource commitments, and actually wish to do so.

A further problem facing organisations in their attempts to satisfy environmental demands concerns their ability to predict what actions on their part will actually satisfy those demands, assuming that they have been identified accurately. Some organisation theorists have identified environmental predictability (or uncertainty) as an important factor to be considered in the design of organisations (e.g. Lawrence and Lorsch, 1967b; Duncan, 1972), but the content of that uncertainty (as perceived by those 'inside' the organisation) is events which take place 'outside' in the environment.

The argument of this chapter is concerned with the predictability of the organisations–environment relationships, rather than with the predictability of the environment per se. The problem is not simply that of predicting what is going to happen 'out there', but of predicting what the effect of particular organisational actions will be on the various sectors of the environment. By implication, it is concerned with the effect of particular actions on the various environmental views of the organisation's effectiveness. But since different sectors of the environment hold different criteria of effectiveness, any attempt to satisfy one sector runs the risk of upsetting another. In many cases, the limits of organisational resources will necessitate making choices between competing demands. It is not enough, therefore, for organisations to strive to satisfy all demands, rather they must make choices about which demands of which sectors are to be heeded.

As a tool to help management make that choice, Pfeffer and Salancik (1978) have proposed a methodology, which, they claim, can 'increase awareness of the contingencies facing an organisation' and 'overcome some of the problems encountered in designing organisational actions'. If these claims are justified, then the methodology provides a means of influencing the behaviour and effectiveness of organisation members in their interactions with the environment, and it can therefore be regarded as an externally oriented form of management control if used regularly and consistently (see Figure 7.2).

THE METHODOLOGY

The steps which constitute the methodology are as follows:

1. The first task is to determine the various interest groups or organisations (environmental sectors) which are necessary for or relevant to the continued survival and success of the organisation. It is suggested that this can be done by considering which resources are critical to the organisation and identifying who provides or affects those resources. Pfeffer and Salancik note that 'Recognising interdependence is not always easy, and a sequential questioning of key actors in the organisation may be a useful beginning.'

   The interest groups or organisations should then be ranked in order of importance. It is suggested that this can be done by asking representatives of each group to rate each other in order of importance for the organisation, and averaging their responses.

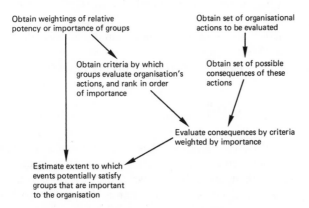

SOURCE: Adapted from J. Pfeffer and G. R. Salancik (1978) *The External Control of Organisations* (New York: Harper and Row) p. 87

FIGURE 7.2 *Methodology for evaluating environmental effects of organisational actions*

2. 'The next task is to determine the criteria or values by which each group evaluates the organisation.' Pfeffer and Salancik suggest that this can be done by examining the perceptions of members within the organisation, and by asking external actors directly. Member's perceptions can be problematic, so obtaining external views would seem to be essential if the process is to claim any degree of objectivity. Indeed if both internal and external views are obtained, any mismatch will indicate the efficiency of the existing management control systems with respect to the environment. The criteria should then be ranked in order of importance, presumably by weighting them with the relative importance of their owning group.

3. Having achieved a ranking of effectiveness criteria, the consequences of potential actions can then be evaluated. Where a variety of actions are possible, the consequences of each, in terms of their effects on the different environmental groups, should be forecast. For each group likely to be affected, the organisation could then assess the extent to which a particular action will or will not satisfy their criteria of effectiveness.

Information about the impact of events on criteria can be usefully incorporated with the information about the groups and their preferred interests. Three things can be derived: (1) estimates of the extent to which a given event potentially satisfies any given interest group; (2) estimates of the extent to which a particular event potentially satisfies some groups while simultaneously dissatisfying others; and (3) estimates of the extent to which the event potentially satisfies groups that are important to the organisation. (Pfeffer and Salancik, 1978, p. 86)

Pfeffer and Salancik infer that an organisation will be effective to the extent that it is able to undertake actions which will satisfy the demands of different interest groups simultaneously, and they describe the methodology as a means for assessing organisational effectiveness. In fact, what they appear to advocate is a means for assessing 'the effectiveness of particular actions', but perhaps the distinction is not important so long as all potential actions are so evaluated.

The methodology advocated by Pfeffer and Salancik appears to be highly rational, but it is in stark contrast with the author's experience in research which is that generally, organisations attend to different environmental demands sequentially one at a time, as they become critical, and then only evaluate the effects of potential actions against the demands of the most prominent externality(s) in each case. The ranking of interest groups in order of importance is a simple concept in theory, but if individuals' ratings differ by much, then the aggregate rating may also be a matter of disagreement. The objection is really that unless there is adequate consensus on this point, then the resultant lack of confidence in the outcome may undermine the benefit of the whole process.

A further concern is the degree to which the organisation is able to evaluate the possible consequences of its actions. Weick suggests that we cannot know the effects of our actions until they are done. 'Only by doing is it possible for us to discover what we have done' (Weick, 1969, p. 64). The message seems to be that we can never predict the complete set of possible consequences, one reason being that other events will be taking place in the environment of which we have no advance knowledge, yet these will affect the outcome of our own actions, and the way in which the environment interprets what we have done.

Despite the practical difficulties mentioned above, the theory underlying the methodology has much to recommend it. As Pfeffer and Salancik remind us so concisely:

> The central questions of organisational action are, we believe: who wants what and how important is it that the demand be satisfied? and what are the implications of the satisfaction of one demand for the satisfaction of other demands?

There can be no doubt that these are critically important issues, or that the methodology provides a means for an organisation to approach these questions in a rigorous and systematic manner. Traditional management control systems do not look outside the organisation, and therein lies the strengh of this one. But, however well the methodology is applied, it cannot solve the problem of managing (and of having to make choices between) conflicting demands. What it can do is highlight the existence of potential conflict where it may be present, and it could help managers to identify the strategic implications of particular actions. Where conflict exists, it remains the task of management to decide on actions in the light of their likely consequences as identified by their use of the methodology. By preventing gross distortions in the perception of environ-

mental demands, it should enable organisations to avoid acting in
ways which are inappropriate or self-damaging.

IMPLICATIONS FOR MANAGEMENT CONTROL SYSTEMS

By the inclusion of this methodology in its management control
strategy, an organisation is better placed to manage its environment
proactively, rather than by simply reacting to external pressures. For
strategic planning purposes, the methodology is a source of rich
environmental data, and it provides assessments of the implications of
certain decisions on external interdependencies. It is a means of constructing the 'predictive model' of the organisation–environment
relationship which Otley (in Chapter 4) argues is central to any control
system. The direct benefit of this is to increase the organisation's
capacity for feedforward control and the avoidance of undesired or
out-of-control occurrences. In order to maintain control, the methodology must be used frequently constantly to monitor the environment and allow for 'fine-tuning' of the predictive model, or where
necessary, rapidly to reflect some radical changes in interdependencies. The inability successfully to achieve the latter appears to be a
common shortcoming of most traditional management control
techniques.

In organisations which have many interdependencies, implementation of the methodology will involve handling a large volume of
qualitative and some numerical data, and would undoubtedly benefit
from computerisation to make that part of the task less wearisome.
However, this is a relatively small part of the total process, and lack of
such facilities should not prevent an organisation from using th
methodology to good effect.

A more serious barrier to effective implementation lies within the
attitudes of senior management towards a resource which is often
underutilised, especially in the UK, that is the contributions of lower
level employees. The methodology involves gathering information
from the environment, but unfortunately it may not always be
possible to do this directly if the issues involved are sensitive or con-
fidential. As has already been argued earlier in this chapter, this
difficulty can be overcome be seeking the views of any employees who
have information which is relevant to an assessment of the expectations and demands of environmental groups, usually boundary
spanners who are in regular contact with 'the environment' (see

Richbell, Chapter 9, for a full discussion of the question of worker participation in management). Even in cases where obtaining information directly from the environment is not particularly problematic, there are advantages to be gained from this sort of worker participation, such as being able to confirm that employee perceptions about the environment accord with the environment's actual expectations, and keeping employees alert to external changes as these affect their own organisation. However, though these advantages seem real enough, and though the concept of worker participation in management is no longer new, managements are often reluctant to engage in such processes (Richbell, Chapter 9).

This may well change after the example of several Japanese companies who now manufacture in the UK, and who have introduced participative approaches to management with a great deal of success (*Sunday Times*, 6 December 1981). These firms do recognise the expertise and knowledge that each worker accumulates whatever his position in the organisational hierarchy, and attempt to make the best use of it. Environmental management is one aspect of management control that this author believes would benefit immeasurably from greater involvement of low-level employees. The methodology of Pfeffer and Salancik provides a suitable vehicle through which this can be achieved.

Part III

8 Motivational Aspects of Management Control

Eugene McKenna

Control is often construed as a process, based on influence, authority and power, in which a person, a group or an organisation intentionally affects what another person, group or organisation will do. Conformity to organisational norms is a normal feature of this type of control (Tannenbaum, 1962). Such a definition of control is too restrictive if we are to do justice to a realistic assessment of management control. This chapter will address itself to an appraisal of management control and its motivational implications.

FRAMEWORK OF MANAGEMENT CONTROL

Though management control manifests itself in different forms, as we shall see later, a fairly conventional view of it would embrace the following features. The control process assists in ensuring the minimisation of idiosyncratic behaviour and the promotion of conformity in accordance with the explicit plans of the organisation (Tannenbaum, 1962); it exists to ensure adherence to rules, or to ensure that activity coincides with expectations contained in policies, plans and targets (Child, 1977; Hopwood, 1974). But control is also concerned with defining what individuals, groups and organisational units are expected to do before establishing criteria against which organisational performance is to be assessed. It provides informational feedback on the way events have materialised and it accommodates a feedforward mechanism so that information based on forecasting can be assessed with a view to making adjustments to plans where necessary. This may be an unnecessarily restrictive view of control, particularly in the light of Richbell's discussion in Chapter 9, which

examines control as a process that does not reside only in management. There is scope in organisations for it to be distributed, but she
acknowledges that the prevalence of diversity in management and
worker groups weakens management control.

From whatever angle one views control it soon becomes patently
clear that significant aspects of motivated behaviour, of both the
controller and the controlled, come firmly into focus. One way in
which control manifests itself is in the form of close supervision.
Work activities are closely supervised at each hierarchical level, and
limits are set on the legitimate discretion that can be exercised by
subordinates. Close supervision can act as a substitute for formalisation – which will be discussed later – as well as reinforcing it (i.e. the
superordinate checks that subordinates are keeping to the rules). The
implications of close supervision might be a low motivational disposi-
tion among subordinates, particularly well-qualified personnel, and
problems of communication might arise because of the hierarchical
emphasis. In addition, if the controls are considered illegitimate or
threatening, the subordinate may be motivated to distort the feedback
reaching the superordinate. Though less close supervision or distant
supervision is often considered desirable in a motivational sense, one
could justify the relevance of close supervision in circumstances where
the coordination of widely disparate types of activities and potentially
diffuse behaviour of organisational members is necessary.

Another way in which control manifests itself is in the form of
procedural control, based to a large extent on formalisation of organisational activities. Formalisation refers to controlling employee
behaviour with a view to making the activities of employees more
predictable in a desired direction (Child, 1977). It is reflected in
written policies and plans against which performance can be
measured, and in procedures, rules and job definitions designed to
prescribe correct or expected action. It can act as a substitute for overt
control though Gouldner (1953) is of the view that it promotes mini-
mally acceptable behaviour rather than effective behaviour. Procedural control would also incorporate the verbal transmission of
rules and procedures as well as those acquired through experience
(specifying, for example, when one has discretion not to accept
authority), and acts as a source of convenience in the sense that the
organisational participant on a large number of occasions is not
motivated to search for an appropriate rule or set of rules. In this way
rules are dominant features of organisational life. Where participants
experience little or no difficulty in sharing the purpose or goals of the

organisation, acceptance of procedural controls is unlikely to be a problem. Where significant differences of opinion exist with respect to the purpose or goals of the organisation, then it would appear that acceptance of procedural controls is very much a function of the provision of suitable rewards, such as money and social recognition, rather than coercion. In most organisational conditions the acceptance of controls is problematic. Procedural controls which purport to demand rigid and conformist behaviour are hardly appropriate in conditions of innovation and a rapidly changing environment (Burns and Stalker, 1961). Should this mismatch prevail, the likelihood of motivational and performance dysfunctional consequences is very real indeed. Likewise a preoccupation with means (operating the control system), particularly when rewarded, to the detriment of ends is also said to promote dysfunctional organisational behaviour (Merton *et al.*, 1957).

Formalisation facilitates greater delegation since it structures work activities, and as a consequence it reduces the amount of close supervision (McKenna, 1978). It is frequently asserted that greater individual effort follows delegation since it permits a high degree of individual freedom, discretion and control; in addition, goal congruence is facilitated in these circumstances. A crucial question to face with respect to delegation is, will individuals whose tasks are interdependent be sufficiently motivated and committed to integrate their activities without centralised direction? If one were to accept Selznick's (1966) view of delegation, at the level of the organisation, the answer would be no. He believes that managers in different departments with different backgrounds develop their own departmental identities and philosophies over time. Their decisions become increasingly based on departmental rather than organisational needs and a parochial outlook makes coordination more difficult. Allied to the notion of delegation is centralisation and decentralisation, though Child (1977) perceives this dichotomy as applicable to the location where a decision is taken rather than the involvement of individuals in the total decision process. Under centralisation the upper echelon retains authority to make most decisions, whilst under decentralisation authority to make decisions is passed down the hierarchy, normally with the proviso that certain limits will not be exceeded with respect to the scope and type of decision. In practice, routine operational decisions are delegated, whilst non-routine and strategic decisions are more likely to be centralised.

Besides control which is inextricably tied up with supervision and procedures, social control and self-control are key ingredients of the management control process. They focus more specifically on the group and the individual. As such they generate important motivational considerations. Social controls arise from shared values and commitments by members of a group and they constitute group norms. A powerful regulatory force emerges when members' performance deviates from the significant norms of the group, though initially disapproval may amount to no more than reminding the culprit that a deviation has taken place. Thereafter disapproval may assume a stricter and harsher form. Group norms, which may exist within a formal system of management control, can relate to work targets, resource sharing and mutual help. They can be affected by prevailing and anticipated happenings and events such as changes in work practices and in the way people perceive and react to employment considerations and economic prosperity. The productivity level of the men engaged in wiring up telephone banks in the celebrated 'Hawthorne' studies was well below what the men could have achieved. A variety of social influences were at work in this group; for example, those who wired up around 6600 connections per day had approval and favours bestowed on them by the others. Those who exceeded this target attempted to conceal it, and those who worked below the productivity norm were shown various forms of disapproval by the group (Roethlisberger and Dickson, 1939). One of the findings in a study conducted by Lupton (1963) confirms the bank wiring room finding, referred to above, but another finding did not. There was a restrictive productivity standard in one factory – Jays – engaged in light engineering, and all employees referred to it as the 'fiddle'. In the other factory – Wye – engaged in the manufacture of waterproof garments each employee sought to maximise his or her earnings. Various explanations were put forward to account for the differences in group standards or norms. Jays operated in a stable market, had a history of union organisation, a predominantly male labour force with interdependent work and relatively low labour costs. Wye operated in a small unstable market, had a weak union, a predominantly female labour force with independent tasks and high labour costs. What appears to be fairly clear is that attempting to maximise earnings in one organisation was tantamount to deviant behaviour, but such behaviour in the other organisation amounted to conformist behaviour. In the latter case social pressure can reinforce organisational rules and procedures. Social control is undoubtedly a complex social process and consequently prediction of behaviour is extraordinarily difficult.

Having considered the nature of social control and how it manifests itself in an organisational setting, we shall now briefly acknowledge the importance of self-control. This is a topic which will be discussed again in the section dealing with human needs. Self-control is exercised from within the individual and is subject to the level of need gratification at a particular time. Normally it is associated with the gratification of higher-level human needs (Maslow, 1954), and rests on the acceptance of strongly internalised norms of competence and control (Child, 1977). The alleged confusion surrounding the meaning of self-control is discussed at length by Thomas (in Chapter 10). Hopwood (1974) states administrative and social controls have to be internalised and operate as 'personal controls' over attitudes and behaviour. He promotes the idea that there should be convergency between individual need gratification, mounted on personal or self-control, and administrative and social controls, otherwise anxious and pressurised individuals will respond insignificantly to formal controls. To achieve this convergency would be an overambitious task, almost doomed to failure from the beginning. For there will be times when an employee will exercise self-control to advance his career within the organisation, or to achieve some short-term benefit, and this could be at variance to a significant degree with the optimum achievement of organisational goals. In a sense Hopwood recognises this dilemma when he points out that 'it is simply unrealistic to presume that the motivations and self-controls of individual managers and employees can be readily marshalled behind the administration controls designed by more senior managers. Conflict and differences in fundamental needs and objectives have to be recognised as basic features of organisational life in democratic societies ... In addition, our knowledge of the means of integrating the different approaches to control remains far from adequate.' Supervisory control is not specifically mentioned but there is no good reason why it should not be considered in the context of convergency. If it was considered, the sentiments expressed above would still stand.

APPLICATION OF MOTIVATION THEORIES

In the light of the above discussion of some motivational implications of management control, an attempt will be made to relate insights derived from motivation theory by using them as an exercise designed to increase or clarify our understanding of the dynamics of management control. It is fair to say that our understanding of human motivation has only reached modest proportions, perhaps less so when we examine the interface between motivation and management control. The discussion will fall under three major headings which denote different approaches – personality, human needs and cognitive – to the study of motivation. Certain themes will inevitably overlap, but this type of classification is likely to be a useful way of developing the discussion.

Personality

Personality is a term used here to denote two motivational schools of thought – psychoanalysis (Freud, 1943) and learning through reinforcement (Dollard and Miller, 1950) – which view behaviour in terms of a reduction of tension in the pursuit of some desirable equilibrium or steady state within the organism. Involvement in this process is said to lead to the development of complexity in ideas and the growth of adaptive behaviour. Both schools speak of the individual as being dominated by two sets of drives. The primary drives consist of inborn and physiological motives and the secondary drives consist of acquired social motives (learning, perception, interactions, etc). In this section the discussion of personality development will be confined to a brief overview of the subject from the perspective of the two schools mentioned above, but hopefully this will be sufficient as a background to the link between personality and management control.

Freud conceives the organism as a mounting reservoir of undischarged energy awaiting release in some form, and social behaviour is merely a sublimation of instinctual discharges. There is the tendency to seek immediate pleasure (minimise tension) by the discharge of instinctual energies, although the ego learns to prevent such a discharge if it is considered inappropriate and out of place at a particular time. Emotions, such as anger and the impulse to attack, are likewise moderated or inhibited and redirected or transformed into socially acceptable impulses. The individual is forced to search the environment to locate stimuli, to gratify his needs, and the search is facilitated by wish-fulfilment (the individual forms an image or hallucination of the appropriate stimulus). It seems highly likely that learning rather than biological inheritance is associated with wish-fulfilment. Freud considered psychosexual development as a key factor in personality development. He attributed a number of personality traits manifest later in life to the unsuccessful negotiation of the different phases of psychosexual development. For example, the individual who failed to negotiate the oral stage (1 year old) is said to be among other things immature and dependent as an adult; the individual fixed at the anal stage (2 years) could be subsequently orderly in his behaviour, and finally, the excessively ambitious type could be a victim of the phallic fixation (3 years).

Dollard and Miller subscribe to the notion of need gratification as a function of the learning process, and they see a repertoire of behavioural responses arising out of the process of tension-reduction. Complex social motives, such as the desire to be liked or to achieve, are assumed to be learnt. In early childhood the child receives expressions of approval and disapproval from parents and adults, and these rewards and sanctions reinforce behaviour. It is suggested that any complex pattern of emotional response, having fear as its root, such as neurotic symptoms and their associated defence mechanisms, can be learnt.

Both schools of personality ignore the fact that social motives assume a certain degree of autonomy and become divorced from their earlier associations; for example, the work motive is functionally autonomous of its primary drive origins (Allport, 1937). It would be ill-advised to view pleasure or satisfaction as merely a reduction in discomfort or pain; for example, certain motives with a primary need origin assume an attraction in their own right (e.g. having a meal). Likewise, there are circumstances when the individual is engaged in behaviour designed to elicit stimulation (e.g. racing driver) rather than the reduction of tension. There are also times when attachment to certain motives assumes overriding importance irrespective of the consequences (e.g. die rather than betray trust).

Early in life and throughout childhood and adolescence powerful socialising and developmental processes are initiated and nurtured in the context of control exercised by teachers, parents and elders upon whom the child is highly dependent. The interactions and interrelationships between personality and control can become charged emotionally and personality dispositions are likely to be affected by the way control is exercised. Inevitably this will have an influence on the way the individual exercises and reacts to control later in life in an organisation. Tannenbaum (1962) recognises two implications of every act of control; one is pragmatic – i.e. what to do and not to do, the area of choice or freedom available to the individual and any general restrictions – and the other is psychological. The psychological implication has relevance for both the controller and controlled and implies feelings of superiority, inferiority, dominance, submission, guidance, help, criticism, reprimand, manliness and virility. This is tantamount to stating that the exercise of control is charged emotionally.

There is some evidence suggesting that the reaction of individuals to patterns of organisational control may be dictated by their personality. This is highlighted in an experiment conducted among female clerical staff in an organisational setting. The clerks were allocated greater responsibility to make decisions about assignments of work, overtime, vacation rosters and so on. Previously these decisions were taken by their superiors. Most of the clerks reacted favourably to greater participation in decisions that affected their group, with the exception of a small number who did not. This minority preferred to be submissive, depend on others, obey the rules and follow directions (Tannenbaum and Allport, 1956). Similar results emerged from a study of male workers in a service organisation (Vroom, 1960). However, Tosi (1970) was unable to replicate the results of Vroom's study.

Preferences for different kinds of control may develop out of early childhood experiences, subsequently mediated by events occuring in organisations. Research on the authoritarian personality suggests that those who experience failure at work, and suffer anxiety as a result, may show a tendency to prefer more structured control situations. In a study of insurance salesmen, conducted by Wispe and Lloyd (1955), productivity was found to vary from high to low from one period to another. In a period of low productivity the salesmen suffered some anxiety. They indicated a desire for interpersonal interaction through the hierarchical structure where decisions were made by the district manager, and they preferred people in authority to act aloof but at the same time to be friendly without being too intimate. When productivity was high the salesmen felt less threatened, and preferred a system of control lacking in hierarchical emphasis with an absence of communication barriers based on status.

Given the potential of personality and early socialisation as factors likely to influence preferences and predispositions of the controlled, to what extent can these factors influence the controllers? There are some speculative answers available. For example, Thompson (1961) feels that some people with strong dominance and status needs aspire to managerial positions; a leader may resort to discipline of a harsh nature in order to express a deep-seated hostility need (Tannenbaum and Massarik, 1963); and a superior may impose autocratic rule as an outlet for aggressions repressed because of his own exposure to auto-cratic rule as a subordinate (Fromm, 1942).

Human needs

The human needs approach, or force-for-growth model of motiva-tion, postulates the view that man strives toward realising his inner potentiality (self-actualisation) and may suffer some personal dis-advantage in doing so. Frequently the adolescent seeks independence and autonomy even though he has a comfortable existence with his parents at home. There are also occasions when a person forfeits comfort and security so as to support an unpopular principle or cause. Maslow (1954) identifies a hierarchy of needs and values ranging from the most primitive – which man shares with the lower forms of life – to those associated with the higher forms. The lowest needs include hunger, thirst and safety and the highest embrace belongingness and love, esteem, cognitive, and aesthetic (e.g. thirst for knowledge and desire for beauty) and self-actualisation needs. The gratification of the higher needs follows gratification of the lower needs, and it is frequently asserted that in western industrialised society the lower needs are reasonably well satisfied for many people most of the time. Since needs which are gratified are no longer determinants of beha-viour, it follows that the higher needs become important for many people in our culture. In a study based on the success of managerial trainees over a five-year period in the American Telephone and Telegraph Corporation, the hierarchy of needs was subjected to an empirical test. The successful group – success being measured in terms of fifth-year income – reported the highest satisfaction of achieve-ment, esteem and self-actualisation needs (Hall and Nougaim, 1968).

Though the 'human needs' approach has been criticised as mystical and value-laden, since it flirts so continuously with the evaluation of man in terms of normative judgements of high and low, advanced and primitive, good and bad (Lazarus, 1971), nevertheless it has made a significant impact on the development and application of work motivation theories. In his later work Maslow (1965), however, expressed a word of caution about the indiscriminate acceptance of his theory. He goes on to say that 'the carry-over of this theory to the industrial situation has some support from industrial studies, but certainly I would like to see more studies of this kind before feeling finally convinced that this carry-over from the study of neurosis to the study of labour in factories is legitimate'. The work of Herzberg

(1966) in an organisational setting is consistent with Maslow's theory. His two-factor theory is based on considerable empirical evidence and is built on the principle that people are motivated towards what makes them feel good and away from what makes them feel bad. Herzberg's research identifies the following factors as producing good feelings in the work situation: achievement, recognition, work itself, responsibility and advancement; these are real motivators and relate to work content. They could also be related to the higher needs. By contrast he suggests that the following factors arouse bad feelings in the work situation: company policy and administration, supervision, salary, interpersonal relations and working conditions. These factors are clearly concerned with the work environment and are referred to as 'hygiene factors', and it is claimed that they differ significantly from motivators in as much as they 'can only prevent illness but cannot bring about good health'. Put in another way, the lack of adequate 'job hygiene' will cause dissatisfaction, but its presence will not of itself cause satisfaction; it is motivators that do this. The absence of motivators will not cause dissatisfaction, assuming the 'job hygiene' factors are adequate, but there will be no positive motivation.

This rigid distinction between hygiene factors and motivators appears somewhat far-fetched in the light of our inherent limitations in constructing any complex form of social reality, such as motivation. Its not surprising that the methodology used by Herzberg has been the subject of a well-articulated attack by House and Wigdor (1967), who claim among other things that respondents' bias and experimenter's evaluation under uncontrolled conditions seriously undermine the results. There is other evidence which is not entirely compatible with the findings of Herzberg. For example, Wernimont (1966) maintains that either 'motivators' or 'hygiene factors' can both cause satisfied and dissatisfied feelings about the job, though he also concedes that motivators are important determinants of satisfied feelings about the job. A group of highly and lowly satisfied technicians mentioned hygiene factors more frequently than motivators as factors influencing both job satisfaction and dissatisfaction (Hinrichs and Mischkind, 1967). The findings of McDougall (1973), which relate to senior executives in a large UK company, indicate that financial reward assumed a position of significant importance as a motivating force, and therefore could be classified as a motivator rather than a hygiene or neutral factor in accordance with Herzberg's model.

Given that motivators are critical factors residing in a job, Herzberg

goes on to suggest that jobs should be enriched in order to accommodate motivators. Job enrichment is an approach to job design which
attempts to make tasks more intrinsically interesting, involving and
rewarding, and it involves both vertical and horizontal loading.
Vertical loading involves injecting more important and challenging
duties into the job, whilst horizontal loading embraces job enlargement
– increasing the number or diversity of activities – and job rotation –
moving people back and forth among different tasks. Herzberg's
approach to job enrichment has merit since jobs have been redesigned
on the basis of it, though with limited success. The underlying belief in
his approach is that satisfaction is an important source of motivation
that leads to better performance, because of an alleged association
between satisfaction and increased productivity which in turn is
assisted by reduced turnover, absenteeism and tardiness. Job enrichment has an affinity with the principle of participative management,
but at this stage a pertinent question to ask is, does every category of
worker respond positively to job enrichment in terms of a more
meaningful and challenging job? There is some evidence to suggest
that the answer is no. For example, jobs characterised as varied,
complex and demanding were associated with low satisfaction for
workers of a particular cultural background (Turner and Lawrence,
1965); and job enrichment may be beneficial for white-collar, supervisory and non-alienated blue-collar workers, but other workers may
not welcome the opportunity to become more involved in their work
and participate in decision-making (Hulin and Blood, 1968). At Luton
Goldthorpe *et al.* (1970) found that workers sought jobs voluntarily
on the assembly line and had previously given up jobs elsewhere
offering interest, status, responsibility and the opportunity to
exercise skill and ability. Because of their instrumental orientation,
they appeared not to be interested in jobs offering only intrinsic
rewards.

A more recent approach to job enrichment, which has not been
extensively evaluated, is propounded by Hackman and Oldham
(1975). The authors focus on five core dimensions of a job – skill
variety, task identity, task significance, autonomy and feedback. In
some respects there is a similarity between this scheme and that of
Herzberg's, for if a job scored high on the five core dimensions it
would almost certainly possess substantial 'motivators'. A high score
would materialise when the job requires the holder to possess a number
of different skills and talents; the job requires the performance of an
identifiable unit of work with a visible outcome; the job has a signifi-

cant impact on the lives and work of other people inside or outside the organisation; the job offers a high degree of freedom, discretion and independence at both the planning and execution stages; and finally, there is available to the job holder direct and clear information about the effectiveness of his performance (feedback) as he is engaged in carrying out the various activities associated with the job. Besides the five core dimensions, three factors mediate the effectiveness of a job enrichment scheme. These factors are employee growth, need strength and current job context. The individual who desires personal growth would respond positively to a job which scores highly on the core dimensions, but the individual who does not place much value on personal growth or accomplishment would find a job with a high score both uncomfortable and a source of anxiety. It is also suggested that if an employee is grossly dissatisfied with contextual job factors – e.g. pay, security, supervision – then a job high on the core dimensions would not be enthusiastically performed. Exploratory research carried out by Umstot *et al.* (1976) supports the Hackman and Oldham model with respect to satisfaction, but not when it is related to productivity.

Earlier different types of management control–procedural, social, supervisory and self-control – were discussed. As a means to structure the link between management control and human needs, we could envisage a crude association between procedural control and the lower needs, between social control and belongingness needs, and between self-control with distant supervision and the higher needs. Two major approaches to creating the type of environment in which the individual has the opportunity to exercise self-control are job enrichment, which we have briefly discussed, and participation. A classic study by Coch and French (1948) showed improved production after the introduction of changes to work practice based on group discussion. But an attempt to replicate this finding was unsuccessful (French *et al.*, 1960). Management at ICI saw three main benefits accruing to participation at the shopfloor level. People's unique knowledge of their work enabled them to identify waste which only they could know about; proposed changes were discussed in a positive cooperative spirit with both parties making suggestions and evaluating them together, as opposed to management making proposals which would subsequently be rejected by the workers' representatives; after formal acceptance, changes took place with speed and without disruption to the life of the enterprise (Daniel and McIntosh, 1972). However, though discussion with shopfloor employees was encouraged, a disadvantage appeared to be the apparent erosion of the middle manager's role. Aiming his discourse at accountants, Parker (1979) advocates participation in some form in the budget process. He believes that 'the budget process is more likely to be improved by each person's contribution of his unique and intimate knowledge of his area of company operations to the planning process and to the investigation of budget variance causes'. He also acknowledges that though this could increase the accountants' awareness of significant information, it could be a time-consuming exercise and unduly delay budget preparation. Some might view this prescription for participation as bordering on manipulation, but I am sure it was not intended to be that way. Involvement in the participative process does not always lead to commitment. Obviously Wallace (1966) recognises this when he emphasises that it is not just task-involvement in the participative process that counts, it is ego involvement that really matters. Foran and De Coster (1974) claim on the basis of an experimental laboratory study that feedback to participants about the acceptability of their proposals is a prerequisite to commitment. It would appear desirable that if proposals advanced by participants in a participative process have to be modified or rejected in the light of extraneous factors, then participants should be allowed to discuss these matters, otherwise they may be discouraged from continuing to participate.

Standards (or targets) in any control process are less likely to be accepted if they are seen as unilaterally set, and this is said to be particularly so if those affected by the standards see the individuals who devised them as not qualified to set standards in the first instance (Porter *et al.*, 1975). Therefore, the argument goes that if you want to foster acceptance of standards some participation in the setting of standards by those affected is desirable. There is research evidence available which indicates that some beneficial consequences flow from participation in the setting of standards. Hofestede (1968), who maintains that we can expect the budgetee's need fulfilment to be fairly high on Maslow's hierarchy of needs, found that higher participation in the budgeting process led to higher budget motivation, though participation in the setting of technical financial standards did not correlate with motivation. Employees participating in setting standards performed better than those who did not (Bass and Leavitt, 1963), though Milani (1975) offers only limited support for this finding. He appears to be of the view, following a field study, that participation is more likely to produce a favourable effect upon attitudes rather than performance.

There is always the danger of devising a control system which appears to give subordinates influence over decisions, but in reality their influence is negligible. Eventually people can see that their suggestions are not heeded or reflected in decisions. This illustration of pseudo-participation is embodied in a classic study conducted by Argyris (1953). He commented on the tactics of the controller who at one and the same time encourages an exchange of opinions and, believing that the line supervisors have not much to contribute anyway, is very keen to get their signatures endorsed on the new budget signifying their approval. The signature is then evidence of their approval. One should note, however, that if supervisors accept half-heartedly a budget target or budget changes, and are bound by their signatures, it will almost inevitably follow that the initiators of the targets or changes will have to be vigilant constantly, pressurising the acceptors of the suggested course of action in order to ensure compliance. This is not a favourable situation to be in for somebody who subscribes to the notion of participation as a motivational tool. There is also a danger of budget biasing taking root in a participatory budget system; this amounts to managers inflating costs or reducing revenue at the budget stage (Schiff and Lewin, 1970). There are other limitations inherent in the participative process. Although generally people would like to exercise some degree of control over their own environment, they may fear that by participating, their integrity and independence will be threatened or that they will be controlled to some extent by other participants. Should the rewards or benefits which accrue as a result of cooperating with others prove inadequate, then withdrawal from the participative process is a likely outcome (Crozier, 1964). It is also suggested that participation might lack appeal for those who do not trust each other, who feel intellectually superior to their peers and who do not have the patience to bother with it (Davis, 1967). With a specific reference to meeting the requirements of the corporate master budget, Parker (1979) feels that the ability of large groups of lower-level personnel to participate in budget planning must be the subject of some doubt for the following reasons. They may lack the interest and expertise required for comprehending the range of factors to be balanced in the planning of sales, production, materials and administration. Likewise, they may be limited in their ability to understand the need for identifying limiting factors and may be unable to co-ordinate their estimates with those of other draft sub-budgets. There may also be difficulties in comprehending the more sophisticated forecasting and simulation techniques as well as a lack of full understanding of the broader economic and other environmental factors affecting operations. Lastly, to finalise a budget with so many people contributing would present many problems for the accountant, and if planning were to start much earlier in order to accommodate this constraint, estimates may be out of date.

When our focus shifts to participating at the macro level, where workers' representatives or worker directors participate in policy formulation or implementation, difficulties arise with this form of power equalisation. Mulder (1971) made some interesting comments on the reality surrounding the operation of Work Councils in Yugoslavia. For example, 90 per cent of the talkers in the council were experts who had received higher education, the workers were inadequately motivated and in evidence was the growth of a 'power elite' and a small circle of competent and responsible people. On the basis of a personal impression of dysfunctional aspects of industrial participation in Israel, Child (1978) makes a very interesting observation.

The role of socialist principles in the establishment of Israeli institutions and, indeed, in the political life of the country even today cannot be overlooked. Bearing these factors in mind, one might conclude that if in that type of society schemes of participation and industrial democracy have on the whole become transmuted into techniques of management and have not substantially modified industrial hierarchy, then in societies where social stratification is more strongly entrenched there is even less prospect that the establishment of formal systems of industrial democracy will lead to any fundamental change of social relationships within industry.

Earlier in the discussion of self-control in the section on the framework of management control, the constraints surrounding any congruency between self-control and other forms of control were mentioned. Likewise, in the above discussion of schemes of job enrichment and participation, where opportunities for the exercise of self-control exist, again we found that constraints could invalidate their effectiveness. Nevertheless, the redesign of work and the involvement of people in decisions affecting their work, on the basis of the principles enunciated above, has much to commend itself in tomorrow's society. If more people wish to express themselves, and use their full capacities at work and they are willing and able to exercise self-control, rather than having to accept control externally enforced, then the concepts of participation and job enrichment have a lot of mileage. It is likely that people will change their ideas on what is legitimate control, in which case those responsible for organisational design will have to modify their concept of control. Over a decade ago Argyris (1964) criticised conventional cost control systems organised on a strict hierarchical basis, and suggested alternative control strategies which he believed would be compatible with the needs of 'mature' individuals. These control strategies are basically group-centred, where the group enjoys considerable autonomy for both the design and operation of the control system with significant discretion over whether or not to pass information on performance up the management structure. It would appear that a useful starting-point for the development of alternative control strategies would be the setting of mutually agreed objectives, whereby responsibility for their achievement would rest with self-managing groups; the self-management process would be assisted by the provision of frequent feedback on progress related to the objectives; and finally, at infrequent intervals the progress of the group would be discussed with higher management.

A real problem appears to hinge on whether it is possible to develop a culture in which mutually agreed objectives can readily take root. Where it is possible to do so, little difficulty will be experienced in reconciling organisational needs and the individual's desire for more involvement and self-actualisation. It is perhaps fair to say that very few organisational conditions lend themselves to the effective exploitation of the concept of self-control. There are of course subtle means by which control can be exercised in order to change the 'values' of the organisation in a direction compatible with self-control. This could amount to instituting recruitment strategies whereby 'appropriate' or the right type of personnel enter the organisation, and by a training and development programme that instils social values and organisational culture congruent with self-control. Before moving on to a brief discussion of the links between other forms of control – procedural and social – and human needs, it is necessary to say a final word on self-control. Child (1977) feels that it is most appropriate in conditions of uncertainty and rapid industrial change (e.g. new markets, techniques, etc). It is the specialist employees with their up-to-date knowledge or information that are effective, and 'traditional bureaucratic formalisation with its built-in delayed action cannot cope with the speed of information processing and response that is required'.

A theory X (McGregor, 1960) view – that people are naturally lazy and unwilling to work, and they must be bribed, frightened or psychologically manipulated if they are to put forth any effort at all – which can be equated with a lower position on the hierarchy of needs, could be reflected in procedural control where rewards and sanctions are of the instrumental type. This is a view reinforced by Caplan (1971) who states that cost accounting systems are still based on assumptions of an authoritarian model of behaviour. Hofestede (1968) admonishes the budget controller by pointing out that attempts at budget motivation by building on the lower-level needs, for people whose need fulfilment is fairly high in the pyramid, will be likely to have either no effect or possibly a negative one. Though it is generally recognised that a strong preoccupation with and attachment to procedural control can lead to diminishing awareness of organisational objectives and a 'red tape' mentality, as well as 'trained incapacity' – where previous training and past skills elicit inappropriate responses to changed conditions (Merton, 1949) – nevertheless, as was stated earlier in this chapter, procedural control facilitates delegation with some desirable motivational consequences.

Finally, social control may assume a position of importance when people are intent on the satisfaction of affiliation or belongingness needs. In the earlier discussion of social controls, particularly with reference to the bank wiring group and Jays, some employees felt it necessary to subscribe to group norms operating within a formal system of management control, and a primary motivation appeared to be the gratification of affiliation needs. It has also been suggested that affiliation needs could be gratified by budgetees tending to develop informal groups who will resist budget pressures exerted by the controller's department (Buckley and McKenna, 1972).

Cognitive

A cognitive approach to motivation has some connection with the tension reduction model discussed earlier, since skills which are relied on to cope with and affect and individual's environment are developed in pursuit of the reduction of tension. We learn about visual forms, how to grasp and let go of objects and coordinate the hands and the eye. Constancy facilitates the stabilisation of our perception, and we develop a cognitive map to guide and structure our behaviour. The individual in his relationship with the environment likes to be active, to explore, to manipulate, to control and to create and accomplish things (White, 1960). A cognitive theory of motivation recognises that many aspects of motivated behaviour arise when people are fully aware of their motives and actions, of the risks involved, and make plans guided by their expectations. There are a number of instances in the life of the individual when he engages in purposeful behaviour by first of all setting objectives or a course of action, then recognising the obstacles on the way to achieving the objectives, and finally overcoming the obstacles and feeling satisfied with the performance. In such circumstances success can lead to the development of greater self-direction.

The setting of goals has received particular attention in experiments connected with studying the level of aspiration (something within our reach), and it appears that we are more likely to be motivated by realistic goals where there is a recognition of the possibility of failure (Atkinson, 1964). Aspiration levels could obviously be set in isolation, but group influences are said to be important when the individual is faced with setting aspiration levels (Lewin, 1964). For example, if one's performance in an activity is better than the average for the group as a whole, this may lead to a lowering of the aspiration level next time round. But equally if one establishes that one's performance is worse than somebody whose standing in the group is low, this could give rise to an upward shift in the aspiration level. As regards the relationship between aspiration level and actual achievement, it is said that if achievement falls far below the aspiration level the individual may subsequently reduce the aspiration level until the disparity level is slight (Child and Whiting, 1954), settling at a level where aspiration level exceeds achievement by a small margin. Stedry (1960) introduces the notion of aspiration level and its impact on results and noted that the best results are associated with high aspiration levels. Apparently, the degree of difficulty associated with a budget target is related to both performance and level of aspiration (Stedry and Kay, 1964). A difficult target can produce a positive or negative effect in terms of performance, the positive effect (good performance) arising when the difficult target is seen as a challenge and when it is adopted as an aspiration level. But where a negative effect (poor performance) followed the imposition of a difficult target, the budgetee seemed to be discouraged, he began to display withdrawal symptoms and failed to set an aspiration level. So success and failure can give rise to variations in the level of aspiration, but changes in a person's confidence in his ability to achieve the target is also critical in this respect (Child and Whiting, 1954). Also, past budget performance is likely to affect future budget targets. According to Lowe and Shaw (1968), managers felt it to be in their interest to agree lower rather than higher budget targets, striking a balance between present job security and increasing future income. These managers, whose track record may be either impressive or wanting, were quite subtle in the manner in which they tried to influence forecasts in order to win short- or long-term approval or personal benefits.

Hofstede (1968) examined the effects on performance as a result of varying degrees of difficulty in achieving the budget. As the budget becomes more difficult to achieve, the budgetee is motivated and aspires to higher levels of aspiration, but performance does not reach the level of aspiration and likewise the budget target is not achieved. Beyond this stage of budget difficulty both levels of aspiration and performance fall because the budgetee does not rate his chances of achieving the budget very highly. This can create negative motivation and result in a deterioration in performance. Similar findings are reported by Otley (1977) who maintains that the budget target which motivates the best performance is unlikely to be achieved most of the time, but it has the advantage of creating the highest aspiration level. Whereas a budget target which is usually achieved – the budget target, aspiration level and actual performance converge – will motivate the individual at a lower level of performance. Otley adds that the use of departmental meetings were found to be useful in facilitating the internalisation of budget targets into a manager's personal goals. He also points out that a manager's reaction to a budget standard is also influenced by personality, organisational and cultural factors.

People who tend to define their goals or targets in accordance with some standard of excellence are said to have a motive to achieve. In developing the concept of the achievement motive McClelland (1967) focuses on the desire of people to be challenged and to be innovative, and he is of the view that the desire for achievement varies in individuals according to personality and other factors. For example, parental expectations and rewards are important socialising influences on the performance of children high in the need to achieve. Likewise, the need to achieve can be developed or modified through a learning programme, lending weight to the view that learning is an important agent in motivation. The centre of attention in any discussion of achievement motivation is invariably the high achiever, rather than the low achiever who presumably does not need a high degree of autonomy or discretion in his job and may feel favourably disposed towards procedural control. The high achiever is said to flourish when tasks are challenging but feasible, when he has a sense of control over what he accomplishes and receives regular feedback on progress. He prefers to work alone where he has control over the outcome of his actions, he dislikes situations where there are no standards to measure his performance, or where the task is too difficult or easy. Extrinsic rewards are viewed more as symbols of achievement rather than as an intrinsic motivating force; it is the desire for success that appears to be the major motivating force. Most organisational conditions would appear not to be compatible with the needs of the high achiever, since managers, particularly in large organisations, frequently cannot act alone. However, an association between achievement motivation and one particular form of management control has been emphasised – 'the most sophisticated budgetary system may be of little practical consequence if it fails to elicit the achievement motivations of a significant number of managers and employees' (Hopwood, 1974).

A useful concept applicable to the supervisory dimension of management control is the 'need for power' which is attributed to Veroff (1953). Unlike the need for achievement, the need for power is a motive that involves other people in the organisation and is closely linked with management styles. One group of managers high in the need for power has been identified by McClelland (1975) as being competitive, with management potential, in search of responsibility and institutional power. Power is often associated with prestige, status, social eminence or superiority, and it can affect an individual's self-concept. Sometimes managers who exercise control in organisations are looked up to with respect because they occupy positions of power, although they might feel uncomfortable if they were told they were high in the need for power because of the traditional link between seeking power and its negative associations (suppression, exploitation and tyranny). It may be argued as a general proposition that members of an organisation may prefer to exercise influence than to be powerless, and it is conceivable that managers and workers are much more likely to feel that they have too little, rather than enough or too much, authority in their work. Certain psychological satisfactions are likely to be derived from the exercise of power, and certain managers get enormous pleasure and satisfaction from influencing the work situation in a way that is compatible with their own interests. In some respects the rationale for certain organisational controls may be embedded in the psyche of the manager. But it is all too easy to become preoccupied with the rewards accompanying power and forget its more unpalatable side. Managers in their role of exercising control can suffer frustration and serious tension as a result of a number of organisational demands. Some of these have been identified by Tannenbaum (1962) as extra responsibility, commitment, loyalty and the burdens of taking decisions. The incidence of psychosomatic ailments among people in positions of control and responsibility is well documented, and has become a topical issue in recent times (McKenna, 1980).

A recognisable development within a cognitive theory of motivation is the emergence of expectancy theory. This theory basically expounds the view that we choose among alternative behaviours after anticipating the possible outcome of various proposed actions. A weighting or value is attached to each possible outcome and the subjective probability that an outcome will follow a course of action will be assessed. Finally, the course of action that maximises expected utility will be chosen. In Vroom's (1964) formulation of expectancy theory, the outcome is split into two, a first-level and a second-level outcome, and the causal relationship between first- and second-level outcomes is called instrumentality. There would be a strong causal relationship if the first-level outcome (a job well done) were to lead to a second-level outcome which is valued (material reward or recognition). The strength of a person's preference for a particular outcome, which can be positive (desired) or negative (not desired), is referred to as valence, and expectancy is the probability that behaviour (effort) will result in a first-level outcome (good performance).

Expectancy theory is placed firmly in an organisational context, with implications for management control, by Porter and Lawler (1968). The Porter and Lawler model is depicted in Figure 8.1.

The factors that will affect the amount of effort a person puts into his work are the value he places on the outcome which he hopes will materialise as a result of his efforts and the probability that reward will follow effort. But effort is not the only consideration, since a person's abilities and traits as well as his perception of his organisational role can affect his performance. Porter and Lawler maintain, on the basis of empirical evidence, that successful managers perceive their roles as requiring the display of inner-directed personality traits (forcefulness, imagination, independence, self-confidence and decisiveness), and other things being equal they are expected to perform better than managers who perceive their roles as requiring the display of other-directed traits (cooperativeness, adaptability, caution, agreeableness and tactfulness). Satisfaction arises when intrinsic rewards (e.g. feeling of challenge, achievement, success) and extrinsic rewards (e.g. pay, promotion, fringe benefits, etc.) are the consequence of performance, but the level of satisfaction depends on how near the rewards are to what the individual perceives as equitable for the services rendered. The closer the fit between actual rewards and perceived equitable rewards, the greater the level of satisfaction experienced.

The feedback loop between satisfaction and reward indicates that rewards associated with higher order needs (intrinsic rewards) assume greater importance the more the individual is rewarded. Apparently the more intrinsic rewards the individual receives the better from the point of view of higher future effort. The emphasis on intrinsic rewards reminds one of Herzberg's motivators; but unlike Herzberg's model, where satisfaction precedes performance, the Porter and Lawler model shows performance leading to satisfaction with rewards and perceived equity serving as intervening variables. But note the weight given to extrinsic rewards, such as pay, in the Porter and Lawler model. Reverting to Figure 8.1, the feedback loop between intrinsic/extrinsic rewards and the perceived probability that effort will lead to reward suggests that, if good performance is rewarded, the perceived likelihood that effort leads to reward will grow stronger.

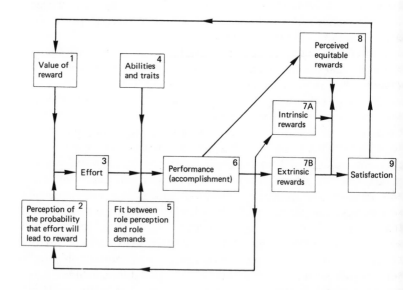

SOURCE: L. W. Porter and E. E. Lawler (1968) *Managerial Attitudes and Performance* (Homewood, ILL.: R. D. Irwin).

FIGURE 8.1   *Porter and Lawler model*

The message conveyed by the work of Porter and Lawler is that not only should jobs be designed or redesigned (job enrichment) so that they pose challenge, variety and autonomy – intrinsic qualities – but also extrinsic rewards, such as pay, should be provided and equated with perceived equitable rewards. In addition, there should be a match between the employees' traits and abilities and the requirements of the job. This has already been recognised elsewhere. For example, Carlson (1969) puts forward the view that where workers' abilities and experience correspond closely to those required by their jobs, job satisfaction will have a high positive relationship with job performance, while in those situations where there is inconsistency the relationship will be progressively lower.

What now remains to be tackled is a consideration of the Porter and Lawler model in the context of management control. Performance standards reflect managements' expectations of what constitutes successful performance, with an implicit understanding that appropriate extrinsic rewards will follow. It is accepted that recognition will be forthcoming if actual performance reaches the standards laid down. Whilst the individual is engaged in subjectively assessing the rewards associated with meeting standards of performance, it would be beneficial if he had access to knowledge or awareness of the set of rewards associated with effective performance. The subordinate's expectancy of future extrinsic satisfaction or utility associated with meeting standards can be affected by the degree to which the manager has recognised past achievements. In fact it is likely that there could be a revision of the expectancy that the meeting of standards gives rise to extrinsic rewards if management have been inconsistent in providing rewards related to performance. The significance of deviations from past standards is important when perceiving the difficulties inherent in achieving standards, and expectations may have to be adjusted accordingly. Apart from the satisfaction derived from achieving standards, there are likely to be occasions when people derive satisfaction from having activities structured and ambiguities minimised along the path to the attainment of goals. The above interpretation of an expectancy approach to control places much emphasis on the superior and subordinate relationship and the provision of extrinsic rewards, but it does not detract in any way from the potency of intrinsic rewards in this process.

The process leading up to performance evaluation (performance measurement), for the purpose of reward, has been the target of attack, particularly in the context of management accounting. Porter *et al.* (1975) believe that confidence in the measuring aspect of a control system is likely to be undermined if the individual feels that some aspects of his performance should be measured but are not. Confidence could also be diluted if the measurement includes items that the individual feels are misleading indicators. It is also suggested that greater trust is vested in measurements where subjective elements – i.e. a superior's informal notion of what constitutes good performance – are minimised or eliminated. Beresford Dew and Gee (1973) found that a significant amount of control data was not used because it related to events outside the province of the manager, it was too detailed or not detailed enough and it arrived too late. Hopper (1979) also reports criticism of management accountants in the budgeting process who failed to present information in an easily understandable form relevant to the manager's responsibilities, and were reluctant to ensure accuracy and realism by sufficient managerial involvement in the determination of the manager's information needs.

Because of the difficulty of measuring non-monetary aspects of performance, the accounting system usually restricts itself to reporting on financial performance. But therein lies a danger in that managers may be motivated to emphasise things that can be measured to the neglect of those that cannot. It is of course possible to create a composite measure of performance, incorporating non-financial measures, but then the priorities and 'value system' of senior management may be ingrained in the weighting each dimension receives. For this very reason it may be considered unacceptable, apart from the difficulty of translating it into numerical form. Frequently in practice attention is focussed on significant deviations from standards, as opposed to the meeting of standards. In such a system it is by and large the unfavourable deviation requiring corrective action that activates a response, whilst it requires exceptional success to attract management's attention and recognition. This type of system may be viewed by subordinates as negative rather than informative, with an emphasis on failure. The consequences may be defensiveness, over-cautious behaviour and other dysfunctional effects (Sayles and Chandler, 1971). Employees may be motivated to distort measurements used for policing purposes so as to present a favourable impression of their performance (Likert, 1961). The motivation to distort the measurements is to a large extent removed, according to Likert, if measurements are supportive and used for self-guidance rather than for policing purposes. In many situations in organisations it is difficult to measure a person's contribution to a set of results, because frequently tasks are interdependent and efforts are joint or inter-personal, where an individual may have only partial control over the outcome of a group's activities. In addition, external disturbances or chance events can invalidate to some extent the performance of even the most skilled operator.

However, though it is suggested that one should separate evaluation from control (Ross, 1957), because otherwise there might be an inclination to distort information and set easy standards to secure personal advantage, there is a link between the outcome of the evaluative process and allocation of extrinsic rewards. Elsewhere in this monograph Richbell points out, quite rightly, that the reward system can be seen as a management control system since it is designed to reinforce desired behaviour, though its effectiveness depends on how people value the rewards. The adequacy of the intrinsic rewards is a function of the role the individual occupies; these rewards originate from within the individual in the form of psychological satisfactions. However, management has some influence in the determination of intrinsic rewards since it can create organisational conditions within which opportunities exist for the exercise of self-control. Perhaps management's influence is even more pronounced in the provision of extrinsic rewards (e.g. pay, promotion, etc.) to reinforce perform-ance. But it is claimed, quite emphatically, by Porter *et al.* (1975) that for differential extrinsic rewards to be effective in motivating performance a number of conditions must be present. These are: (i) the organisation can offer important rewards; (ii) rewards can be varied widely depending on the individual's current performance; (iii) meaningful performance appraisal sessions can take place between superiors and subordinates; (iv) performance can be measured objec-tively, including all relevant measurable items; (v) it must be possible to publicise how rewards are given; (vi) superiors are willing and able to explain and support the reward system in discussions with their subordinates; (vii) trust is high; and (viii) the plan will not cause negative outcomes to be tied to performance. The condition which refers to objectivity in performance measurement would be difficult to meet, but this would hardly invalidate the effectiveness of a scheme that satisfies most of the conditions. Finally, the equitable nature of reward is important. We are all inclined to compare each other's inputs and outputs, consciously or otherwise, and if we perceive our input as justifying a larger output or if, on a comparative basis, we feel we are unfairly treated, feelings of inequity can arise (Adams, 1963). Perhaps some of us would also feel uncomfortable if we were overcompensated. A feeling of inequity could influence the level of satisfaction and the amount of effort put into a job.

CONCLUSION

A process of management control incorporating procedural, social, supervisory and self-control was suggested as a framework to examine the motivational impact of control in organisations. This framework provided the scene within which three perspectives extracted from motivation theory – personality, human needs and cognitive – were identified and related to broad issues raised by management control.

What appeared to emerge from the discussion is that firm hierarchical and procedural methods of control in a traditional sense, though not without some virtue or significance, may not altogether be the most appropriate forms of control.

However, there are discernible developments which tend to suggest that the application and widespread use of microtechnology could contribute to an increase in central control of a direct interventionary nature (Cosyns *et al.*, 1981). This would be brought about by an increase in information held by senior management as a result of developments in microelectronics. The interpretative function performed by middle management would no longer be required, and the discretionary elements of middle managers' jobs are likely as a consequence to be restricted because of the direct flow of information to senior managers. In fact the jobs of middle managers could be put at risk. Although there is likely to be large-scale deskilling of jobs, and a shift from direct to impersonal control by automated regulatory systems, certain groups of workers will need higher-level skills. Therefore in selective circumstances the potential for the exercise of discretion and self-control still remains.

A control system which facilitates the development of employee autonomy, where group acceptance and equitable rewards prevail, has much to commend itself, more so in the likely future turbulent conditions in society. A consequence of its adoption could be the enhancement of organisational adaptability and responsiveness. But a formidable constraint surrounds the effective implementation of this type of control system. The problem is basically, can we develop an organisational environment or culture, modified if necessary at the transitional stage because of differences in motivational dispositions, which is supportive of and compatible with man's yearning for greater autonomy? Here lies the challenge facing us!

9 Management Control and Worker Participation in Management

Suzanne Richbell

INTRODUCTION

Many studies of management control accept implicitly, if not explicitly, the traditional hierarchical structure of most organisations. Yet, an increasing number of organisations are adopting some form of worker participation in management where this traditional structure is changed. In view of this, it would seem appropriate that studies of management control should be concerned with the implications of such developments for control. It is recognised that whether an organisation chooses to adopt participation or not is based on value judgements. However, in this chapter, the rationale behind examining the relationship between participation and control is that worker participation in management is a phenomenon which is operating in many organisations today and on this basis merits study.

The chapter is in two main parts. The first discusses the concepts of participation and control and examines, at a theoretical level, the potential that participation holds for *increasing* management control of human resources. The second part adopts a more critical approach and examines some of the major human constraints which in practice may limit the success of participation in increasing such control.

WORKER PARTICIPATION IN MANAGEMENT

Definitions of worker participation have varied from workers actually sharing in the managerial decision-making process to an emphasis on workers 'influencing', 'taking part in' or 'being involved' in the management function (see for example, Walker, 1975, and Guest and Fatchett, 1974). More recently, Wall and Lischeron (1977, p. 38) have stressed that participation is not a unitary concept but consists of interrelated elements. They argue that participation 'refers to influence in decision-making exerted through a process of interaction between workers and managers and based upon information sharing'. This broader definition is able to accommodate the wide spectrum of participative schemes which have developed and is adopted here.

A classification of the types or levels of decision-making incorporated in the process of management is offered by Thomason (1973, pp. 138–9). He identified the 'directive' decisions concerned with determining the organisation's objectives and policies, the 'administrative' decisions which focus on devising methods and procedures for achieving the organisation's objectives and the 'executive' decisions which are the more day-to-day implementation decisions concerned with securing fit to the circumstances. Similarly, Wall and Lischeron (1977, pp. 41–2) offer a threefold classification of 'Distant, Medium and Local' levels of participation. While such classifications are helpful tools in analysis, in reality these levels of decision-making need not be clearcut and may overlap.

A further distinction is necessary between direct and indirect forms of participation. Direct participation covers situations in which the workers themselves participate in decision-making, while indirect participation includes those situations in which representation is used. Wall and Lischeron (1977, p. 42) point to the use of worker directors, shop stewards, works council representatives as examples of indirect participation. Gowler and Legge (1978, p. 171) argue that it is in larger organisations and those characterised by mechanistic structures that there is a greater tendency to indirect participation. The level of decision-making at which participation is to take place also influences the form of participation. In all but the smallest organisations, there are practical difficulties in attempting to involve everyone directly in decision-making above the executive or local level.

The possible combinations of levels of decision-making and forms of participation are presented in Figure 9.1. The shaded areas represent the combinations most commonly found as the ensuing discussion illustrates. The pecked lines emphasis the fuzziness of the boundaries between levels of decision-making. Within an organisation, worker participation in management need not be restricted to one level or form. A more complex illustration of possible combinations of these relationships is provided by Reilly (1979, p. 13).

Examples of worker participation at the 'executive' or local level of decision-making may include simple meetings between a work group and its manager to decide work arrangements. This form of participation may be formally structured or may result from a particular manager's leadership style. A more formal example of participation at this level is the establishment of autonomous work groups where, within certain constraints, work groups undertake self-management. A classic example of the establishment of autonomous work groups is found in the Volvo experiments (Aguren *et al.*, 1976).

Participative schemes involving the 'administrative' level of decision-making are concerned with how policy is to be implemented. Much British participation has centred at this level and, except in very small organisations, has tended to operate through a representative system, usually a trade union system. Major developments in the introduction of participation at this level were seen in the 1960s when some major companies adopted a participative approach to the formulation of productivity agreements. Examples of such agreements include the classic one at Fawley (Flanders, 1964) and in later years at Stanton and Staveley (Shaw, 1967). These participative agreements reflected a change in approach to the formulation of agreements from the pure conflict process of distributive bargaining to the joint problem-solving one of integrative bargaining (Walton and McKersie, 1965).

In Britain, participation at the policy or 'directive' level has proved to be a controversial subject as witnessed by the divergent responses to

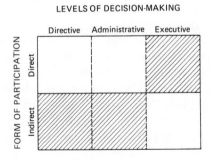

FIGURE 9.1 *Forms of participation and levels of decision-making*

the Bullock Report (1977). There are very few British examples of workers sharing in decisions at this level, one exception being the worker-director scheme of the British Steel Corporation. A notable contrast is provided by Germany where *Mitbestimmung* provides for employee representation on supervisory boards which determine policy and by Sweden where employee directors on boards have proved popular with both industrialists and trade unionists.

Not all participative schemes extend to the actual sharing of decision-making. Some allow only for employees to 'influence' managerial decision-making, usually through a process of consultation. This form of participation was found to be widespread in Britain in the late 1940s, although it has since declined significantly (Reilly, 1979, p. 14). In contrast 'workers' control' is a system where management is ultimately responsible to the workforce rather than some outside body. However, the degree to which workers participate in the management process may vary. In some cases, the process may be entirely carried out by workers elected to various committees while in others a professional management may be appointed by the workforce.

Although this chapter considers the relationship between participation and control, it would be unwise to suggest that all advocates of participation are concerned with increasing control within the managerial decision-making process. While many have favoured participation on the practical grounds of securing greater cooperation between workers and managers or as a means of enriching jobs and developing greater personal involvement, others have given their support on political or ideological grounds. As Brown (1972, p. 5) has argued 'various groupings who want "some participation" will, in fact, all be seeking different objectives varying from extreme ideas . . . through to quite mild measures'. Walker (1974, pp. 4–8), emphasises how controversial the subject of participation is and how it may be viewed in several different ways. However, he points out that underlying all the debate on worker participation in management are three basic issues: (i) how power is to be shared between managers and workers; (ii) how greater cooperation is to be achieved between the two parties; and (iii) how the personal involvement of the workers in their work and the enterprise is to be secured.

Attention is now directed to the concept of control and in particular to Tannenbaum's theory that there is potential to *increase* management control of human resources embodied in the process of sharing decision-making (Tannenbaum 1968).

CONTROL

The complex nature of the concept of control has merited growing attention and is implicit in the development of this collection of papers studying its many perspectives and dimensions. As early as 1920, Tawney declared that control was the most ambiguous and least self-explanatory of concepts. Machin (see Chapter 2) adopts a smilar stance but argues that, 'it is necessary to have a fuzzy concept to represent fuzzy managerial reality'. In spite of these difficulties, attempts have been made to define management control as 'the process by which managers assure that resources are obtained and used effectively in the accomplishment of the organisation's objectives' (Anthony and Dearden, 1976). However, this definition has been regarded as incomplete. For example, Lowe and Puxty (1979) point to its omission of the effects of an organisation's environment. Such criticism serves to emphasise the wide-reaching perspectives embodied within the concept of control and highlights the need for this chapter to state clearly its perspective on control.

This chapter addresses itself primarily to work organisations. It adopts an internal focus on the organisation and its prime concern is with management control in relation to human resources. Put into the context of Anthony and Dearden's definition, its focus is the process by which managers assure that human resources are used effectively in the accomplishment of the organisation's objectives. It is argued that the above process is fundamentally a process of decision-making and implementation. In this context, and under the more traditional autocratic model of organisation, the essence of management control over human resources is seen as the ability of those with managerial roles to secure the compliance of those with non-managerial roles with decisions made by managers and to ensure their implementation through a process of directing and monitoring human behaviour. Indeed Tannenbaum (1968) discusses control in terms of any process in which one party intentionally affects the behaviour of another. However, as the paper is concerned with organisations which have adopted a participative approach to management, the terms 'managerial' and 'non-managerial' roles are less appropriate as, under participation, both 'management' and 'workers' become involved in the managerial process and hence both parties take on, to some degree, managerial roles. Admittedly, the extent to which all organisational members take on managerial roles will vary greatly depending on the form of participation that is introduced. Under the participative approach, management control over human resources becomes the ability of all organisational members to secure the compliance of each other with their shared decisions.

Within the framework of worker participation in management, this chapter examines the perspective of Tannenbaum and Kahn (1957) which questions the traditional concept of a 'fixed' amount of control within an organisation. They put forward the idea of a variable amount of control and emphasise the possibility of increasing the total amount of control within an organisation by sharing the decision-making process among the different organisational members. This perspective is a break from the more established view of control depicted by the autocratic or oligarchic model, where formal or legitimate control is allocated according to position in the organisational hierarchy with the most control being at the top and the amount decreasing with descent of the hierarchy.

It must be acknowledged that managerial control as defined here is not the only form of control within an organisation. Groups or individuals may exhibit forms of behaviour which challenge and indeed sometimes overrule managerial decisions. The growth of restrictive labour practices in Britain is a prime example of how groups of workers have increased the amount of control they hold within organisations. But this is a win/lose situation in that where workers exhibit strong restrictive labour practices, then management will have less control over implementing decisions which involve the workforce. However, where the philosophy underlying management–worker relationships is changed from one of imposing decisions on workers to one of sharing in the same decisions, then the possibility of increasing the total amount of control exists, as both groups are united in a common activity.

If the exercise of control is viewed as an exchange of some valued resource by one party in return for compliance on the part of another, then the total amount of control in an organisation may be seen as a function of the amount of exchange involving compliance. The traditional managerial approaches involve workers in an exchange of compliance for pay while, under the participative approach, there is an exchange of workers' compliance for some managerial compliance in addition to pay. In this latter joint decision-making process, the total amount of compliance or control is increased as the situation is no longer of a win/lose nature. Tannenbaum, who has developed the concept of a 'polyarchic model' of control where all groups have important influence, argues for more concentration on increasing the total amount of control rather than concern with its distribution within organisations.

A diagrammatical representation of the polyarchic model is provided in Figure 9.2 through the use of a control graph which was introduced as a descriptive technique by Tannenbaum and Kahn (1957). They define the graph of the polyarchic model as a curve which remains high (i.e. control is high) for all hierarchical levels. Figure 9.2 also illustrates the contrasting curve under the autocratic model which is described as a curve which falls (i.e. control decreases with descent of the hierarchy). The shaded area represents the amount of control in each model.

The key to how participation may in Tannenbaum's terms increase the total amount of control within an organisation, lies in its potential to create attitudes of involvement and commitment to the organisation among all members. The argument for this potential is based on the view that individuals will feel more responsibility for carrying out decisions in which they have been involved and from this will stem a form of self-generated control at both the group and the individual level. Management surrenders its right to unilateral decisions which may be disregarded by the workforce and shares the decision-making process to increase the likelihood that the decisions made are carried out. In this way, participation offers a means of uniting diverse groups through a common role in managerial decision-making.

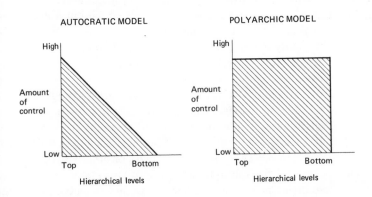

SOURCE: A. Tannenbaum and R. Kahn (1957) 'Organisation Control Structure', *Human Relations*, vol. 10, no. 2, p. 130.

FIGURE 9.2   *Control curves*

In terms of Etzioni's (1961) power/involvement matrix, this would accord with a shift in emphasis from calculative involvement based on utilitarian power towards a moral involvement based on normative power. Although in organisations where human resources are hired rather than acquired on a voluntary basis, some degree of calculative involvement is likely to remain. At a theoretical level it might be argued that a successful move in this direction would result in less of a need for control systems in the form of rewards such as higher pay/ promotion, as the development of a greater commitment to the organisation generated its own propensity to meet organisational objectives without the inducement of rewards. In this sense, participation might be seen not only as a means of increasing control but also, through its existence as a continuing exercise, as a mechanism for maintaining control which may come to replace more traditional motivational mechanisms.

The participative approach may be seen as giving workers more control over their tasks as they are given a chance to enter the decision-making machinery surrounding these tasks. However, by sharing in the managerial process they also become part of management and ultimately the process offers more control over tasks for the new, enlarged management body. In the same way, participation at the policy level provides workers with more control over goals but also through the shared decision-making process provides a greater consensus within the organisation. However, while participation may offer the possibility of increasing control over uncertainty surrounding the human resource factor, its potential for providing control over organisational outcomes is extremely limited. Control over uncertainty surrounding external factors such as technology, the market, the economy cannot be secured solely through an increase in compliance between the labour force and management.

In directing attention to Tannenbaum's polyarchic model and its potential to increase management control over human resources in organisations, there is the implication that such an increase is desirable. It is recognised that this implication is open to question and that differing opinions exist on the desirability or otherwise of such an increase in control for the individual, the organisation or society at large. These differences reflect varying value judgements and beliefs about the way society should be ordered. It has already been shown that many advocates of worker participation, which is the practical reality of the polyarchic model, may not base their support on any concern for increasing management control over human resources.

Other more radical schools of thought may oppose attempts to increase management control over human resources on the grounds that it is a means of preventing change in the present order of society. In line with this latter perspective, it might be argued that increasing management control through participation is helping to promote the present inequalities by bringing about modifications which aid the maintenance of the existing social order (Fox, 1974). Alternatively, it might be claimed that participation is a move from within the existing social order in the direction of redressing the current imbalance by giving workers the opportunity to take part in managerial decision-making and hence to achieve some control over the management process.

CONSTRAINTS ON PARTICIPATION

The second part of this chapter takes a more critical stance in relation to the potential of participation to *increase* management control as postulated by Tannenbaum (1968) and focuses on the extent to which certain essential human requirements for the successful operation of participation may exist within organisations. The three main areas of investigation are:

1. the degree to which there is a *willingness* to participate among organisational members;
2. the degree to which organisational members have the *ability* to participate;
3. the degree to which it is possible to develop an *organisational perspective* which organisational members will bring to bear in the shared, decision-making process.

Willingness

Although many participative schemes have been managerially initiated, this does not necessarily mean that the entire managerial team is in favour of participation or indeed has actually been consulted on its introduction. Brewster, Gill and Richbell (1981) distinguish within the management team those who formulate policy or the 'instigators' and those who carry out policy or the 'implementers'. The instigators are usually a small group of senior managers/directors while the main body of management are referred to as the implementers and it is the latter's actions or lack of actions which are reflected in the policies followed in practice. Instigators often assume that implementers will automatically adapt to whatever policy is presented to them. This misconception is particularly important in the case of participation where the policy relates more to the development of a general style of management rather than to the completion of specific tasks. Unless managers share a common understanding of the meaning of participation and internalise its values, then the extent to which management control over human resources increases will, at best, be extremely limited. In some cases such control may even decrease where the introduction of participation has resulted in the development of certain employee expectations of managerial style which are not met in the day-to-day work experience. Brannen *et al.* (1976, p. 47) provide evidence of differences in understanding of the meaning of participation between directors and managers concerned with the British Steel Worker Director Scheme.

Not all managers may find it easy to accept the participative approach. For example, some may see it as threatening as it allows a platform for others to question their decisions and ultimately their expertise. Managers accustomed to a traditional, autocratic structure may regard participation as an abdication of responsibility or as a formalised admittance of a loss of management control. Others may see participation as an imposition on their time and ability to meet other specific targets especially where its introduction is not accompanied by a corresponding reduction in their other duties.

Such unfavourable attitudes are not exclusive to managers but may be shared, although for differing reasons, by members of the 'worker' or 'non-managerial' categories. These individuals may find it difficult to accept the idea of engaging in an joint problem-solving approach with management especially where management–worker relationships had previously been based on the conflict model of distributive bargaining (Walton and McKersie, 1965). Where a participative scheme has been managerially initiated, workers may be suspicious of management's real intention and view the participative approach as a possible manipulative technique. Workers who belong to organised groups such as trade unions may fear participation as an attempt to undermine the power of such groups. This form of apprehension may lead to discord between various groups of workers as indeed was illustrated in Britain by conflicting views generated by the Bullock Report over whether worker directors should be elected through trade union channels. Other workers may simply not wish to take on the additional responsibility of engaging in managerial decision-making or may regard participation as a form of exploitation in that management involves workers in additional activities without paying for their services.

Such examples serve to illustrate the varying degree to which a willingness on the part of both management and workers to participate in managerial decision-making exists. But such a willingness is not the only requirement for a realisation of the increase in management control over human resources postulated by Tannenbaum. There is also a need for the ability to participate and it may be unrealistic to assume the existence of such ability.

Ability

In the case of management, and because of the very nature of their work, a certain level of competence or expertise in managerial decision-making might realistically be considered present. However, management's ability to use this expertise through a participative approach may be questionable. Many managers may need careful training in this sensitive area, if a successful change to a participative style is to be achieved.

In contrast, the extent to which the 'non-managerial' or 'worker' category hold the necessary skills and expertise to engage in managerial decision-making may be variable. It may be unwise to initiate participative schemes before representatives of the various parties involved have a sufficient level of ability in terms of managerial knowledge and skills. In many cases there is an obvious need for training in managerial skills, if worker representatives are to be effective particularly where participation is at the higher levels of decision-making.

The net result of a lack of ability to participate may be an output of shared decisions which may be regarded as 'poor' in the sense that they may occasion the organisation to fail in meeting its shared objectives or even threaten its continued existence. Where, through a lack of ability, workers or their representatives have misjudged issues which have resulted in adverse effects on them, then this may lead to a decrease in the amount of compliance workers are ready to exchange with management and so ultimately to a decrease in the amount of management control over human resources.

A futher barrier to the ability of both management and workers to engage in participation may arise from a failure to restructure organisational processes such as the communication system and the representative system to facilitate the change to participation. Indeed, limitations on ability due to organisational barriers or lack of training have lead to much useful prescriptive advice (see for example Bell, 1979) but such advice cannot provide for all forms of ability.

Organisational perspective

The third main area of investigation involves the potential constraint on the successful long-term operation of Tannenbaum's polyarchic model which seems to be inherent in the pluralistic nature of organisations. For the total amount of management control over human resources to be increased through the polyarchic model, it can be argued that it is necessary for the many organisational interest groups to approach the shared decision-making activity with an overall, general concern for the organisation reflected in an organisational perspective. In view of this, the extent of the diversity of subgroups within work organisations deserves further exploration.

It must be admitted that this chapter has been guilty of masking the degree of such diversity by referring to 'management' and 'worker' categories of organisational membership. While such terms may be helpful in an explanation of the broad principles of participation, it is necessary to acknowledge that they are blanket terms which imply an unrealistic degree of homogeneity within each of these two main groups. An examination of some of the bases for distinguishing various interest groups within each of these broader categories reveals the prevalence and entrenched nature of diversity and its inherent potential for conflict.

In the case of the 'management' category, previous discussion has cited Brewster *et al.* (1980) who distinguished between the 'instigators' and the 'implementers' on the basis of their role in relation to policy and indicated the potential conflict which may arise when implementers are presented with policies without prior consultation and/or which they find difficult to accept.

The strict hierarchical levels found in many organisations tend to separate groups of managers. In a similar way many managers internalise the values and culture generated in their particular functional area whether it be, for example, sales, production or finance. This leads to a tendency to approach organisational processes with a specific functional perspective rather than a more general organisational one (Selznick, 1966). The potential for conflict between line management and specialist departments was emphasised by Dalton (1950) in his research on line-staff tensions. Other examples of diversity may be found in informal coalitions of managers when there are clashes over values or orientations. Ultimately, any analysis must recognise diversity at the individual level. Variations in personal characteristics and motivational needs may act as a further restriction on any collective concept of managerial control over human resources.

Traditionally, under the autocratic model of organisation, any conflict which arises through diversity within 'worker' or 'non-managerial' groups is a restriction or attack upon the management control process over human resources but is essentially outside that process. However, under worker participation in management, the threat to management control from such conflict comes from within the management process.

Occupational categorisation represents one form of diversity within the 'worker' group as terms such as professional, white-collar, craft and manual are used to distinguish and unite certain workers. Trade union membership forms a further significant basis for differentiation and, although such groupings may serve to promote feelings of solidarity among members of the same union, they may also become a point for dividing those belonging to different unions. Individuals also hold membership of smaller, primary work groups. These may be formal (Sayles, 1957, pp. 131–45) but there is also a tendency for informal groups to develop whose activities may be different from those required by the organisation. The bank wiring room experiment (Homans, 1951) provides a classic example of the strength of informal group norms and the subsequent loss of management control over human resources.

This analysis would seem to confirm that group diversity is an inherent feature of organisations and that it may lead to conflict. Indeed, such conflict forms a critical part of Cyert and March's (1963) behavioural theory of the firm. In view of this, the pertinent question in relation to the introduction of participation, or in theoretical terms the operation of the polyarchic model of control, is whether it is possible to develop a unitary, organisational perspective within all members of the organisation which will supersede sectional interests. The extent to which this is possible must be a major constraint on increasing the exchange of compliance between organisational members and hence in Tannenbaum's terms of increasing management control over human resources. Indeed Tannenbaum (1968) recognises this constraint but argues that although factionalisation or intraorganisational conflict may imply special subgroup loyalties, these need not contravene the loyalty of the members to the organisation itself.

Closely related to the reassertion of a sectional perspective is the subgroup's perceptions of the distribution of control over human resources under participation. Whether a move to Tannenbaum's polyarchic model results in an increase in total control will depend on the extent to which various groups perceive themselves as having the opportunity to influence the managerial decision-making process. These perceptions are highly subjective, and Richbell (1976) argues may be based more on whether a decision affected the group in a favourable or unfavourable way rather than whether an opportunity to influence the decision-making process was provided.

The degree to which group diversity may be overcome in favour of the development and maintenance of an organisational perspective may be further influenced by the particular circumstances of each organisation. Internal factors such as the extent and form of participation introduced and the amount of training both in practical skills and attitudinal change will affect the perspective adopted. The previously discussed factors of a willingness and ability to participate are important determinants of perspective. Similarly, the influence of external factors which the organisation may have little or no control over may ultimately have a major impact on the perspective adopted. In periods of uncertainty, when particular interest groups feel threatened, it would seem likely that sectional or subunit interests would reassert themselves and take precedence over any general organisational concern (Richbell, 1979). Conversely, an organisational perspective may develop when the survival of the total organisation is threatened.

It would seem inevitable that although worker participation in management may be a means of stressing commonalty between groups, such groups will still remain and continue to be diverse. This diversity represents the continuing presence of a potential constraint on the development of an organisational perspective in the shared decision-making activity of participation.

CONCLUSION

At a theoretical level, Tannenbaum and Kahn's (1957) concept of the polyarchic model implies that the introduction of worker participation in management may lead to an increase in management control over human resources. However, at a practical level, it would appear that there may be limitations on the degree to which the polyarchic model can be operationalised. This chapter has identified certain possible human constraints on the functioning of worker participation and hence its capacity to increase management control over human resources. Clearly, in reality, participation does not necessarily achieve the high level of management control over human resources that Tannenbaum and Kahn postulate as possible. It would also seem that because of the dynamic nature of organisations, the amount of such control is constantly subject to change.

10 Self-control

Andrew P. Thomas

INTRODUCTION

A useful classification of the types of control in organisations is that by Dalton and Lawrence (1971) (see Table 2.2, p. 35) and Hopwood (1974) which relates to administrative control, social control and self-control. However, this has certain limitations in that administrative controls are socially constructed and executed, both administrative and social controls are exercised through individuals, and individual behaviour occurs in a social context. Furthermore, as Hopwood suggests:

> administrative, social and self controls ... can never be considered independently of one another. For if one type of control is working at counter-purposes with another, the potential power of each is considerably reduced and their joint outcome can often be problematic. The administrative controls of an enterprise may, for instance, be designed to reward productivity increases, but they may have little effect if the employees have developed their own social controls which place restrictions on productivity improvements. Or alternatively, the most sophisticated budgetary system may be of little practical consequence if it fails to elicit the achievement motivations of a significant number of managers and employees. (Hopwood, 1974)

What this, of course, takes for granted is some generally accepted idea of the nature of organisational control and each of these three types of control. As will be shown this is far from clear in the case of self-control. For the purpose of this chapter the author will adopt a somewhat narrow but fairly conventional definition of organisational control as a process based on influence, power and authority by which senior management ensure that subordinates execute prescribed formal duties, adhere to laid down rules, and accomplish certain objectives in accordance with given policies and plans.

Perhaps surprisingly a definition of the nature of self-control seems almost as difficult as defining organisation control. This is because it raises questions relating to the existence or otherwise of free will, it has been used as a synonym for system regulation, in addition to confusion about the nature of goal congruence, internalisation and self-direction.

The principal aim of this chapter is to identify and analyse the variety of uses of the term self-control in the literature with a view to clarifying its nature. This is a response to the emphasis given to the concept by writers on management such as McGregor (1960) and Dalton and Lawrence (1971) and, what concerns this author most, its comparatively recent introduction into the management accounting literature (Hopwood, 1974; Parker, 1977) with little regard for its nature and the conditions under which it may be an effective means of organisational control.

This author is forced to conclude that the concept of self-control has frequently been used as a misnomer for either social control or self-direction, and that in its uncorrupted sense may have limited applicability as a means of organisational control in business enterprises.

CONCEPTS OF SELF-CONTROL

A literal interpretation of self-control implies the control which individuals exercise over their own behaviour in contrast to the influence that is exerted by others or the environment. This raises philosophical issues relating to the existence or otherwise of free will. The first section of the chapter therefore addresses the question of the philosophical meaning of self-control in terms of individual free will.

The concept of self-control has crept into systems approaches to control to describe the tendency of social systems generally and organisations in particular to be 'in control' despite the absence of formal control processes. The second section of the chapter thus examines the systems theory meaning of self-control in terms of system regulation.

Most of the references to self-control, however, relate to the behaviour of individuals and usually lead to a consideration of human needs: 'Any understanding of the control which individuals exert ove their own behaviour must . . . be based on a knowledge of needs (Hopwood, 1974).

The third section of the chapter therefore discusses the psychologi cal meaning of self-control in terms of its motivational characteristics and some suggestions are given relating to the conditions under which it may arise.

This raises questions concerning the relationship between organisa tional goals and administrative control, and self-control. The fourth section of the chapter thus investigates the sociological meaning o self-control in terms of the process of internalisation.

The remaining references to self-control in the literature seem to equate self-control with what this author would call self-direction where the individual exercises choice over his own actions. However this may not be conducive to the achievement of organisational objec tives; that is, there may be a lack of organisational control. The penultimate section of the chapter therefore examines the distinction between self-direction and self-control in the light of an ideal type that arises out of the preceding discussion.

Finally, the insights gained from this reassessment of the nature o self-control are used to evaluate its possible role in corporat budgeting.

The existence or otherwise of free will

In view of the conflicting theories in philosophy, probably the firs question that should be asked is whether self-control in the sense o individual free will exists, or the extent thereof. Behaviourists such a Skinner (1973) would have us believe that all individual behaviour i socially determined and thus management control would presumabl consist of an organisational . version of the principles of 'societa operant conditioning' expounded in his *Beyond Freedom and Dignity* Given this perspective, self-control might be said to be merely a misnomer for social control. Despite its failings, behaviourism ha played a significant part in the development of disciplines concerne with learning, social interaction and behaviour control.

At the other extreme of opinions about the extent of free will ar religious views and existentialist philosophers such as Sartre (1957 who claim that there is no limit to our freedom except that we are no free to cease being free. The implication of this being that ultimatel all control resides within the individual. It is this type of thinking tha lies behind modern organisation theories where 'the essence of management control is the willingness of other participants to *accept* the authority of management' (Caplan, 1971).

It is important to appreciate that none of these theorists are claiming that human choices do not take place; at most they are only suggesting that choices are constrained by basic needs and factors outside the individual's control. The debate thus seems potentially reconcilable along the lines that man has freedom of choice (or self-direction) and certain basic needs and instincts which act as constraints on behaviour. As one of the founding fathers of sociology put it:

> While everyone holds that, in the matter of marriage, his will is, in the ordinary sense of the word, free; yet he is obliged to recognise the fact that his will, and the wills of others, are so far determined by common elements of human nature as to produce these average social results (Spencer, 1873).

System regulation

An approach to control where the term self-control is sometimes tossed around perhaps too casually is systems theory. Otley and Berry, for example, state: 'Social systems in general and human organisations in particular often appear to exhibit remarkable tendencies towards self regulation *and self-control* with no apparent conscious attempt to devise and apply control processes' (Otley and Berry 1977; italics added). This author finds it difficult to see how social systems exhibit self-control in the sense of being anything more than internal/informal regulation. It may be that the use of the term self-control in relation to social systems is just poor terminology in view of its implied individualistic meaning. However, if we take it to mean that human social systems contain mechanisms for maintaining order that are functional to its survival, two such mechanisms may be identified, namely instincts and social norms. Thus social systems may be said to be *regulated* by inherited instincts and/or social norms that are learnt through imitation, operant conditioning, or whatever. It may be argued with some justification that if social norms are internalised[1] they result in self-control by the individual. However, the internalisation of social norms does not of itself constitute 'system self-control'. System control occurs by virtue of the communal nature of social norms and the existence of means of ensuring compliance, which may be through internalisation though not necessarily. Thus when examining the use of the concept of self-control in the context of systems theory this author is driven to the conclusion that it can only refer to either some biological process or social control.

Motivation theories and goal congruence

The concept of self-control which probably stands out above all others is that in the classic work of McGregor who argues:

> The aim is to further the growth of the sub-ordinate: his increased competence, his full acceptance of responsibility (self direction *and self-control),* his ability to achieve integration between organisational requirements and his own personal goals . . . Selling management a program of target setting, and providing standardized forms and procedures, is the surest way to prevent the development of management by integration and self-control . . . Often such a development of management by integration and self-control begins with an individual who develops his own strategy and discovers its value. (McGregor, 1960; italics added)

The two most important factors in McGregor's conception of self-control seem to be commitment to organisational objectives and the higher motivational needs of man:

> External control and the threat of punishment are not the only means of bringing about effort toward organisational objectives. Man will exercise self direction *and self control* in the service of objectives to which he is committed . . . Commitment to objectives is a function of the rewards associated with their achievement. The most significant of such rewards, e.g. the satisfaction of ego and self actualization needs, can be direct products of effort directed toward organisational objectives. (McGregor, 1960; italics added)

Self-control thus appears to depend on the individual being motivated primarily by the self-actualisation need which produces commitment to organisational objectives. It follows that if any other need in Maslow's (1954) hierarchy is dominant the individual is unlikely to be committed to the organisation's objectives, and thus his actions may not be conducive to the achievement of those goals. A number of studies such as that by Goldthorpe *et al.* (1970) have shown that many occupational groups are not primarily motivated by the self-actualisation need.

The need for commitment to corporate objectives has been absorbed into the management accounting literature under the heading of goal congruence, and is regarded as a first priority in designing systems of responsibility accounting such as budgetary control. What is probably the biggest selling textbook on management accounting claims that: 'The first question to ask in appraising a system is: *Does goal congruence exist?* That is ... does the system specify goals and subgoals to encourage behaviour such that individuals accept top-management goals as their personal goals' (Horngren, 1977). Other authors define goal congruence as follows:

> to create situations in which each individual, in attempting to satisfy his own needs will be making the greatest possible contribution to the accomplishment of the goals of the organisation. (Caplan, 1971).

> the MCS should be structured so that the goals of participants so far as feasible are consistent with the goals of the organisation as a whole. (Anthony and Dearden, 1976).

The term goal congruence has thus been used to refer to the acceptance, alignment and consistency of goals, each of which have different meanings. It is partly the variety of uses of the term goal congruence that has led to the confusion which surrounds the concept of self-control. Furthermore, and what is particularly worrying, is that 'goal congruence' has been taken by accountants as a condition for designing management accounting systems without regard to whether it is suited to the kind of involvement that might be expected from a manager. A clarification of the concept of goal congruence would thus seem to be fundamental both to ascertaining the nature of self-control, as well as identifying the circumstances in which this may be an effective means of organisational control in business enterprises.

Three ideal types of congruence may be identified which arise from differing human needs and the kinds of involvement that these are likely to produce. This is depicted in Table 10.1 which also integrates the existing literature relating to Dalton and Lawrence's types of control (1971) and the kinds of power and involvement suggested by Etzioni (1961).

The analysis is intended to suggest that:

TABLE 10.1 *Variables associated with the types of control in organisations*

Variables	(a) Administrative control	(b) Social control	(c) Self-control
Operative human needs	Physiological, safety	Belonging, social esteem	Self-esteem, self-actualisation
Kinds of involvement	Calculative	Gregarious	Moral
Types of congruence	Goal alignment and behaviour congruence	Goal congruence	Internalisation of goals, values and beliefs
Kinds of power	Remunerative	Normative	Ideological
Rewards	Monetary, job security, promotion, etc.	Group membership, peer approval, status, etc.	Increase in self-esteem, and fulfilment of self-actualisation need
Sanctions	Monetary, dismissal, demotion, etc.	Disapproval, ostracism, etc.	Loss of self-esteem, feelings of failure, and guilt
Behaviour and performance standards	Rules, procedures and standards	Group norms, and (significant) others' expectations	Aspiration levels

1. Physiological and safety needs produce a calculative kind of involvement which given appropriate rewards and administrative controls results either in *goal alignment*, where in attempting to satisfy his own needs the individual makes the greatest possible contribution to the accomplishment of the goals of the organisation, or *behaviour congruence* where the individual's actions conform with the organisation's rules and procedures. This is said to be characteristic of shopfloor workers and lower supervisory levels.

2. The needs to belong and for social esteem produce what might be called a gregarious kind of involvement characterised by conformity to group norms of behaviour and commitment to group aims. Almost by definition, the existence of social norms gives rise to what this author has labelled a normative kind of power which relates to the coercive nature of group norms and sanctions. Herein lies the nature of *goal congruence*: several authors suggest that organisations are coalitions of participants and that goal-setting is a bargaining process (Cyert and March, 1963). This occurs in a social context exhibiting many of those characteristics described above. The result is a compromise among the various groups such that the goals of the participants are compatible with each other, and control over efforts to achieve agreed goals is exercised primarily through social controls.

3. Following McGregor, self-control is seen as dependent on the individual being motivated primarily by self-esteem and self-actualisation needs. This is likely to be accompanied by a moral kind of involvement characterised by the individual's perception of the similarity between his own values and beliefs and those of the organisational culture. The existence of both the self-actualisation need and a moral kind of involvement may produce a type of congruence such that individuals accept top-management's goals as their own personal goals. The author has labelled this the *internalisation of goals*. Internalisation is discussed further in the next section. It may also be noted that a moral kind of involvement gives rise to the possibility of an ideological kind of power where senior management are able to influence the individual's behaviour by appealing to his values and beliefs. Much of the above is usually said to be characteristic of universities, charities, religious and political organisations, etc. However, senior and middle managers in business enterprises who tend to identify with the organisation may also exhibit these features.

Internalisation

More recent authors on self-control stress the importance of internalisation[1]:

> Ultimately, all forms of control must be expressed through the actions of individual managers and employees ... ; the administrative and social controls have either directly or indirectly to be *internalised* by the members of the enterprise and operate as personal controls over attitudes and behaviour ... It is for this reason that many administrative controls attempt to elicit personal needs for material well-being and social acknowledgement. (Hopwood, 1974; italics added).

This view of self-control contrasts radically with McGregor's as being where 'an individual develops his own strategy'. Furthermore, Hopwood's suggestion that rewards aimed at any need in Maslow's hierarchy will result in internalisation is inconsistent with McGregor's view that commitment is primarily a function of the satisfaction of the self-actualisation need.

However, it does seem to this author that the concept of self-control, independent of any moral questions, hinges on internalisation. At this point it might be useful to consider an example. A few years ago a major UK company instituted a scheme at some of their depots whereby if all the employees in a work group lost no time as a result of injuries at work over a calendar month they received a bonus. Many individuals that lived through the 1930s who proudly boasted of never having been absent through illness found this most repugnant. The reason seems obvious: attendance at work was a value they had internalised during their socialisation. For the younger generation however a monetary inducement backed up by group pressures was apparently necessary to achieve the desired behaviour. The point, which is one of the main considerations of this chapter, is whether both of these generations were exercising self-control or whether in the case of the younger generation the outcome was a direct result of administrative and social controls. Thus while as Hopwood says 'ultimately all forms of control must be expressed through the actions of individuals', it does not necessarily follow that 'administrative and social controls *have* ... to be internalised' (using the sociological definition) to be effective. If they are (through whatever need is operative) then the resulting behaviour might be said to constitute self-control, and the individual may be left to 'develop his own strategy'. Alternatively if administrative controls are not internalised, senior management will have to monitor performance to ensure behaviour congruence or goal alignment. This is developed further in the last section on corporate budgeting.

Self-direction

The remaining references to self-control in the literature have a discernable thread which seems to equate self-control with self-direction: 'the control which individuals exert over their own behaviour' (Hopwood, 1974); 'self control affects everything which a manager does' (Machin, Chapter 2); 'self control . . . might be seen as a matter of accountants realising that it is lower level employees who really exercise control over their own activities' (Parker, 1977).

At the risk of being perverse these strike this author as simply being truisms in that no one would deny that at the level of the individual it is the individual who exercises 'control' over his own behaviour. In slightly different terms, as discussed in the earlier section on free will, few would claim that human choices do not take place. However, there is a fundamental difference between an individual's discretion over his own behaviour (i.e. self-direction), which may not necessarily be conducive to the achievement of organisational goals, and self-control that results from the internalisation of organisational goals and values as shown in Table 10.1. Furthermore self-control is not the panacea that some authors seem to suggest. In the absence of the internalisation of goals there is no alternative but to resort to administrative and social control. As McGregor puts it: 'it is clear that authority (as against self control) *is* an appropriate means for control under certain circumstances – particularly where genuine commitment to objectives cannot be achieved' (McGregor, 1960).

SELF-CONTROL AND CORPORATE BUDGETING

According to Parker:

> What may prove advantageous is a diminished emphasis by accountants upon the budget as a higher management control device and its replacement by a broader set of budget purposes of which lower level management self control is but one. This might be

seen as a matter of accountants realising that it is lower level employees who really exercise control over their own activities ... ; the accountant might well reconsider variances to be a decision tool of operating personnel themselves rather than of higher levels of management. In this context the accountant can still offer the traditional services of the 'budget group' ... The budget becomes a web of social and legal relationships and a network of communications. Herein lies the basis of a redefinition of the role of the corporate budget as being a mechanism available to all levels of personnel in the company for the purpose of planning, decision making, communicating and monitoring progress. The role of monitoring progress of operations could be viewed as a redefinition of the control role itself with a greater allowance for the possibility of self control by line managers. (Parker, 1977).

Once again one is led to wonder whether the reference to self-control is really appropriate for some of the reasons already discussed. First, Parker implicitly assumes that budgets will be used by managers which is inconsistent with McGregor's criterion of 'the individual who develops his own strategy'. Secondly, the quotation refers to the budget becoming a web of social relationships which suggests it forms a basis for social control. This, together with the view of budgeting as being a bargaining process, provides further support for the conditions associated with social control as depicted in Table 10.1, rather than those associated with self-control. Thirdly, Parker equates self-control with the discretion that individuals have over their own activities and the use of variances as a decision tool of operating personnel themselves. This only constitutes self-direction and knowledge of results. It says nothing about the conditions under which self-control is an effective means of organisational control. Indeed Parker does not discuss the question of congruence or the internalisation of goals.[2] The bulk of his article is devoted to the now well established negative aspects of the use of budgets as rigid, punitive, pressure devices, and little consideration is given to how self-control would be integrated with organisational requirements.

The self-control issue however raises some interesting questions relating to the role of budgets as a means of control. Accountants in industry acknowledge the existence of either one or both of the roles of budgetary control as being to enable senior management to monitor progress and/or as a feedback device for line managers to improve their own performance. The monitoring of performance by senior management provides an input into the process of formulating administrative and social controls that are likely to produce the desired responses by line managers; and the feedback to line managers indicates the means by which this may be achieved. It is this latter use of budgets that Parker describes as 'self-control' which really relates to their use by line managers in decision-making rather than by senior management as a basis for applying sanctions. Decentralised decision-making has obvious benefits to firms facing environmental uncertainty and changing technologies, the literature on which is fairly extensive (Bruns and Waterhouse, 1975; Waterhouse and Tiessen, 1978). However, the question of rewards and sanctions is a separate issue. The problem here is to encourage managers to whom discretion has been delegated to make decisions that are consistent with organisational objectives. The feedback of information to line managers does not automatically guarantee this and is thus not synonymous with self-control as this author has defined it.

SUMMARY AND CONCLUSIONS

A number of authors on both management (McGregor, 1960; Dalton and Lawrence, 1971; Otley and Berry, 1977; Machin, Chapter 2), and accounting (Hopwood, 1974; Parker, 1977) cite self-control as a type of control in organisations, and many suggest that greater emphasis should be given to it in designing organisational control systems. Most of these authors either take for granted some generally accepted idea of the nature of self-control, which is far from clear, or only define it loosely. The chapter therefore examined the variety of uses of the term self-control with a view to clarifying its nature and the conditions under which it may be an effective means of organisational control in business enterprises.

Five meanings of the concept of self-control were identified. The first, which relates to individual free will, was shown to refer to the exercising of freedom of choice subject to the constraints imposed by basic human needs and instincts. The second concerns system regulation where it may be that self-control has been used as a misnomer for social control. Thirdly, self-control appears to depend on the individual being motivated primarily by self-esteem and self-actualisation needs, and the internalisation of organisational goals and values. In this context an analysis of the various types of control in organisations based on differing human needs, kinds of involvement and types of goal congruence, was suggested. This leads to a fourth consideration which is whether self-control refers to the internalisation of administrative and social controls. It was shown that while self-control appears to hinge on internalisation it does not necessarily follow that administrative and social controls have to be internalised to be effective. Finally, many authors equate self-control with the 'control' which individuals exert over their own behaviour. This merely relates to exercising freedom of choice or self-direction, and may not be conducive to the achievement of organisational objectives.

This author is forced to conclude that self-control has frequently been used as a misnomer for either social control or self-direction; and in its uncorrupted sense, which depends on the individual being motivated by the self-actualisation need and the internalisation of organisational goals and values, may have limited applicability as an effective means of organisational control in business enterprises.

NOTES

1. Internalisation is usually defined by sociologists in terms of the acceptance by an individual as part of his own self of an attitude, belief or value held by another person.
2. He does however direct the reader's attention to an earlier article (Parker, 1976) in which he presents a convincing argument that goal congruence may be 'mis-directed in its basic conception and unsuitable for practical application' on the grounds that 'it is doubtful whether a single dominant goal can be found for any company ... in the absence of [which] ... the accountant who is asked to encourage goal congruence might ask congruent with what?' He further argues that 'the maintenance of goal congruence is not necessary for the efficient functioning of the corporate budgetary system'. This assertion however is founded on a definition of budget coordination as referring to 'a temporary agreement among personnel to settle for certain targets as the outcome of a bargaining process until they can re-enter the bargaining process at the end of the budget period', and a definition of goal congruence based on 'imposing top management goals upon other company personnel'. While this author sympathises with the suggestion that such a conception of goal congruence is misdirected and impractical, budget coordination has a separate technical meaning; one can, for example, coordinate budgets which have not been agreed by line managers. What Parker defines as budget coordination, i.e. the agreement arising out of the bargaining process, relates to the goal-setting process as described by modern organisation theorists which broadly equates with this author's definition of goal congruence.

Part IV

11 A Communication-based Methodology for Research into, and Development of, Management Control Systems

John L. J. Machin and Charles H. S. Tai

INTRODUCTION

Communication is a vital part of the management control process. If one wishes to cause things to happen as a result of the actions of others, communication is essential – organised or coordinated activity is impossible without it. It follows that the quality of communication in a work group is critical and that effective communication is a necessary (though obviously not sufficient) condition for effective management control.

Communication is so all-pervasive in work groups that the volume of communications, the diversity of the contents of communications, and the multiplicity of possible communication channels in organisations have combined to present a challenge to researchers which in the past significantly exceeded the data-gathering and handling resources and technology available. During the 1970s this technology became increasingly available, and during the 1980s its availability will be commonplace and its cost negligible.

This chapter presents and reviews a communication-based methodology which takes advantage of modern information technology and has been designed specifically for use in the field of management control systems. The methodology, known as the 'expectations approach' (EA) has been developed with the help of more than 2500 managers from over 40 organisations. In the course of its development the methodology has been used for two quite distinct (though obviously related) purposes:

1. To research the efficiency and effectiveness of the interpersonal communication generated by the management control systems currently in use in an organisation.
2. To provide a managerial information and communication system to support the processes of planning and controlling managerial activity.

The material in this chapter is presented in three main sections:

Section A. A short description of each of the 7 steps in the EA methodology.
Section B. A review of results obtained from using the EA methodology.
Section C. An assessment of the extent to which the EA methodology meets, and/or throws light on, the criteria for the design of management control systems postulated by Machin in Chapter 2 of this book (see Figure 2.5, p. 42).

SECTION A.   A DESCRIPTION OF THE MAIN STEPS IN THE EA METHODOLOGY

Whatever the disagreements surrounding the subject of management control systems, virtually every author (both in this book and elsewhere) describes the management control process as cyclical. The seven main steps in the EA methodology were developed to deal with the key communication elements in the managerial planning and control cycle (see Figure 2.4, p. 33). The first three steps in the methodology offer a way of assessing the present effectiveness of the management control systems in an organisation and can therefore be used either for research purposes, and thus be an end in themselves, or as the first steps in the development of an information and communication system to help managers to attain, and thereafter maintain, a higher level of managerial performance.

Managers can participate in research using the first three steps in the

EA methodology without it necessarily affecting their performance and without any presupposition that they wish to be more effective than they are currently.

The last four steps in the methodology represent the steps necessary to complete the cyclical process of management control. Managers undertaking these steps in the EA methodology are likely to be affected by the process, since the clear purpose of undertaking them is to improve the managerial effectiveness of those taking part.

Step 1. Documenting the direction and contents of interpersonal job-related, expectations

The first step in the EA methodology requires each individual in the participating group (which may be a whole organisation, a part of an organisation, or a number of organisations) to itemise two different kinds of expectations; those which they actually hold of their colleagues (known not surprisingly as *actual* expectations) and those which they think their colleagues hold of them (known as *perceived* expectations).

Each expectation takes as its 'subject' the person who is expressing the expectation, and has as its 'object' the person of whom the expectation is held. This first step in the methodology calls for each participant:

1. To identify from amongst the other participants those of whom he actually holds expectations.
2. To document as precisely as he can the expectations that he actually holds of the individuals identified in (1) above.
3. To decide which of the other participants hold expectations of him.
4. To document as accurately as he can just what he perceives each of the other participants identified in (3) above to expect from him.

In this manner each participant is documenting the inputs to his job (i.e. what he actually expects from his colleagues) and the outputs from his job as he sees them (i.e. what he perceives his colleagues to want from him).

Once all participants have completed the documentation of their actual and perceived expectations the data so produced can be used to provide information with which to assess the efficiency of communication within the participant group.

Step 2. Assessing the efficiency of communication of interpersonal, job-related expectations

A report is produced for each participant which presents, in the four-block layout shown in Figure 11.1, the data collected in the first step of the methodology, for every interpersonal communication channel which features the participant concerned as the 'subject' manager.

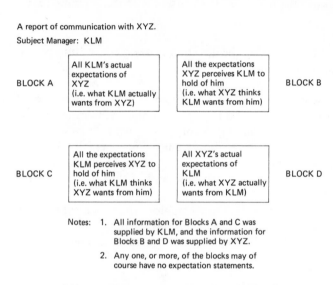

A report of communication with XYZ.

Subject Manager: KLM

BLOCK A — All KLM's actual expectations of XYZ (i.e. what KLM actually wants from XYZ)

BLOCK B — All the expectations XYZ perceives KLM to hold of him (i.e. what XYZ thinks KLM wants from him)

BLOCK C — All the expectations KLM perceives XYZ to hold of him (i.e. what KLM thinks XYZ wants from him)

BLOCK D — All XYZ's actual expectations of KLM (i.e. what XYZ actually wants from KLM)

Notes: 1. All information for Blocks A and C was supplied by KLM, and the information for Blocks B and D was supplied by XYZ.

2. Any one, or more, of the blocks may of course have no expectation statements.

FIGURE 11.1   *A diagrammatic presentation of one page of an EA communication audit report*

The efficiency of communication of desired activity by and within the group can now be measured by comparing the contents in the corresponding blocks of expectations in the report, i.e. whether the contents of the expectations in Block A *means* the same as the contents of the expectations in Block B, and whether the contents of the expectations in Block C *means* the same as the contents of the expectations in Block D.

The assessment involves comparing the *meaning* of the contents of the expectation statements, and not simply the words.

Each participant audits his own communication audit report in respect of both the *channels* of communication, and the *contents* of communication. Initially each participant checks for *broken channels* of communication by identifying:

1. Every situation where somebody of whom he holds actual expectations fails to perceive him to want anything at all (i.e. where there is at least one expectation in Block A but none at all in Block B).
2. Any situation where people perceive him to want something from them but where in fact he has no such expectations (i.e. where there is at least one expectation in Block B but none in Block A).
3. Any situations where people actually expect things from him but he has not perceived them to do so (i.e. where there are expectations in Block D but none appear in Block C).
4. Any situations where he perceives people to want something from him but they do not in fact do so (i.e. where there is something in Block C and nothing in Block D).

Each of the above types of broken communication channel clearly indicates less than effective managerial performance.

After identifying every broken channel of communication, participants then proceed to assess the accuracy with which the contents of the expectations have been communicated.

Broadly speaking, an expectation, if it is to stand a chance of being met, needs to have a content, quality, quantity and timing expressed within it. Each participant therefore assesses the following:

1. The clarity and precision of actual and perceived expectations (both those he expressed himself and those expressed by others).
2. The match that is apparent (in respect of every person with whom he interacts) between the contents of the expectations in Block A and the contents of the expectations in Block B (which represents for the participant an expression of his input needs).
3. The match that exists between the contents of the expectations in Block C and the contents of the expectations in Block D (which constitutes the output expected from the participant by others).

In a research application of EA the results of this step in the methodology give an indication of the efficiency of communication within the participant group. In a managerial application of EA the results of this step in the methodology pinpoint areas where the communication of the participants is in need of improvement.

Step 3. Classifying the nature of expectations

By the end of the second step of the EA methodology, each participant's job inputs (i.e. the participant's actual expectations of others) and job outputs (i.e. colleagues' actual expectations of the participant) are fully documented. The database so created is both large in size and rich in potential for both research and managerial insights into the managerial task and the ways in which different managers carry it out.

The classification of expectations enables researchers and/or managers to focus their attention on particular attributes of the managerial task. Thus researchers may ask participants to classify 'output' expectations in terms of:

1. Expectations the participant finds it enjoyable to try to meet
2. Expectations the participant does not find it enjoyable to try to meet
3. Expectations the participant finds it easy to meet
4. Expectations the participant finds it difficult to meet.

Management development specialists may ask participants to check those output expectations where the participant feels he is in need of training to enable him to generate the required level of output.

Managers using EA operationally usually choose ways of classifying expectations which have a direct bearing on job performance, e.g. by classifying expectations in terms of their relative priority:

E = absolutely essential, must be performed.
N = necessary, should be performed but if it appears possible that it will not be performed the holder must be notified as soon as possible.
D = desirable that this should be performed, but only after E and N have been completed.

The three steps in the methodology described so far provide a useful research tool for those seeking to understand the present state of management control within a given organisation. They also serve as the first three steps in the development of an effective managerial information and communication system to support managerial planning and control. Later in this chapter the authors demonstrate and document the results of using the first three steps for each of these purposes. This section, however, completes its presentation of the steps in the EA methodology by describing the final four steps.

Step 4. Validating the organisational appropriateness of the contents and direction of interpersonal, job-related expectations within the participant group

In every organisation where the EA methodology has been used, the reports produced in Step 2 of the methodology have included a significant number of broken communication channels, and many, many examples of poor communication. Managers have found that the reports produced in Step 2 of the methodology form an excellent basis for interpersonal discussions to improve communication within the participant groups. Participants discuss instances of poor communication with their colleagues, decide exactly what should be expected by one participant of another, and alter the EA database accordingly. Thus by the end of the second step in the methodology in a *managerial application* (as opposed to a research application) of EA, actual and perceived expectations have usually been improved to the point where they match in meaning.

If, during Step 3 of the methodology, managers rate expectations in terms of priority, and subject and object managers discuss and resolve any cases where they differ significantly in their view of the relative importance of an expectation, then they will have established by the *end* of Step 3 a database which carries most of the information necessary to support effective managerial performance.

In the first three steps of methodology, the development of the database is purely individual oriented. Such a process leaves two concerns for the organisation. The first is that individuals may wilfully decide to waste organisational resources – i.e. two individuals may agree with each other to expect *nothing* from one another, and thus actively contrive to lead quiet and peaceful lives making little, if any, contribution to the achievement of organisational purpose. The second concern is that individuals may, completely inadvertently, arrange to waste organisational resource. Individuals may perceive what they are doing to be completely in line with organisation purpose and may simply be unaware of the fact that what they are planning to do duplicates the effort of others in different parts of the organisation for example.

Step 4 in the EA methodology, therefore, requires either 'someone in authority', or 'someone with the appropriate knowledge', to decide whether or not each of the expectations documented in the database is actually organisationally appropriate, i.e. likely to contribute in the most effective way possible to the achievement of organisational purpose.

Step 5. Negotiating agreement to meet expectations

Once the organisation has ensured that all the expectations in the database are organisationally appropriate, the next step is clearly to seek to encourage all members of the participant group to attempt to meet the expectations that are held of them.

The fifth step in the EA methodology requires the participants to reach agreement between themselves that each will undertake to try to supply what is expected.

At this stage in the development of the EA management system there is no need to continue with the twin concepts of 'actual' and 'perceived' expectations. Once actual and perceived expectations have been brought into line, so that their contents match, there is an unnecessary duplication of statements in the database.

The systems and procedures that have been developed for the fifth stage in the EA methodology are extremely simple. Each participant selects from the expectations that are held of him those that he agrees to undertake to try to meet. At the same time, he chooses what he sees to be the most appropriate, clear and precise statement of what is expected (this requires a choice between either his perception of what is expected, the actual expectation that his colleague holds of him, or a new expectation which both he and his colleague feel expresses more clearly and precisely what is actually expected).

Effectively, this halves the size of the database because it now includes only 'agreed' expectations. The previous database including both actual and perceived expectations, whilst of interest to organisational analysts, is of no further use as a basis for a management control system.

To recognise the switch from a database made up of 'actual' and 'perceived' expectations, to a database of 'agreed' expectations, there is a change in the nomenclature for 'subject' and 'object' manager.

The person who holds an agreed expectation of another is called the *holder* of the expectation. The person who undertakes to meet the agreed expectation is called the *contractor* of the agreed expectation.

At the end of the fifth step in the EA methodology, each participant within the group receives two reports which contain his planned input, and his planned output, respectively.

The participant is the *holder* of his planned *input* report which includes all the agreed expectations he holds of his colleagues, together with the relative priority ascribed to his needs by his contractors.

The participant is the *contractor* for his planned *output* report, which includes all the agreed expectations held of him by others, together with his rating of their relative priority in the context of his job.

After some period of time (and the most appropriate length of time will obviously vary from organisation to organisation, and frequently from level to level within the same organisation), participants need to obtain, and to give, feedback on the extent to which agreed expectations are being met. The sixth step in the EA methodology covers this process.

Step 6. Reporting on the extent to which agreed expectations are being met

The first five steps in the EA methodology are normally carried out in a relatively short period of time as directly consequential steps. The sixth step in the EA methodology is usually undertaken some months after the completion of Step 5 (Reid, 1980).

Each participating manager rates, as *contractor*, the level of performance that he believes himself to be achieving in meeting the needs of his colleagues. At the same time each participating manager rates, as *holder*, his colleagues' performance in meeting the agreed expectations that he holds of them.

The systems and procedures developed to support such reporting can be tailored to the facilities available within an organisation. Those with ample VDUs available may find the quickest and easiest method of reporting performance is for participants to enter their ratings directly.

For those organisations without those facilities the EA computer programs permit batch processing of turn-around documents where a manager merely tears off a specific slip from his contractors' or holders' report, which has space on it for ticking the performance level he wishes to ascribe to each expectation.

The performance reports supplied to a manager by the EA methodology are the most detailed and objective provided by any system currently available. The contractor's performance report and the holder's performance report for each participating manager have two distinct attributes in the expectations approach methodology:

1. Agreed expectations are rated in respect of their performance both
   by the contractor and by the holder – i.e. by both the supplier and
   the receiver.
2. Because the expectations approach methodology makes no pre-
   suppositions about hierarchical relationship, the performance
   reporting facility is omnidirectional (thus in one organisation the
   managing director was reporting on the tea-queen in respect of the
   quality of her tea, and the tea-queen was reporting on the
   managing director's ability to remember to have the right money
   on a Friday).

The reader can no doubt immediately bring to mind some organisations that would welcome the opportunity of using such an effective
system and others where certain members of the organisation would
be appalled by the facilities offered by EA.

Otley, in Chapter 4, makes the important distinction between
feedback reporting and feedforward reporting. The authors of this
chapter believe the latter to be much the more important in the
planning and control of managed cost. Their belief has been reinforced by the observation of managers using the EA reporting procedures as a way of obtaining information which might help them to
plan their future performance more effectively, rather than as information on which to base discussions about who was more (or less)
effective in the past.

Managerial jobs, and the demands that are made of them, are
changing rapidly. Indeed, one of the main contentions of all the contributors to this book is that society and technology are changing so
fast that management control systems theory needs to be thoroughly
reviewed. The manager's job itself will change enormously over the
next fifteen to twenty years, and if that change is to be handled and
incorporated inside organisations in a planned manner, management
control systems in the future must be able to respond rapidly to
significant changes in the managerial job. It necessarily follows that in
any planning and control cycle there must be a step devoted to
reviewing the extent to which each managerial job requires modification and change over the following year to ensure that the manager
concerned is trying to meet the needs of the next year, rather than the
needs and the environment of the previous year.

Step 7. Reviewing and re-planning the participants' jobs

Each participant checks through his holder's report to decide which expectations need modification in the light of changing demands on the participant and on his job. Changes may be brought about by new technology, new colleagues, new skills which he has recently acquired, etc.

Each participant checks through his contractor's report discarding items that are no longer wanted, seeking new items to produce which will give him greater job satisfaction, and negotiating changes with his work group which are likely to give rise to higher group performance overall as a result of changing the distribution of tasks in the group.

The EA computer programs and procedures allow that to be done simply and with the confidence that re-routed expectations will have an identified contractor, whose responsibility it will be subsequently to agree to meet the expectation.

The EA management information and communication system derived from the methodology described in this section of the chapter can help any organisation in which managers are seeking to improve managerial job design by improving the match between individual skills and task requirements.

The number of communication channels in use in even small organisations is very large. (In one organisation researched using EA, there were 25 managers and therefore 600 communication channels. Of these channels, 315 were actually in use! (Craven, 1981). In a large organisation the number of communication channels is virtually infinite. Only with modern information technology was it possible to develop a system which could enable managers to discover whether they were communicating efficiently (in the sense that what they wished to communicate to others was received and understood by others in precisely the way intended), and effectively (in the sense that what they wished to be done for them by others was actually done).

The same modern information technology has made it possible for researchers to study the communication which takes place in management control. The results obtained by researchers studying the data collected by the EA methodology form the subject of the next section of this chapter.

SECTION B. A REVIEW OF RESULTS OBTAINED FROM USING THE EA METHODOLOGY

The EA methodology has been tested in more than 40 organisations. The present authors can do no more than select a few key conclusions from this wealth of research which is listed and fully annotated in Brookes *et al.* (1982).

The documentation of interpersonal job-related expectations which constitutes the first step in the EA research methodology produces an immense volume of data, the very richness of which poses problems for the researcher. Because each participant documents his input and output expectations in the detail, and in the manner, that he wishes, the personality of each participant comes through strongly from even the most cursory reading of the expectations in the database (Machin and Tai, 1979).

In most *research* applications of EA, participants have been given no guidance on, and presented with no constraints as to, the kinds of expectations that they should document. Participants have reacted to that common trigger mechanism in a wide variety of ways. Some have documented only those expectations which were specifically to do with the tasks associated with their jobs. Others have documented in great detail the expectations they hold of their working colleagues in respect of relationships, i.e. friendships, and what could best be described as the 'group norms' affecting the working group.

The pattern of communication

Analysis of the expectation data shows that there is a close relationship between the *direction of communication* and the *content of the material communicated* in expectation statements. Three fairly recognisable patterns of communication within participant groups have emerged:

1. *Hierarchical.* Expectations carrying communication concerning policy, plans, objectives, goals, targets, and control, tend in most participant groups to be hierarchical, i.e. expectations carrying such information follow the lines of the organisation chart.
2. *Omnidirectional.* Communication of expectations concerned with the processes whereby individual participants achieve their objectives (e.g. expectations concerned with advice, information, coordination, cooperation, providing, agreeing and negotiating etc.) tends to be omnidirectional, i.e. lateral and diagonal communication in respect of these items, is quite as frequent as (and in many cases far more frequent than) vertical communication.
3. *Focal person.* Communication of expectations about a particular specialist skill (e.g. statistics, safety, manpower planning, etc.), tends to concentrate on a particular specialised focal person.

Sometimes the analysis of EA data shows the inappropriateness of managerial titles. In one senior management team which included an 'information manager', the only specialist, 'focal person' expectations in respect of that individual were about statistics! Expectations concerning information were spread omnidirectionally throughout the group and did not in any way converge on the 'information manager'.

Volume of expectations per person

The volume of data obtained by the first step in the EA methodology is awesome. Despite the volume – both of expectations and of research applications – it has been impossible to identify in a significant manner the factors which affect the number of expectations which a manager will document. There is some indication that the number of expectations exchanged within a participant group is affected by the organisational structure. Within matrix organisations the number of expectations documented seems appreciably higher per participant than in traditional line structures. In senior management groups the number of expectations documented per participant has ranged from a low of approximately 100 expectations in a traditionally structured organisation to well over 200 expectations per participant in a matrix-structured, senior management team.

Any such figures are relatively meaningless as an indication of the volume of communication necessary for effective managerial performance within a senior management group however, because the number of expectations documented by participants is undoubtedly affected by the size of the participant group and by the research being carried out. In those organisations where the whole of the participant group was keen to audit their communication, the number of expectations documented was significantly higher than in those organisations where only a limited number of members of the participant group were activitely keen to use EA methodology to help them to become more effective.

In virtually every application of EA, however, the volume of expectations impacting on managerial job-holder has exceeded 100 and in some jobs has risen above 300. At the very least, the EA methodology provided managers for the first time with a checklist of such expectations as a help in day-to-day job planning. It is difficult to see how managers could keep *effective* control of such a volume of expectations without such a checklist.

Contents of expectations

The analysis of the contents of expectations statements is beset by all the problems associated with any analysis of free structure written language. Given the volume of data to be analysed, researchers have developed a methodology for analysing content that works in a number of progressively more sophisticated steps:

(i) Key words (or rootstocks)

Researchers have found from reading the thousands of pages of managers' EA reports which so far have been produced, that certain key words appear to be used consistently, not only within a given participant group, but in any participant group. Words such as 'policy' and 'plan' seem to mean approximately the same things in any participant group.

Words like 'advice' tend to mean the same thing in most participant groups though sometimes participants use the word 'advise' to mean something almost synonymous with 'inform'. Equally, an expectation worded: 'Please advise me on . . .' and an expectation worded: 'Please give me advice on . . .' clearly mean virtually the same and for the purpose of initial data-analysis the use of the word rootstock ADVI is preferable to the use of either 'ADVISE' or 'ADVICE', since only the rootstock 'ADVI' will capture both expectation statements.

The word used for a given concept can vary enormously from participant group to participant group and in respect of some concepts many words may be used for the same concept within a given participant group. The influence of management by objectives, for example, has been neither total nor uniform. Even within a given participant group the words 'goal', 'target', 'objective' and 'aim', may be used by different people to mean the same thing – and by a given participant to mean different things.

Using a single key word (or rootstock), the initial analysis of an EA database can identify areas of potentially poor or inadequate communication where more detailed analysis is needed, either to correct what turns out to be an incorrect view of what is going on, or to confirm it!

Two examples will be given to illustrate such analyses. The first (Table 11.1) shows the volumes of expectations containing *'advi'* written by, and of, each of the ten participants in a senior management team.

TABLE 11.1   *Individual communication content summary – 'ADVI'*

| | Input to subject manager | | Output from subject manager | |
Subject manager	Actual wants	Colleagues perceive him to need	Perceives colleagues to need	Colleagues actual wants
JMG	12	24	14	14
WJW	7	25	29	18
GWI	4	15	0	8
CHS	1	8	18	14
RJG	0	7	24	8
AKH	12	9	5	5
TJP	2	16	5	1
EWB	10	16	2	1
SJO	4	15	8	1
NRA	19	14	44	1
Total	71	149	149	71

The numbers shown indicate the number of actual and perceived expectations respectively which contained the rootstock 'ADVI'.

Thus: Manager JMG holds 12 actual expectations of his colleagues containing 'ADVI'.
JMG's colleagues collectively wrote 24 expectations in which they perceived JMG to want 'ADVI'.

The information set out in Table 11.1 gives a fascinating insight into the different ways in which members of that senior management team offer, and look for, advice from their colleagues. The respective totals of actual and perceived expectations are likely to confirm the reader's own managerial experience. Within this team overall, the propensity to *offer* advice is twice as great as the propensity to *seek* it! RJG sees himself as having no need for advice but offers a great deal (24 expectations worth) to others. GWI, on the other hand, does not think that anyone would want to receive advice from him yet quite a lot (8 expectations worth) is in fact wanted.

This senior management team included four people with ostensibly identical jobs. TJP, EWB, SJO and NRA each carried broadly equivalent responsibility for four different geographic areas. Quite clearly, although they were doing similar jobs, they had very different attitudes to the offering and seeking of advice.

(ii) Groups of key words

A more sophisticated analysis of the contents of expectations state
ments can be achieved by carrying out an analysis which looks for one
or more of a group of cognate words, rather than just a single key word

The results of such an analysis for the same team of managers is
shown in Table 11.2. In this case the analysis was for: goal, target
objective.

Again, Table 11.2 gives an interesting insight into the quality o
communication with the team in respect of 'GOAL, TARGET, OBJ'
Four members of the group had no actual expectations at all con
cerning any of those words, yet every member was perceived to expec
something in connection with them (mostly by the chief executive
JMG!).

Six members of the group perceived none of their colleagues to
expect anything of them in respect of those words.

TABLE 11.2   *Individual communication content summary: GOAL,*
TARGET, OBJ

	Input to subject manager		Output from subject manager	
Subject manager	*Actual wants*	*Colleagues perceive him to need*	*Perceives colleagues to need*	*Colleagues actual wants*
JMG	5	5	24	5
WJW	6	6	5	4
GWI	0	3	0	1
CHS	0	3	0	0
RJG	0	2	0	3
AKH	1	3	0	0
TJP	0	4	0	2
EWB	1	4	0	2
SJO	5	4	4	2
NRA	3	4	5	2
Total	21	38	38	21

The numbers shown indicate the number of actual and perceived expectation
respectively which contained one or more of the following: GOAL, TARGET
OBJ.

It is a reflection on the effectiveness of management control within the team that four managers, GWI, CHS, RJG and TJP did not use any of those three words in *any* of the expectations they wrote.

Analysis of the contents of expectations enables researchers to understand more clearly both the style and the processes of management control within a working group. For example, the relative frequency of use of words like 'direct', 'direction', 'instruct', 'instruction', can be compared with the frequency of use of words such as 'assist', 'assistance', 'advise', 'advice', both in respect of each individual's communication and in respect of the participant group as a whole. Such information is usually of interest both to the researcher and to the participants, who may well turn to the management development personnel within the organisation for advice or training when this seems desirable in the interests of more effective team performance.

Assessing the efficiency of communication within the participant group

An important factor affecting the effectiveness of managerial performance within a participant group is the extent to which there is *agreement* about the most appropriate control style and the most effective management control interactions that should exist in the group – i.e. whether the content of an actual expectation is both *appropriate* and *matched* by the content of the relevant perceived expectation. If an individual is seeking 'advice' but is being offered 'instruction', for example, it is unlikely that fully effective performance will result. Researchers are, therefore, interested not only in the contents of the expectations statements produced by the first step in the EA methodology, but by the extent to which the contents of such expectations are found to be reciprocated during the second step of the methodology when individuals assess the efficiency of interpersonal communication within the participant group.

Researchers can only go so far in assessing the efficiency of interpersonal communication within a participant group through the analyses of actual and perceived expectations statements. Only the two managers involved in a dyadic pair can make a completely accurate assessment of whether a specific actual expectation and a specific perceived expectation mean the same thing to both the 'subject' and 'object' managers concerned. As with the analyses of the contents of expectations statements, however, analyses can be carried out at many different levels of detail, and the researcher can always work from a fairly general analysis through to the precise detail of particular expectations, if the former shows that the latter analysis is desirable. In particular, a researcher concerned to assess the efficiency of inter-personal communication within a participant group can gain consider-able insight into the group's effectiveness from analysing the usage of communication channels before assessing the match of actual and perceived expectations being sent along any one channel.

(i) Unreciprocated channels of communication

Where one participant within the group actually expects one or more things from a colleague and the latter does not perceive the former to expect *anything at all*, there is clear *prima facie* evidence of inefficient communication. Computer analysis of the EA database can identify broken channels at the same different levels of sophistication of analysis as were described above in connection with contents analysis.

Analyses of communication channels can be carried out: for all communication; for single key words; and for groups of cognate words. Thus, for example, the communication channel matrix for 'ADVI' in the same senior management team is shown in Figure 11.2.

A summary of the information presented in Figure 11.2 shows that of the 90 interpersonal communication channels in the group, 19 are not used at all ('/.), 24 are reciprocated (P/A) and no less than 47 are unreciprocated. Of these 34 channels carry a perception that ADVI is wanted when in fact it is not (P/.) and 13 channels carry a request for ADVI which is not perceived to be wanted ('/A).

It is difficult to believe that the management control systems in use in an organisation are really effective when interpersonal communica-tion at the top includes such a high number of unreciprocated channels in respect of such an important element of the senior management job.

The results shown in Tables 11.1 and 11.2, and Figure 11.2 are *typical* of the results in all 40 organisations in which research has been undertaken. (See Machin 1983 for more detailed research results.)

(ii) How matched is the contents of interpersonal communication?

The analysis presented above on broken channels dealt with the entire participant group.

Where the *contents* of expectations are concerned, however, the

SUBJECT MANAGERS OF PERCEIVED EXPECTATIONS

		Senior managers		H.O. Department managers				Area managers			
		JMG	WJW	GWI	CHS	RJG	AKH	TJP	EWB	SJO	NRA
JMG		•	P / A	• / A	P / A	• / A	• / A	P / •	P / •	P / •	P / •
WJW		P / A	•	• / A	P / A	P / A	• / •	P / •	P / •	P / •	P / •
GWI		P / A	P / •	•	P / A	P / A	• / A	• / •	• / •	P / •	P / •
CHS		P / •	P / •	• / A	•	P / •	• / •	• / •	• / •	• / •	P / •
RJG		P / •	P / •	• / •	P / •	•	P / •	• / •	• / •	• / •	P / •
AKH		P / •	P / A	• / A	• / A	P / A	•	• / A	• / A	• / A	P / A
TJP		P / •	P / •	• / •	P / A	P / A	P / •	• / •	• / •	P / •	P / •
EWB		P / A	P / A	• / •	P / A	P / A	P / A	• / •	• / •	P / •	P / •
SJO		P / •	P / •	• / A	P / A	P / A	P / A	• / •	• / •	• / •	P / •
NRA		P / A	P / A	• / A	P / A	P / •	P / •	• / •	• / •	P / •	• / •

SUBJECT MANAGERS OF ACTUAL EXPECTATIONS (left vertical axis)

OUTPUT FROM (right vertical axis)

INPUT TO

P   P is printed when the manager on the top axis has written one or more PERCEIVED expectations about the manager on the left axis.

A   A is printed when the manager on the left axis has written one or more ACTUAL expectations about the manager on the top axis.

•   • is printed when no expectations have been expressed.

FIGURE 11.2   *Communication channel analysis: channels carrying expectations containing ADVI*

researcher will usually also wish to study each individual participant's communication both to identify the contents of the job they do, and to ascertain the extent to which the job as seen by the role-holder equates with the way his job is seen by his colleagues. It is difficult to believe that a manager can achieve an effective level of performance if the job he is actually trying to do is significantly different from the job that his colleagues would choose to have him do.

EA research data can be analysed to present two contrasting profiles – the profile of the job as the role-holder sees it, and the profile of the job as his colleagues see it.

The EA database, of course, contains documentation of both job *inputs* and job *outputs*. As a result, the EA job profile for any one individual has four elements in it, as shown in Figure 11.3.

The managerial job profile shown in Figure 11.3 is based on the fundamental elements of the managerial planning and control cycle. Clearly, researchers can vary the horizontal axis of the job profile to satisfy their own research interests. Once a job profile axis has been settled upon by a researcher there is virtually unlimited scope for comparing the profiles of similar jobs in different organisations, or of different jobs within the same organisation.

Researchers have also been concerned to study the way in which the job is carried out. A managerial planning and control job profile was shown in Figure 11.3. A managerial actions and styles job profile for the same manager is shown in Figure 11.4.

The authors wished in this section to demonstrate the flexibility of the analytical tools available with a communication based methodology as well as the results obtained from using them.

In the course of doing so, the authors hope that they have shown EA to be a contingent methodology which generates large quantities of complex job-related data which can yield rich insights into the contents, style and state of management control in an organisation.

In the following section the authors review the effectiveness of the methodology when all seven steps of the methodology are used in a regular manner.

SECTION C.   AN ASSESSMENT OF THE EXTENT TO WHICH THE EA METHODOLOGY MEETS ITS DESIGN CRITERIA

The expectations approach methodology was designed to meet the 11 criteria listed in Figure 2.5 on p. 42 of this book. This section of the chapter describes briefly how the system based on that methodology meets those 11 criteria, and then discusses some of the questions that have been raised in respect of those criteria as a result of its operational use.

Criterion 1

The system must permit clear links to be developed from planned organisational purpose to operational activity.

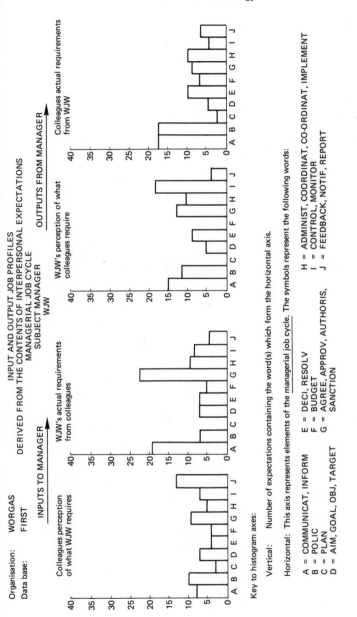

FIGURE 11.3 *Input and output communication profiles. Managerial job cycle. First database. Manager WJW*

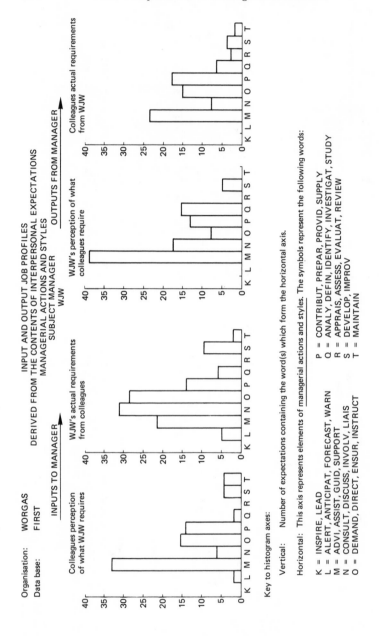

FIGURE 11.4 *Input and output communication profiles. Managerial actions and styles. First database. Manager WJW*

If all managers within a working group use the 7 steps of EA methodology in a committed manner it must necessarily follow that those concerned with the determination of organisational purpose are linked through communication channels that are analysable, visible and traceable through to operational activity. In fact the boundaries of an organisation can be (and have been) crossed using EA and it is then possible to check whether the assumptions made by those concerned with planning organisational purpose about the expectations of external groups, e.g. customers, pensioners or shareholders, are in fact true. In a number of organisations those concerned with interfacing customers have actually shown them what they perceived the customers to expect of them and asked them to verify whether or not that was the case. In one retail outlet, those employed there put up on the wall a statement of what they actually expected of their customers. This statement formed a discussion point which, incidentally, led to some of the employees actual expectations of customers being reformulated. (See Chapter 7 by Wilkinson for a thorough consideration of the role of boundary-spanning information in management control systems.)

In relatively small organisations it is usually possible to trace directly the links from a statement of corporate purpose to operational activity. Where such links cannot be traced, it calls into question either the appropriateness of the statement of purpose or the linkages in the chain. In the reverse direction, it should be possible to trace each element of operational activity to part of the organisation's purpose. If it is not possible so to do there must be cause to seek the reason why the operational activity is being carried out.

In large organisations, tracing these links has been impossible, practically. For any given manager, one output expectation may require for its generation a range of input expectations (frequently not using all of any input expectation, but using some of a variety of input expectations).

Therefore, whilst the expectations approach methodology obviously provides for links to be developed from planned organisational purpose to operational activity, links are rarely clear, and it is therefore usually impossible for an outsider to judge whether the links are the most effective possible.

Criterion 2

The system must be able to assist managers both when planning purpose and when controlling its achievement.

The EA methodology (particularly Steps 5, 6 and 7) provides the basis for doing specifically that. The chief advantage offered by EA is that the same database is used when planning purpose and when controlling the achievement of purpose. The EA database contains detailed documentation of both inputs and outputs. When a manager is defining the purpose of his job (which in most systems is only defined in terms of output) using EA he is also negotiating his expectations for input from his 'contractors' to ensure that he will get what he needs to enable the achievement of the outputs required from him.

Performance reporting as described in Step 6 regularly informs a manager of the extent to which his contractors are meeting his expectations and therefore enables him to monitor the inflow of the resources necessary for the achievement of his own purpose.

Criterion 3

The system must be designed to help a manager deal with the actual complexity of his job.

Each manager using EA decides for himself what expectations he will document. Not only has he total freedom to set down expectations containing the level of detail he deems to be appropriate for his job, but he can include expectations, if he so wishes, to deal with the full range of influences that affect the way he plans and controls the achievement of his job's purpose. Managers in different organisations have varied in the extent to which they wished to document the actual complexity of their job. In some organisations the methodology has been used specifically to concentrate on interpersonal relationships, rather than on interpersonal tasks. In one organisation the managers themselves chose to differentiate between those expectations that were associated with the role (and would continue when the role incumbent changed), and those expectations which were held of a given individual because of who he was, rather what he was. It was recognised that these 'relationship' expectations would change when the role incumbent changed.

No EA user has found that the methodology has been unable to deal with the actual complexity of his job. Even the word expectation has not been seen as a constraint. It spans the full spectrum from 'I expect a high level of cooperation in joint decision-making from Smith' to 'I expect Smith to be as obstructive and unhelpful in the future as he has been in the past'.

Criterion 4

The system must not be dependent for its successful operation on any particular organisational structure and, therefore, must be capable of being used successfully in matrix or even fluid structure.

There is no doubt that EA meets this criterion because it has been used in such structures. It has been used within family units by parents and children, it has been used in a multinational, matrix-structured organisation and the methodology is clearly independent of structure. No assumptions are made within the methodology that communication either should or will travel along particular lines. The EA methodology (and the computer-based systems supporting the methodology) allow each participating manager to write either actual or perceived expectations about any or every other member of the working group. Each individual user thus has control over the direction in which his or her expectations travel, and the contents of those expectations. It is therefore inevitable, given the methodology, that the EA managerial information and communication system meets Criterion 5.

Criterion 5

The system must be open in the sense that it will accept omnidirectional communication patterns.

Criterion 6

The system must not be dependent for its successful operation on the nature of the output generated by a manager, and, therefore, must be capable of being used successfully by managers whose organisational output may range from the concrete to the abstract.

The expectations approach methodology has been tried out by over 2500 people from more than 40 organisations. These organisations include small, medium and large profit-seeking organisations and small, medium and large non-profit-seeking organisations. In that enormous spread of users no one has yet said that they felt constrained in any way by the expectations methodology when setting down their interactions with others within the group. Clearly 2500 users is not a large number relative to the numbers currently using managerial control systems world-wide. Nevertheless, the signs so far are that this criterion has been met.

Criterion 7

The system must not be dependent for its successful operation on a particular philosophy of managerial interaction and, therefore, must be capable of being used successfully by managers whose approach may range from the completely dictatorial to completely self-effacing, group participation.

It all depends on what you mean by 'successful operation'. If by successful operation the reader would mean that the system of itself, and inevitably, leads to improved managerial effectiveness, then almost certainly the answer is 'The EA system does not meet this criterion.' If by successful operation the reader means that a system used by a manager with a distinctive style should enable him to implement that style more successfully, then EA almost certainly does work. It has been used by some chief executives who were absolutely determined to tell their subordinates exactly what they should expect of each other. It is a marvellous system for allowing a dictatorial senior manager to audit the expectations of everyone in the organisation (if he has the time and the determination) and to delete from the agreed expectations those that he perceives to be unnecessary, frivolous or a waste of organisational resource.

Using a system in a dictatorial manner does not necessarily improve either individual or organisational effectiveness. On the other hand, without some validating mechanism it is always possible that two people anywhere in an organisation could agree to expect nothing of each other when in fact they should. Personal animosity or sheer laziness could well lead to situations where hopelessly ineffective expectations were agreed between 'consenting couples' which represented subnormal performance from almost any point of view! Not only could two people agree to expect very little of each other, they could also agree to expect quite the wrong things of each other. It is easy to envisage how in a particularly lax organisation it would be possible to 'empire build' or to establish bureaucratic procedures which might be diametrically opposed to the needs of an effective organisation.

Consideration of the extent to which EA meets this particular criterion highlights the value judgements that underlie the design of management control systems. The key question is whether the control system *of itself* should be concerned to bring about managerial effectiveness, or whether the system should be inert and thus capable of helping those who wish to bring about organisational effectiveness as well as it helps those who wish to undermine organisational effectiveness. It is an absolutely critical question.

There are undoubtedly some who believe that a management control system should be purposeful in the sense that the system *of itself* should contribute to organisational effectiveness, even if some managers do not wish to achieve it.

There seems little doubt that EA cannot force a manager to be effective if he does not wish to be. It may well provide information which would enable such an individual to be more readily identified by others, however, and thus EA raises the question specifically addressed by Willmer in Chapter 13; 'Who controls whom?'

Undoubtedly when using the EA management control system those in authority need to think very carefully about verification procedures if they are not to find that the system is used against them on some occasions by people within the organisation. There is nothing new in managers learning either to avoid systems or to use them for their own ends. The expectations approach methodology appears to enable them to do that more successfully, in exactly the same way as it helps managers who wish to be more effective to achieve that more successfully. In one organisation the chief executive when writing down his actual expectations of his colleagues paused for only a moment when contemplating what he expected of the chief accountant and actually wrote down the seven-letter word 'Nothing'. Whatever one makes of the sentiment one cannot deny that it has a distinctive style.

The designer of the expectations approach methodology designed it to produce a purposeless managerial planning and control system, i.e. a system whose use mirrored the purpose of the user. In that sense there is no doubt that it meets Criterion 7. In so doing it raises critical value judgements and it must be the reader who determines whether or not the system meets Criterion 7 in the way in which the reader would wish.

Criterion 8

The system must enable a manager, who so wishes, to ascertain exactly what output is expected of him and by whom.

Steps 1, 2 and 3 of the EA methodology so completely and obviously meet this criterion that no further statements are needed.

Equally, Step 6 in the methodology ensures that the EA management control system meets Criterion 9.

Criterion 9

*The system must enable a manager to obtain information on the
extent to which he is generating the output which is expected of him.*

In fact it does a great deal more! It enables each manager to compare
the extent to which he believes he is generating the output which is
expected of him, with the views of the intended recipients of his
outputs. The expectations approach methodology therefore enables a
more balanced supply of information both to the manager concerned
and to his peer group (or his superior or anyone else who receives a
control report on him) of the extent to which he is generating the
appropriate output in the appropriate manner.

Criterion 10

*The system must enable a manager, who so wishes, to explore his
actual responsibility, his actual authority, and his actual accountability within the organisation.*

At one level it may be that the reader believes the expectations
approach methodology as so far described enables the system to meet
this criterion. It obviously does in terms of the contents of expectations that relate to responsibility, authority and accountability.

In one organisation the managers chose to develop the EA methodology further to enable this particular criterion to be mapped more
accurately. In particular they wanted to trace actual authority in those
areas where there was disagreement between holder and contractor
about whether or not an expectation should be met. Wherever there
was such disagreement, the holder and contractor each specified the
individual within the organisation who held the *sole authority* to
decide whether or not the expectation should be met. If the holder and
contractor specified the same person as holding that authority then,
self-evidently, there was no problem. Where the holder and contractor
specified *different* people as holding the sole authority to decide
whether or not the expectation should be met, the process had to be
repeated until ultimately either the appropriate person was identified,
or the responsibility was given to someone for the first time.

This was one of the few cases where the expectations approach
methodology, of itself, raised problems that the organisation concerned did not have before! The omnidirectional nature of communi-

cation means that the verification of any one manager's input and output expectations may involve verifying expectations between 30 or 40 people and will almost certainly involve verifying expectations that span at least four (and sometimes more) levels in the hierarchy. An organisation reared on management-by-objectives, with a discussion between superior and subordinate about a set of objectives for the subordinate, will find that their procedures and systems are simply inadequate to cope with EA's detailed documentation of the inputs and outputs for the subordinate, particularly given the normal position that the superior is the contractor for some of the subordinate's expectations.

Criterion 10 begs many questions in using a word like 'actual'. Dalton and Lawrence (1971) distinguish between formal and informal authority and the latter is quite as 'real' in organisational activity as the former. No studies based on the EA methodology have been carried out to ascertain whether its use enhances or undermines informal authority; it seems difficult to believe that the 'public' identification and discussion of informal accorded authority would not affect it in some way. If it does, participants may well not be prepared to include informal authority, responsibility and accountability in a formal managerial control system. If they do not, it will clearly no longer meet Criterion 10; a participant who wishes to use EA in a way which would achieve the criterion's objective could easily be blocked from so doing if his colleagues did not share his aspiration. The same problem affects the final criterion.

Criterion 11

The system must be designed to enable each manager to develop the contents of the system to meet his own particular needs.

In one sense the expectations approach methodology meets this criterion. Each individual participating manager writes down expectations in his own words, and chooses what he will write about and what he will not write about. In some organisations participating managers have used Step 1 and Step 2 to express themselves fully and openly, not only about tasks but about relationships. Other participating managers, on the other hand, have written exclusively about tasks and only when they have discovered that their colleagues have written about relationships, and that those expectations are discussed in a supportive and helpful environment, have they tentatively started to include relationship expectations in their own database. In those organisations where relationship expectations have been handled in an unsupportive manner, such expectations have tended to be deleted from the database. In that sense therefore, the content of the database in respect of any given participating manager is completely within his own control and he can develop the contents of his part of the database to meet his own particular needs, both *managerial* and *psychological*.

In another sense, however, the methodology does not meet Criterion 11. At the same time as one participating manager is trying to develop the database to meet his own needs so are all his colleagues within his work group. If the needs of some of his colleagues are significantly different from his own then they will be supplying information to the database which might be quite different from that which he would choose to see inserted. During the verification procedure the verifier may (and probably will) begin to specify the kinds of expectations that should be included and the contents of the system may be increasingly designed to meet the needs of the verifier rather than that of the user manager.

Thus the system designer is brought full cycle to the fundamental question 'Is a management control system to help the user to control himself and other resources – or is it to help someone else to control him?' In most organisations, the authors believe the answer is, and should be 'Both'. The verifier, and the participant, and the participant's colleagues are all users, and the implication is that the wording of the 11 criteria should be altered to recognise that no one user should determine the attributes of a system used by many.

CONCLUSION

The previous sections of this chapter have demonstrated the extent to which the EA methodology meets each of 11 criteria which have been postulated (Figure 2.5, p. 42) as necessary attributes of an effective management control system. The volume of research undertaken using the EA methodology (documented in Brookes *et al.*, 1982) testifies to the acceptability of the methodology to managers at all levels in a wide range of organisations. The prototype managerial control systems developed from the EA methodology therefore show that communication-based systems are both technically feasible and psychologically acceptable to managers. Communication-based systems will not render systems based on cost, cash or number obsolete, but they will offer managers in managed cost responsibility centres an information system which enables them to plan and control in an effective way the appropriateness, quality and quantity of their own work inputs and outputs, rather than just their cost.

Research using EA has shown that a communication-based management control system could provide a useful addition to the range of systems currently available to help managers to manage more effectively (Machin and Kokkalis, 1979a, b). In the course of the EA system's development, however, a number of questions have been raised which need to be resolved before such systems can achieve their full potential.

Who should communicate with whom?

Many managerial groups who cooperated in EA research because 'we have a problem with communications' discovered that the problem was not primarily the *process* of communication *per se*, but the different *attitudes* within the group about who should communicate with whom. EA was designed to carry messages as easily laterally and diagonally throughout a group as vertically, i.e. up and down the lines of the formal organisation chart. Some managers see this facility as helpful and use it, others find it a challenge to traditional, information-based authority and resent it.

In some organisations, policy questions were raised for the first time about the degrees of freedom that people should have to communicate with others. This may appear to be an incredible question, but in some organisations the use of EA has produced definitive communication policy statements, e.g. 'a person may not expect anything of somebody more than two levels above them'. The reader must decide for himself whether he finds that a sensible policy or an unwarranted restraint on personal freedom. A communication-based methodology for a managerial planning and control system calls for a *publicly* articulated communication policy. In many organisations researched in connection with the expectations approach, a policy on interpersonal communication had never even been considered previously, despite the fact that effective communication is a necessary condition for effective managerial performance.

Who should have access to the information in the system?

Criterion 8 and Criterion 10 both include within them the phrase 'who so wishes'. There is no doubt that the system does enable those managers '*who so wish*' to ascertain exactly what output is expected from them. It also, however, forces exactly that kind of information on managers who do not wish to know exactly what is expected of them. It can be used inexorably to present to public gaze within an organisation the performance rating of any manager whether or not he wishes to be effective and whether or not he wishes to be rated by colleagues in respect of his performance.

A fundamental question therefore concerns access to the information in the database. It is possible, within the systems as they are so far developed, for anyone in a participating group to sit at a VDU and call up on to the screen the totality of any other individual's job within that group and, moreover, the performance rating in respect of that individual, both by himself and by his working group. Some chief executives have expressed welcome for the idea that anyone on the shopfloor could see both the contents of their job as chief executive and the performance rating that others have given them in respect of each part of their job. Some chief executives might well regard such an idea with some reluctance or even horror.

What communication should a 'formal' information system carry?

Communication is a highly personal process. It is personal not only in the sense that each individual has their own particular set of language and phraseology, it is also personal in terms of the contents of communication that is carried. Within any working group with which the authors have been associated the 'grapevine' has been absolutely essential for personal survival and personal enjoyment of the working environment. It is questionable whether all the information that goes through an individual's grapevine will be included by that individual in his expectation database. It might well be contrary to his own personal interests for him to do so.

Friendships and relationships are an important part of the working environment, yet very few people would choose to see every one of their friendships or relationships documented and then made publicly visible to everyone else in the organisation. At a more general level of concern (and using Dalton's classification of 'organisational control', 'group norms' and 'individual motivation'), there is no doubt that the expectations approach methodology represents an organisational system. On the other hand its communication-based nature (and field research experience of seeing managers document relationships as well as role expectations) indicates that it has shifted the boundaries of 'organisational control' in a significant manner. If it has previously been the case that what has been included in an organisational system was 'formal' communication and that communication concerning group norms has been 'informal' communication, then there is no doubt that the expectations approach methodology is including within its formal (i.e. organisationally supported) system much communication that has been previously informal. In shifting that boundary it is certainly doing much more than just documenting such informal communication, it is quite clearly changing the nature of it in terms of its impact on the recipient (Archer, 1981).

SUMMARY

The EA managerial planning and control system described in this chapter was developed, using modern information technology, to meet eleven design criteria. Now the system is available, it is time to refine the criteria. Throughout the development of EA, researchers have worked side by side with managers. The authors believe this to be an effective way of developing new and better management control systems. In the light of their experience they believe that the goal for management control systems researchers should be to work with managers to develop improved and better criteria, and, thereafter, to try to develop the systems to meet them.

The development of the EA methodology first as a research tool and then subsequently as an operationally viable managerial planning and control system reinforces the authors' view that one of the more exciting new perspectives in management control systems design lies in the development of progressively better communication-based systems and methodologies. The pace of future development is likely to be dependent (as Anthony (1965) so presciently forecast) on the skill of social psychologists in helping managers to come to terms with both the nature of the information held in the database, and the psychological implications of using such 'open' systems on a day-to-day operational basis.

Above all we need to recognise that modern information technology will not just assist us to develop better systems for helping the managerial control process to be carried out effectively – it will actually change the contents and nature of that process. That is why the study of management control systems which has been compulsively interesting, challenging and rewarding over the last decade will retain that fascination over the next decade. What we study is changing rapidly and by our study we both affect and accelerate that pace of change.

12 Convention in Financial Control

Kenneth P. Gee

The purpose of this chapter is to look at the role of convention in financial control. In the first two sections of the chapter, the conventions focused upon are social in nature, and have to do with the pervasiveness of allocation procedures in financial measurement for divisions of an enterprise. Since financial measurement is no more than a precondition for financial control, the chapter proceeds to examine how current or prospective financial outcomes may be evaluated in relation to non-financial outcomes occurring at the same time. The interpretation of financial outcomes is seen to be dependent upon the way in which the management control system is bounded and structured, which gives rise to an examination of the conventions employed in visualising the consequences of a business decision. Particular attention is paid to multiattribute utility analysis as being a technique for visualising a rich variety of interrelated consequences. This, too, proves to be subject to convention, but examination of a case study indicates that the application of the conventions required by multiattribute utility theory may not limit the usefulness of its results any more than they have already been limited by difficulties associated with the availability of data. The conclusion takes the form of a plea for a less global approach reflecting cost-benefit considerations in the visualisation of management control systems.

INCORRIGIBILITY IN DIVISIONAL PERFORMANCE MEASUREMENT: PROFIT

The commencing proposition of this chapter is that profit as currently measured represents no more than the surplus of sales revenue over a cost figure determined largely by social convention. It is social convention that dictates what constitute acceptable bases for amortising the costs of long-lived assets, for allocating service department costs to manufacturing departments and for absorbing manufacturing department costs into the products passing through those departments. Judgements about bases of cost allocation over time and between products turn on notions of equity and are consequently incorrigible, where this word has the meaning given it in modern philosophy, i.e. 'not open to verification; incapable of being proved true or false'. Since cost is incorrigible, so also must be the profit figure obtained by matching cost against revenue; indeed, revenue recognition itself is also a matter of convention. (A glance, for example, at the range of alternative practices employed concerning the recognition of revenues due on partially-completed building contracts makes this point very well.)

UK businesses of substantial size are typically segmented into semi-autonomous units called divisions; the divisional chief executives having authority over purchasing, credit granting and the payment of debtors. They cannot, however, authorise on their own anything more than small outlays by way of capital investment, and their authority to make financing decisions on behalf of their divisions is even more restricted. Finance is supplied to divisions by means of advances from a corporate bank account, to which they remit the receipts from divisional operations.

An important question arising from the incorrigibility of profit concerns the measurement of divisional financial performance. How far is it possible to go in designing a measure of financial performance for divisions which restricts incorrigibility through the incorporation of market valuations? The importance of this question stems from the use made of financial performance as a criterion for assigning rewards or penalties to divisions and their managers. If a measure of financial performance entering into a reward–penalty system contains many elements which are incapable of verification by reference to market prices, disputes concerning the equitable treatment of these elements are likely to be widespread. Such disputes are often exacerbated by the tendency for perceptions of equity to have their roots in managerial self-interest.

Some progress can be made in designing market-verifiable measures of divisional profitability, but then fundamental problems begin to appear. It is possible to compute, by reference to factor market prices prevailing at the date of sale of a product, the replacement cost of the inputs which can be shown to have been committed exclusively to that product. A difficulty may arise in determining the current entry price of an input which has not recently been purchased, but it is susceptible to solution through index adjustment (Gee, 1979). The first real problem arises with the treatment of overhead costs. No market-verifiable way of absorbing these costs into products exists, yet the alternative of writing them off as period costs violates the matching principle within replacement cost accounting. This principle depends upon a comparison of sales revenue against replacement cost as at the date of sale, with the sum of the differences between these two magnitudes constituting a period's operating profit. But the usage of overhead items cannot by definition be linked to acts of sale, save by means of the arbitrary allocation–absorption process serving to associate particular expenditures on overheads with specific units of product. If this arbitrary process is to be avoided, though, it leaves indeterminate the date at which the replacement cost of an overhead item should be calculated for matching purposes. This indeterminacy can be resolved only by reference to some arbitrary (and therefore contentious) assumption. For example, the assumption implicit in treating overheads as a period cost would involve deeming the pattern of sales activity to be such that it was appropriate to match the mid-period replacement cost of overheads against sales revenue through-out–underestimates and overestimates of replacement cost for individual transactions by coincidence cancelling.

This problem of overhead cost measurement is common to all efforts to design market-verifiable measures of profitability, whether or not these are conducted in a divisionalised context. Much more specific, though, is the problem posed by the market-verification requirement for the capital charge. The view is widely held (Amey, 1975, pp. 62–3; Tomkins, 1975, p. 163) that a capital charge should be imposed upon divisions reflecting the cost borne by the parent company in financing divisional working capital balances. However, financing costs are actually imposed by the postponement of *cash* receipts and the acceleration of *cash* payments; they are entirely unrelated to the dates at which revenues and expenses are recognised in accruals accounting. It has been argued (Gee, 1977, p. 54), for example, that stocks should be valued at historic cost for the purpose of computing a capital charge, on the grounds that the cost of financing stocks consists of interest upon the historic cost of purchasing them. But since historic cost for stock may be determined by any of a variety of conventions, this line of argument has the curious implication that a division could change its working capital balance and therefore its capital charge simply by switching from one stock valuation convention to another, for example from FIFO to LIFO. This position falls far short of market verifiability as a goal, and it begins to seem indeed as if market verifiability and the measurement of divisional profitability net of a capital charge may be fundamentally incompatible.

INCORRIGIBILITY IN DIVISIONAL PERFORMANCE MEASUREMENT: NET CASH FLOW

Superficially, it would appear that changing from an accruals to a cash flow basis would both facilitate an appropriate treatment of the capital charge and obviate most if not all of the incorrigibilities discussed in the previous section. Disbursements and receipts of cash for goods and services bought and sold are computed as the product of quantities transacted multiplied by unit prices; since no allocations are involved, the cash flows of an entire enterprise can be wholly verified by reference to the market. Unfortunately, incorrigibility creeps in as soon as attempts are made to disaggregate cash flows from the level of the whole enterprise to the level of the individual division. A simple illustration of this is provided by stock relief.

Consider the form of relief proposed by the Inland Revenue (1980) and partially implemented in the March 1981 Budget; decisions about the final form of its implementation being deferred until after the Corporation Tax Green Paper due in late 1982. Bear in mind also that this form of relief is being used only as an example. Although the credit restriction upon which the example depends is not to be introduced in 1981–2, 'the Government ... remain of the view that there is a case in principle for a credit restriction' (*Financial Times*, 11 March 1981, p. 19). This chapter therefore adopts the Inland Revenue's 1980 proposal, letting:

S_j represent the value of corporate stocks at the beginning of year j, less £2000.

I_j represent the 'all stocks' index value at the beginning of year j.

B_j represent the amount of corporate borrowings at the beginning of year j.

A_j represent the total value of corporate assets at the beginning of year j.

Then the amount of stock relief for year j, R_j, is given by:

$$R_j = S_j \left(\frac{I_{j+1} - I_j}{I_j} \right) \left(1 - \frac{B_j}{A_j} \right) \qquad (1)$$

In the computation of taxable profit, the amount R_j is deducted from trading profit. Suppose that a divisionalised enterprise is earning trading profits, and that the managers of the divisions have (as is customary) discretion over the level of stock they should hold.[1] The problem then arises of how to allow in divisional cash flow statements for the reduced corporate cash outflow on tax which has arisen because of the relief stemming from the beginning-year value of stock within a particular division. This is problematic because of the credit restriction represented by the right-hand bracket within equation (1). The amount of this restriction depends on total corporate borrowings B_j and total corporate assets A_j. But both borrowings and assets can be divided into divisional and corporate components. Let:

B_{kj} represent the (trade credit) borrowings of the kth division at the beginning of year j.

A_{kj} represent the total value of the kth division's assets at the beginning of year j.

S_{kj} represent the value of the kth division's stocks at the beginning of year j.

Then R_{kj}, the stock relief *traceable* to the kth division for year j, is given by:

$$R_{kj} = S_{kj} \left(\frac{I_{j+1} - I_j}{I_j} \right) \left(1 - \frac{B_{kj}}{A_{kj}} \right) \qquad (2)$$

For an enterprise made up of m divisions, $\sum_{k=1}^{m} R_{kj} \neq R_j$. If all stocks are held by divisions, this inequality must be entirely attributable to the existence of corporate borrowings. (i.e. debt raised by the enterprise as a whole) and to the presence of centrally held (non-stock) assets. No market-verifiable method exists of allocating to divisions the difference between $\sum_{k=1}^{m} R_{kj}$ and R_j, but divisions by their existence plainly influence the magnitudes of corporate borrowings and central asset holdings. A numerical measure of the influence of any one division upon these magnitudes (and therefore upon R_j) can be arrived at only by recourse to incorrigible procedures. Since the influence of a division upon R_j cannot be market-verified, neither can a division's influence upon the corporate tax saving obtained by deducting tR_j from tax payments (where t is the Corporation Tax rate, expressed as a decimal). Thus the reduced corporate cash outflow on tax arising from the beginning-year value of stock in the kth division can be arrived at only by recourse to incorrigible procedures – and once one line of the divisional cash flow statement is shown to be incorrigible, the total magnitude of divisional net cash flow must be incorrigible as a consequence.

VISUALISING DECISION CONSEQUENCES: A SYSTEMS CONTEXT

The lack of market verifiability shown in the previous section as characterising both accruals and cash flow measures of divisional financial performance may go a long way towards explaining why such measures have proved so controversial. But the mere measurement of performance does not of itself enable managers to make control judgements. Control can be exercised only after comparing actual or forecast performance against some notion of the level of performance which ought to be present. It is to this context that attention must now be turned.

Under conditions of uncertainty, an attractive-seeming approach to financial measurement for control involves specifying *ex post* what the optimal set of actions would have been, and then performing a variance analysis assigning deviations of actual from *ex post* optimal performance to their causes. This approach has, for example, been applied to the purchasing decision under inflation (Gee, 1977, ch. 4). Here, the EOQ in the face of a price increase of unknown size involves balancing the extra net carrying costs[2] of larger stocks against the holding gains upon these larger stocks that will arise as replacement cost increases. An *ex post* optimal budget may be drawn up showing what purchases would have been optimal had the size of a price increase during the budget period been known in advance. Deviations from optimality may then be assigned into those arising from failures to anticipate the price increase correctly (forecasting errors) and those arising from failures, once the price increase has taken place, to adapt the quantities purchased to the EOQ associated with the new price (adaptation errors).

There are, however, two problems here. First, the *ex post* optimal budget is optimal only for the period to which it refers. It may be, for example, that a price increase is anticipated at the beginning of the next period, but stocking up in preparation for it would appear simply as an adaptation error in this period's budget. This problem would be particularly acute in the presence of highly uncertain lead times to delivery, since these might well result in stocking up taking place considerably in advance of the anticipated date of a price increase.

A second, and equally fundamental, problem is represented by the fact that optimality here relates only to current profitability, being defined exclusively in terms of cost minimisation. Now the cost-minimising set of purchases may involve a large cash outlay immediately prior to a price increase, and in doing so may give rise to an unacceptable performance as regards liquidity. To generalise, it is apparent that *ex post* optimal performance should not be computed for a single aspect of an enterprise's activity in isolation, but rather across all aspects simultaneously.

This assertion represents a good starting-point for an analysis of the 'systems school' of thought, in that this school makes a particular point of regarding financial control as representing the control of a subsystem within the broader system of management control. However, the very breadth of the systems approach, while apparently its strength, may in fact constitute its most serious weakness. The crucial question here may be phrased as follows: How is the boundary around a management control system to be mapped out? This boundary should in principle be such as to partition variables into endogenous and exogenous categories; only the former lying inside the control system. For a variable to be exogenous, it must in changing its value cause one or more of the endogenous variables to change their values, while remaining itself unchanged by movements in any of the endogenous variables. That is, there can be no feedback loop between an exogenous variable and any of the endogenous variables.

But the more effort an enterprise puts into scrutinising its environment, the more feedback loops it will recognise between itself and that environment. Of particular importance is the fact that *it will never know when it has recognised all the loops*. The more the number of recognised loops grows, the more difficult it will become to find a basis upon which one state of the management control system may be said to be preferred to another. Any preference for a state S_1 over a state S_2 has to be based upon a comparison of the values taken by a limited number of variables in each state – but any preference can be called into question simply by recognising a further feedback loop and thus 'importing' another variable from the environment into the comparison.

To avoid this indeterminacy, some restriction must be placed upon the search for enterprise–environment feedback loops, splitting the environment into what is perceived to be the 'relevant' environment (from which loops are recognised) and the 'irrelevant' environment (from which loops are not recognised). In order to do this, it is necessary to perform a pre-systematic task of selecting out certain interrelated variables that appear to be of relevance to a particular decision, and henceforth to treat those variables as containing within themselves the 'relevant environment'. A second pre-systematic step is then required, involving the reaching of a conclusion as to which of the complications inherent in the maintenance of control (including financial control) fall to be emphasised in relation to a specific decision.

Four major complications are implicit in trying to predict (and therefore control) the consequences of a business decision, namely that such consequences are uncertain, dynamic, multiattributed and interactive. The first two of these are self-explanatory, while what is meant by a business decision being multiattributed is that its consequences will have a number of properties measured on different scales (market share, labour turnover, current profitability and so on). In relation to a business decision, the term 'interactive' means that the probability distribution of outcomes for an attribute in a time-period will depend upon *either* the values assumed to be taken by other attributes in that period *or* the values actually taken by the attribute concerned in previous periods *or* both. Analyses of business decisions which explicitly treat their consequences as being uncertain, dynamic, multiattributed and interactive are rare. Few studies face all four complications simultaneously; one of the closest approaches is to be found in the study by Lee (1977) referred to below.

Having selected a convention as to which of the four complications are to be emphasised and which suppressed, it is often necessary to take a final pre-systematic step by imposing restrictions upon relations among the endogenous variables which have been chosen as composing the system for analysis. A particularly good example of the imposition of such restrictions is provided by the multiattribute utility approach to financial control. In this approach, the problem to be addressed is seen as one of maintaining control over the range of future financial outcomes which may arise, while bearing in mind that the acceptability of any one of these outcomes will depend upon the values of the non-financial outcomes with which it is associated.

CONVENTION IN MULTIATTRIBUTE UTILITY ANALYSIS

The first stage of the multiattribute utility approach involves devising measures applicable to those aspects of performance most directly affected by the decision requiring resolution. Thus in the case of Consumers Power Co. building a 765 kV electrical transmission system across the Lower Peninsula of Michigan, performance in relation to social responsibility was measured in terms of 'number of complaints regarding transmission noise received in the first three years of system operation'. Relationships between this attribute and three attributes relating to cost were then explored in resolving the question of which transmission conductors to select for the system (Crawford, Huntzinger and Kirkwood, 1978). This exploration involved first constructing von Neumann–Morgenstern utility functions over the possible range of outcomes for each attribute separately, and then asking questions about the trade-offs that would be acceptable between the different attributes, so as to be able to compute scaling constants integrating each of the conditional utility measures into a measure of multiattribute utility. The mechanics of this process are not of direct concern here;[3] what does matter, though, is that once the number of attributes under consideration exceeds three it becomes impossible with current knowledge to derive a multi-attribute utility function unless a preferential independence condition limiting the interaction of the attributes within the system is satisfied (Keeney and Raiffa, 1976, p. 298). This condition may be said to be conventional in the sense that it pertains to an agreement on social practices or conventions – specifically here relating to practices as regards the evaluation of multiattributed alternatives.

The preferential independence condition can best be illustrated by the use of algebraic notation. Denote the four attributes under consideration in the Consumers Power Co. study as X_1, X_2, X_3, X_4 in any arbitrary order. Let the value of attribute X_1 be represented by x_1, while the value of X_i ($i \neq 1$) is represented by x_i. Consider two pairs of values of attributes X_1 and X_i, denoted as x_1' and x_i', x_1'' and x_i''. All other attributes apart from X_1 and X_i are referred to as the the complement of X_1 and X_i. Let the values of the complement be held constant at $\overline{x}_{1i}^+$. Finally, introduce the symbol $\gtrsim$ to mean 'is preferred or indifferent to'. Then X_1 and X_i are preferentially independent of their complement if:

$$[(x_1', x_i', \overline{x}_{1i}^+) \succeq (x_1'', x_i'', \overline{x}_{1i}^+)] \Rightarrow [(x_1', x_i', \overline{x}_{1i}) \succeq (x_1'', x_i'', \overline{x}_{1i})] \quad \text{for all } \overline{x}_{1i}$$

In words, for preferential independence to hold as between X_1, X_i and their complement, if one pair of X_1, X_i values is preferred to another pair of X_1, X_i values for a *particular* set of values of their complement $\overline{x}_{1i}^+$, then this preference must hold for *any* set of values of their complement $\overline{x}_{1i}$. The preferential independence condition required for the construction of a multiattribute utility function in the Consumers Power Co. case is simply that each pair of attributes (X_1, X_i) must be preferentially independent of its complement for $i = 2, 3, 4$.

This convention regarding the interaction of attributes is imposed in the interests of tractability (as suggested in the previous section). To illustrate the constraint it imposes, reference may be made to Lee's (1977) study of marine sand and gravel mining. This involved among other attributes the NPV of mining (X_1) at three alternative sites together with the percentage loss of plankton (X_3) and of fish catch (X_5) arising from water turbidity caused by mining. Application of the preferential independence condition had the consequence that the rate at which the decision-maker was willing to trade off loss of plankton for NPV was assumed independent of the turbidity effect on the fish catch. Representing the best possible outcome for fish catch (in which turbidity actually *increased* it) by x_5^*, and the worst outcome by x_5^0, then with the symbol $\sim$ representing 'is indifferent to', the condition for X_1, X_3 and X_5 can be written compactly as:

$$[(x_1', x_3', x_5^*, \overline{x}_{135}^+) \sim (x_1'', x_3'', x_5^*, \overline{x}_{135}^+)] \Rightarrow$$
$$[(x_1', x_3', x_5^0, \overline{x}_{135}^+) \sim (x_1'', x_3'', x_5^0, \overline{x}_{135}^+)]$$

What is being said here is that the decision-maker would accept a reduction in plankton from x_3' to x_3'' in exchange for an increase in NPV from x_1' to x_1'' just as readily in an environment in which turbidity damage to fish catch was at its worst (x_5^0) as in an environment in which there was no turbidity damage at all (x_5^*). This would seem implausible in circumstances in which plankton were valued mainly in so far as they served as fish food, i.e. as a means to an end of fish-catch facilitation. If this was the case, then the decision-maker would seem unlikely to accept the same plankton–NPV trade-off in both the x_5^* and the x_5^0 situations. He would almost certainly take a more serious view of a given percentage reduction in fish food stocks where the damage inflicted directly upon the fish catch by turbidity was severe than where it was not severe. Consequently, he would be less willing to trade off plankton for NPV in x_5^0 conditions than in x_5^* conditions. The application of a convention which excludes from consideration this interdependence of preferences may still represent the most appropriate mapping of reality, though, for reasons which will be explained below.

Having obtained the decision-maker's multiattribute utility function, his preferences over the three mining sites and the alternative of not mining at all can be obtained in a deterministic fashion. To do this involves looking separately at the probability distribution of outcomes for each attribute at each site, and choosing between alternatives by reference to the value of the utility function obtained when the mean attribute values for each alternative are inserted in it. This decision procedure is of course oversimplified, in that the outcome for each attribute is subject to uncertainty. To allow for this uncertainty, however, it would be necessary to take account of probabilistic interdependence among attributes. Here, the presence of percentage loss of lobster catch (X_4) as one of the attributes not so far mentioned serves to complicate the situation. Because plankton, fish and lobsters are related in an ecosystem, the incorporation of uncertainty demands more than just Monte Carlo sampling from a single probability distribution of outcomes for plankton, one for fish and one for lobsters. The probability distribution of outcomes for fish catch seems likely to change in shape and position depending upon the plankton loss outcome, and since lobsters eat fish there will be a consequential modification of the probability distribution of outcomes for lobster catch.

It thus turns out that nothing short of a complete model of the marine ecosystem at the feeding level for each mining site would suffice if uncertainty were to be incorporated in the decision analysis. Such models were simply unavailable in the context of Lee's study, and their unavailability raises this chapter's final question. Since it proved impossible to model the way in which (for example) the fish catch outcome depended on the plankton loss outcome, how much was the quality of the analysis further impaired by the failure of the preferential independence condition to incorporate the extent to which preferences for plankton as against NPV depended upon turbidity's effect on the fish catch?

This failure has to be seen in a context in which *nothing* is known about the dependence of (commercially-caught) fish upon plankton foodstuffs at any of the mining sites. Since the decision-maker has thus *no basis* upon which to estimate the effect upon fish catch of a given percentage plankton loss, does it not become reasonable to apply a convention treating him as possessing a constant plankton–NPV trade-off rate unaffected by the magnitude of the turbidity effect upon fish catch? After all, for the decision-maker to regard a given percentage plankton loss as being more serious for a larger percentage decline in fish catch through turbidity than for a smaller one, he must be able to infer *something* about the 'secondary' effect of this plankton loss upon fish catch through food shortage. If this effect is only small, then it will not be worth sacrificing increasing amounts of NPV to avoid the same percentage decline in plankton as the effect on fish catches of turbidity deteriorates from x_5^* to x_5^0. But the larger the 'secondary' effect is, the more the decision-maker's plankton–NPV trade-off will vary with the loss of fish catch through turbidity. However, the blunt fact is that *nothing* is known about the magnitude of the 'secondary' effect for any of the mining sites under consideration. Consequently, a preferential independence condition which asserts that the plankton–NPV trade-off does not vary at all with changes in the turbidity effect does no more than pick up one assumption (that the 'secondary' effect upon fish catch through plankton diminution is negligible) *which may be as valid as any other*.

The thrust of this argument is directed against the overambitious specification of systems. Whether or not it is worthwhile acquiring information about the interaction of particular variables within a system is an economic question, depending for its resolution on the relationship between the expected cost of acquiring such information and the expected benefits from improved decision-making arising from its possession. But in the last analysis all systems as perceived by people represent simplifications, and conditions such as preferential independence restricting relationships within systems are entirely permissible where there is no information available on economically acceptable terms concerning the relationships which those conditions restrict. More broadly, the act of bounding a system must involve treating variables which are known (or suspected) to be endogenous as if they were exogenous because the cost of suboptimal decision-making arising from this error is perceived to be less than the cost of elaborating the model to avoid it. This balancing of cost as between suboptimisation and model elaboration serves to delineate the boundary between the 'relevant' and the 'irrelevant' environment for decision-making. Over time, this balance will change and the size of an enterprise's 'relevant' environment will shrink or expand correspondingly. For example, as the expected cost of not investigating a variance increases, so a wider environment is searched[4] to locate its cause(s).

A difficulty here is that to derive the expected cost of not investigating a variance it is necessary to assign probabilities to the outcomes 'variance caused by endogenous variable and therefore correctible' and 'variance caused by exogenous variable and therefore not correctible'. There are also problems in dealing with variances which appear to indicate an in-control state but in fact stem from the compromising of some separately-measured objective such as product quality.[5] Notwithstanding these difficulties, approaches defining the size of the 'relevant' environment by reference to an error-learning process do seem more likely to be fruitful than approaches which assume that the environment is always all-embracing.

NOTES

1. For empirical confirmation of the wide range of discretion exercised by UK divisional managers over the level of stock held, see Tomkins (1973, pp. 171–9).
2. These extra carrying costs are computed net of the lower ordering costs consequent upon making fewer orders, each for larger quantities.
3. For a study of multiattribute utility techniques in the context of capital budgeting, refer to Gee (1980).
4. Put in other terms, the size of that portion of the environment from which management is willing to recognise feedback loops, i.e. the 'relevant' environment, increases.
5. The ambiguity inherent in this latter type of variance serves as an argument for the construction of control systems based upon value functions over the attributes (here) of cost and product quality. For techniques used in deriving multiattribute value functions, see Keeney and Raiffa (1976, ch. 3).

13 The Contribution of the Cybernetic Approach to Management Control

Michael A. P. Willmer

INTRODUCTION

The term 'control' with respect to the management of organisations has many shades and nuances and these have been thoroughly explored in other chapters in this book. Otley and Berry (1980) explore the applicability of a cybernetic model of control to human systems and they suggest that the following four conditions have to be satisfied before any process can be said to be controlled in the cybernetic sense:

1. the system under consideration must have an objective
2. it must be possible to measure the results in terms of the dimensions defined by the objective
3. a predictive model of the system must exist
4. there must be relevant alternative actions available to the controller

When applied to physical systems it has often been found that the cybernetic approach has enabled highly sophisticated control mechanisms to be developed. Without such mechanisms many military weapons would lose much of their effectiveness.

The basic idea of the approach is illustrated diagrammatically in Figure 13.1. The situation under consideration is one in which there is a system whose state can be determined by the values of a given number of variables, where there is a desired state for each variable, where the errors can be determined and where the inputs to the system can be modified to reduce the errors. Thus

1. the objectives of the system are clear – the elements of the vector i_0 can be defined unambiguously
2. the elements of the output of the system, i, can be measured, and
3. when the error vector $e = i - i_0$ is determined suitable adjustments to the internal input control variables can be made so as to reduce e.

As far as technology is concerned there is no doubt that developments of this model of control have been extremely successful in both civil and military spheres of operation. Perhaps because of this outstanding success, management scientists have tried to apply the same basic control model to social systems.

In considering the areas in which cybernetic-based control models may be effective it is convenient to categorise processes according to whether they are:

1. routine or non-routine
2. have or have not a clearly defined output

The majority of management situations, of course, do not fall neatly into any of the four groups so obtained but lie somewhere in between. The range of possible situations may be illustrated diagrammatically (see Figure 13.2). It is assumed that two axes can be defined: one representing the lack of routineness that exists in a given case, the other the level of objectivity associated with the output. Clearly the

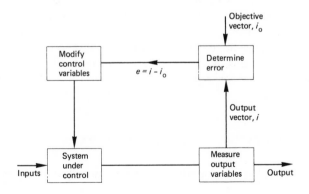

FIGURE 13.1 *Diagrammatic representation of a simple control system*

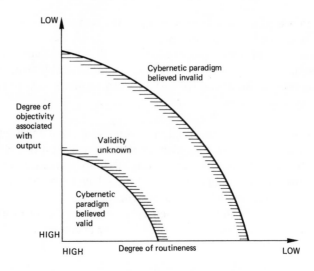

FIGURE 13.2   *Diagrammatic representation of the possible areas of the validity of the cybernetic paradigm*

top right-hand corner of the diagram is the domain where paradigms such as the political paradigm may be appropriate. Similarly the bottom left-hand side is the domain where the cybernetic-based paradigm may be the natural basis of a control philosophy. This leaves the ground in between. Should the cybernetic paradigm be rejected for situations falling in this area? Would such a policy be akin to 'throwing out the baby with the bath water'? The potential of the cybernetic approach is great and it would be imprudent to reject it if a good proportion of the potential can be realised or until sufficient empirical evidence has demonstrated that an alternative is better. This chapter looks at this middle ground and attempts to put the problem of the acceptance or rejection of the cybernetic philosophy into perspective.

THE VALIDITY OF THE CYBERNETIC PARADIGM

The system under consideration must have a well-defined objective

In the case of a purely technical process such as the automatic guidance of a missile the control system is programmed to know the objective, e.g. to hit a particular piece of hardware or landscape. At any moment the navigation equipment of the system has information about its position and the position of the target. From this data an error signal is computed and the control system adjusted accordingly. If the navigation instruments are sufficiently accurate and the control system sufficiently sensitive a 'finely-tuned' system can be obtained. Any deviation from the desired course is quickly corrected.

When an organisation which includes human beings is considered in the same way three important points should be noted. First, the system does not have an objective: it is the individuals within the system who have objectives which may be very different. Nevertheless it can sometimes be convenient to think of an organisation as if it did have one. Not only can the concept be useful when interactions between large organisations are considered but it can also be used for internal control purposes by providing a way of giving individuals an indication of the way others in organisations feel about various matters of mutual interest. Such concepts, however, are meaningful only as long as the personal objectives of those inside the organisation permit them to be so.

To non-members an organisation is often associated with ideal or imputed objectives. These objectives may or may not correspond to those of the individuals within it. Such imputed corporate objectives may be derived from an organisation's public relations literature, from popular mythology and traditional beliefs and may be totally divorced from those held by the individual members of the organisation. The founder of a company may have stated that his empire's objective is to improve the lot of mankind: fifty years later the directors and workforce are concerned primarily with improving their personal standards of living. In the public sector, traditional belief may suggest that the objective of the detective is the pursuit of truth, whereas in reality the average policeman may simply be striving for a given number of arrests to keep his superior happy. Similarly university dons may squabble and fight about research funds and career prospects, whilst many outside the system believe such institutions to be the guardians of good scholarship and learning.

In terms of the cybernetic paradigm the effect of ambiguity and uncertainty about objectives means that there is no clear single standard against which the performance of the organisation can be compared. However each individual can determine a standard corresponding to their own objectives and these standards can be used by the individuals concerned to adjust those inputs under their control to achieve their aims or, if these are too ambitious, to reach modified objectives. Similarly groups of individuals outside an organisation can adjust certain inputs to bring its performance more in line with the imputed or ideal objectives.

Clearly the greater the variety of objectives and hence the greater the number of different standards of organisation performance in use, the less the chance that it is meaningful to talk of an organisation being controlled in the cybernetic sense.

It must be possible to measure the output in terms of the dimensions defined by the objective

The second major difference between human and purely technical systems is concerned with whether or not a common set of measures is used to evaluate the performance of the organisation. In the operational control of a routine industrial process there may be considerable agreement amongst those concerned that the objective is production. Furthermore there may also be widespread agreement that the production system can be in one of a number of different states, each state being defined in terms of the production levels achieved. In addition the mechanism used for counting the number of items is considered by all to be reliable. In such a situation when the recording mechanism indicates that the production system is in a particular state, say S_i, all those concerned interpret the information in the same way.

In contrast for a non-industrial process such as the keeping of the Queen's Peace, many may agree with Beer (1970) that eudemony is the appropriate measure of the public sense of security and that the performance of the law enforcement system can be in one of a number of different states, each state being defined in terms of the level of eudemony achieved. In this case, however, there will be many different views on what constitutes the various states in terms of the variables involved. Although many will agree that murder is a serious offence, there would be less agreement on such offences as illegal parking and driving with more than a certain amount of alcohol in the bloodstream.

By processing the data which reaches him an individual forms an opinion of the state of a system. Some of these data will correspond to values of continuous or approximately continuous variables such as the number of crimes reported, the number of births or deaths in a large region and various financial factors; others will correspond to discontinuous variables, being based on essentially qualitative rather than quantitative factors, e.g. whether the state of affairs under consideration possesses or lacks some attribute. Since individuals have different objectives and value systems, the same data may be interpreted in a variety of ways so that there is confusion about the state of the system and how it could change.

Furthermore, in order to be able to obtain precision in the control of the system, the mechanisms which provide the data which measure the performance of the system must be reliable. This reliability has been obtained in many technical systems which facilitate operational control. In management control processes such reliability is often lacking. This lack stems from two major difficulties which must be overcome to achieve high information reliability: counting and classification. Compared with operational systems, people engaged in managerial processes often have much greater discretion regarding both *what* is recorded and *how* items are recorded. The use of this discretion can sometimes be used to spread misleading information about the true state of affairs under consideration.

To some extent the chances of such errors occurring can be reduced by all those concerned agreeing to follow the same counting and classification procedures and having the discipline to obey them conscientiously. However, even if this was to be the case, recipients would still have different interpretations of the information unless they had a common set of objectives and a common value system. Unreliable information creates ambiguity: different objectives and measures of system performance make it worse. The greater the ambiguity, the less certain a receiver of a message is about its meaning. Consider a system which can be in one of N possible states and let

$P_i(j)$ = the probability that the system is in state j given that the information received about the system suggests that it is in state i.

The larger the ambiguity the wider the spread of probabilities over the N states. The uncertainty associated with the system given that a message has been received to the effect that it is in state i has been called the entropy by Shannon and Weaver (1949), and defined by

$$E_i = -\sum_{j=1}^{N} P_i(j) \log P_i(j)$$

When objectives are the same and where no misunderstandings regarding the interpretation occur, information which suggests that a system is in state *i* means that the recipient may accept with complete confidence that the system is in state *i*, i.e. $P_i(i) = 1$, $P_i(j) = 0$ for all $i \neq j$. In other words the entropy is zero, there is complete certainty. Ambiguity causes a greater spread of the probabilities and hence an increase in the entropy.

It must be possible to reduce the different between output and objective by suitable adjustments to the internal control variables

The third major difference between operational control and managerial control processes concerns the question of whether or not the feedback is usable. In other words, when the error vector has been calculated, can it be meaningfully used to adjust the control of the system in order to modify its performance in the required manner. 'It is no use closing the door after the horse has bolted' illustrates the type of situation where the above condition is clearly not satisfied. 'One-off' projects, like most major investment projects, are of this type. Review procedures may exist but once a project has been started the relevant error information normally comes too late for corrective action to be taken. Perhaps, therefore, it is not surprising that often there is a lack of interest by managers in such reviews (Hagg 1974). In a similar way, planning is a form of control without feedback: it is after a development is well under way that the error signal begins to indicate that something is wrong. The social faults associated with high-rise buildings only became generally accepted after they had been constructed and lived in for some time. In dealing with decisions which are essentially strategic, how often is it found that the whizz-kid who obtained fame and glory following the initial success of a project has moved to higher things by the time the unfortunate consequences of his decision become apparent?

The control problem describing such situations is represented diagrammatically in Figure 13.3. This again assumes that the system under consideration can be in one of N possible states, $\{S_1, S_2, \ldots, S_n, \ldots, S_N\}$. Suppose too that at the time an important decision is to be taken the system is in state, S_n, and that M control options are available, $\{C_1, C_2, \ldots, C_m, \ldots, C_M\}$. Let C_m be the control option at present, its selection would represent a no-change policy. Since the future cannot be foreseen with complete accuracy the transition matrix, which describes the way the states of the system are inter-

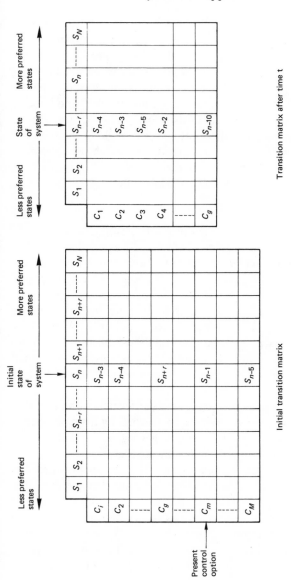

FIGURE 13.3 *Illustration of the change in the transition matrix with respect to a typical strategic decision*

related should the various control options be adopted, has through necessity to be based on a combination of fact, hearsay, prejudices and broad assumptions. The prudent decision-maker is, of course, aware that much of his forecasting is guesswork when he makes his control decision. However, after due consideration, suppose that he decides to adopt C_g as the new strategy because it offers the hope of transforming the system from S_n to the more preferred state S_{n+r}. The figure shows that all the other options are thought likely to lead to less preferred states. The types of situation for which the cybernetic approach is unlikely to be helpful are therefore those in which after a period of time, say t, following the introduction of control option C_g it is found that

1. the system has been transformed into a less preferred state S_{n-r} instead of into the more preferred state S_{n+r} as predicted, and
2. the control options which might have been able to redeem the situation, say $C_{g+1}, C_{g+2}, \ldots, C_m$, are no longer available.

For example, in the pursuit of greater farm yields nature's delicate ecological system may unknowingly become polluted. When these unforeseen consequences become undeniably established it may no longer be possible to switch to a strategy to give even the original yields – the basic underlying mechanisms having been irreparably damaged.

Even more difficult control situations occur when it is thought that the desired state for a system cannot be reached by a single control change but will require two or more changes. In terms of the above illustration, the transition matrix may indicate that it is necessary first to switch to C_{g-1} before changing to C_j in order to transform the system into the state S_{n+r}. Ashby (1956) gives an example of such a situation in which the transition matrix is known with certainty in order to illustrate how the cybernetic approach can provide a solution to the control problem. However the less routine, the less the degree of objectivity associated with the output, the more the transition matrix is immersed in a cloud of uncertainty and hence the less useful the approach.

Although many non-routine processes with low output objectivity are such that the decision-maker's initial assumption about the nature of the transition matrix later turns out to be in error, the second condition, that many of the control options are no longer available when the need for a further control change arises, is often not satisfied. Such situations can occur when a traditional control policy is changed. Suppose, for instance, that a company has for years pursued one policy with regard to the detection and prosecution of pilferers. How the workforce are likely to respond to more 'hawkish' or 'dove-like' strategies is unknown although there will be many opinions amongst the managers and officials. Nor will criminological data be very helpful in predicting the consequences of various possible changes in policy. If therefore the management wish to make a change their transition matrix will be based mainly on guesswork. If a change is made the effects will become known whilst most of the control options are still available. Then by a series of changes a deeper understanding of the true nature of the transition matrix can be obtained. Experiences with a computer simulation of a factory (Willmer, 1976b) have shown that many managers do not make the best use of the information as it is obtained. There is a large amount of luck in choosing the optimum strategy initially when so much is based on guesswork. The advantage of applying the cybernetic approach to such situations is that it enables the maximum benefit to be derived from the feedback information thus reducing the time and the extent to which the system is not under control!

The cybernetic approach will only really work well when the controller knows accurately the present state of the system he is trying to control, the state that he wishes it to be in and the effects of the various control options open to him. As these conditions are rarely if ever satisfied in managerial situations, it is not surprising that many doubts have been expressed about the effectiveness of the approach when applied to the problems of management control. Several years ago the 'conference circuit' was crowded with enthusiastic cyber-neticians proclaiming the potential benefits that could be obtained from the adoption by management of such an approach. Some claimed that their models would enable production managers to have 'finely-tuned' production systems, although in most cases the claims were based on essentially theoretical reasoning. Despite the world-wide enthusiasm amongst academics for these theoretical models there were some who were not convinced. At the Third European Meeting on Cybernetics and Systems Research held in Vienna in 1976 Professor Checkland (1976) reminded delegates of the words of Sir Isaac Newton who once wrote with reference to navigation problems: 'if instead of sending the observations of seamen to able mathematicians at land, the land would send able mathematicians to sea, it would signify much more to the improvements of navigation and safety of men's lives or estates on that element'. Reporting on the conference Willmer (1976a) noted:

> In many of the sessions . . . one was left wondering whether some of the work presented would not have been improved if the cyberneticians involved had followed this advice: most papers seemed to be of a very theoretical nature with empirical data being conspicuous by its absence. Nowhere was this more true than in the section dealing with management. Management is concerned with people. Nevertheless in papers describing theoretical models of control systems for complex processes involving men and machines, the behavioural factors tended to be overlooked. Does it really make sense to talk about the 'fine tuning' of a control system of a production process without considering such factors as the wage payment systems used and the ways in which the workers can influence the structure of control samples?

The evidence of studies which have investigated the ways wage payment systems affect employee behaviour suggest that this aspect of the production process cannot be ignored. For instance, Yetton (1979) reports on a study of the efficiency of a piecework incentive payment system and notes some of the strategies adopted by the workers. Perhaps, however, the most comprehensive study of wage payment systems generally is given in the work described by Warmington, Lupton and Gribbin (1977) where the complexities of the reactions of employees and their supervisors are discussed in depth. This work demonstrates clearly that it can be imprudent to talk of 'finely-tuned' production systems without consideration of the behavioural aspects involved.

Probably the most serious criticism of many management control systems has been expressed by Hofstede (1978) who attributed their ineffectiveness to the cybernetic philosophy on which they are based: 'A distinction is made between routine industrial-type processes for which a homeostatic paradigm is more suitable, and non-routine, non-industrial-type processes, for which a political paradigm is recommended. Attempts at enforcing a cybernetic paradigm on the latter process, like Program-Planning-Budgeting Systems (PPBS) and Management-By-Objectives (MBO) are bound to fail.'

The reference cites in support of this view the opinion of other research workers: 'PPBS has failed everywhere and at all times' (Wildavsky, 1975); and with respect to MBO: 'One of the greatest management illusions' (Levinson, 1970).

The criticisms of other writers have been less scathing. Ford (1979) considers examples of flaws in the theory in discussing the question: 'MBO: An idea whose time has gone?' and Dennison (1979) views the rise and fall of PPBS as an example of management development in government resource allocation.

THE UNRELIABILITY OF MANAGEMENT CONTROL INFORMATION

Besides the difficulties associated with the collection and interpretation of data in human systems further problems arise as information is transmitted from one part of the system to another. At each link of the communication process information is received, processed and transmitted so that there is always a possibility that it will become lost, distorted or misunderstood. The existence of a good management information system may help to minimise this possibility but does not guarantee the causes will be entirely eliminated. Any system may suffer from faults of design and operation and the most common are discussed in Revans (1969). For this reason managers will find it prudent to remember therefore that their communication channels are unlikely to be completely reliable and as a result they may be:

1. more uncertain about the true state of affairs then they should be. This increase can be thought of as noise and it has been found convenient to distinguish between two types; (see Willmer, 1970)

   Internally generated noise – that due to information becoming lost or distorted inside the organisation or because insufficient use is made of information already obtained, and

   Background noise – that due to the organisation not receiving the information in the first place.

2. more certain about the true state of affairs than they should be, bearing in mind the data available. When there is competition or conflict between groups or individuals it may be to the benefit of one party to manipulate the information received by others to mislead rather than to inform. In Willmer (1978) this effect has been called 'pseudo-certainty'. To illustrate, suppose that the information available to a manager when interpreted correctly gives

an uncertainty or entropy level of E_A. Suppose too that a subordinate presents the data in such a way that he misleads his superior into believing with complete confidence that the system is one particular state. His entropy level is therefore zero so that the degree of pseudo-certainty appertaining is given by E_A.

A method for illustrating this situation diagrammatically is described by Willmer (1978). Here it is assumed that a system can be in one of three states, S_1, S_2, S_3 and a receiver on interpreting the information available believes that the probabilities associated with each state are P_1, P_2, P_3 respectively. As there are only three possible states these probabilities lie on a triangle in probability space defined by the equation

$$P_1 + P_2 + P_3 = 1$$

with $\qquad\qquad 0 \leqslant P_i \leqslant 1 \qquad\qquad (i = 1, 2, 3)$

In this triangle lines of constant entropy or uncertainty may be drawn, see Figure 13.4. The centre of the triangle is the point $P_i = P_2 = P_3 = \frac{1}{3}$, i.e. all the states are equally probable and the entropy is a maximum. The figure also shows that the closer the point, (P_1, P_2, P_3), is to one of the apexes, the lower the entropy.

Consider as well the following two points:

1. P_a – the point corresponding to the set of probabilities $\{P_a(i)\}$ where $P_a(i)$ is the probability that the receiver of information believes the system is in state i based on his interpretation of the information which actually reaches him.

2. P_c – the point corresponding to the set of probabilities $\{P_c(i)\}$ where $P_c(i)$ is the probability that the system will be in state i when all the relevant information received by the organisation has been faithfully transmitted to the receiver and correctly interpreted on arrival. It represents therefore the most reliable result that can be expected from the information available to the organisation – there are no errors due to information becoming lost or distorted as it is sent from one part of the organisation to another or from messages being misunderstood or misinterpreted.

Willmer (1978) pointed out that, if a series of lines emanating from the central point were considered, the distance between a typical P_c and a typical P_a consisted of two components:

1. ΔE = a change of entropy or uncertainty, and
2. M = a movement along a line of constant entropy (or a surface of constant entropy when four or more dimensions are considered)

Further, when considering the difference in entropy, it is helpful to consider the situation from the point of view of a true signal being masked by noise. The entropy level of the point P_c can thus be thought of as background noise. When the entropy difference is positive it can be thought of as internally generated noise. On the other hand, when the entropy difference is negative, it indicates the degree of pseudo-certainty appertaining.

One of the aims of a good manager is to ensure that his interpretation of the state of affairs is as accurate as possible. Distorted unreliable information increases the difficulty of this task. Much of the distortion is caused unintentionally rather than by design and by

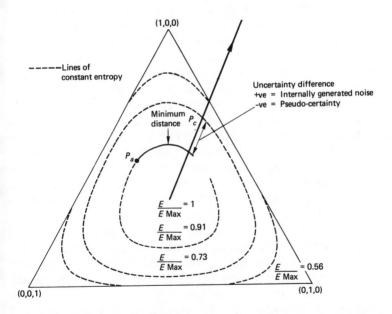

SOURCE: M. Willmer (1978) 'System Uncertainty and Leadership Strategy', *4th European Meeting on Cybernetics and Systems Research* (New York: Hemisphere Publishing).

FIGURE 13.4 *The plane of feasible probabilities*

studying the organisation's communication problems, making employees more aware of each other's difficulties, introducing better or more appropriate equipment the level of unintentional distortion and the number of misconceptions can often be considerably reduced. Often too there is a clear requirement in a company for the development of an effective and fully integrated business intelligence system to enhance the performance of existing information activities and processes (see Pearce, 1976).

The structure of an organisation can also play an important role in reducing distortion, especially where one section is dependent on another for information. A production department may rely on their sales and marketing colleagues for data about prospective customer needs. If care is not taken to structure the organisation appropriately it is possible this link may generate more distortion and misunderstanding than need be the case, (see Willmer, 1977). In this reference it was assumed that the production and marketing people had different objectives and that it was essentially lack of concern which caused errors to occur in the information that was transmitted: the distortions were not deliberately nor maliciously introduced.

Deliberate distortions can be expected when there are major differences of objective between people in an organisation. They have been noted in connection with budgets by Williamson (1964) and Schiff and Lewin (1970) – where it was found that managers will understate revenues and overstate costs in order to obtain slack budgets. The propensity for information bias among middle managers has been considered by Lowe and Shahin (1980). Line managers have been found to behave in a similar way by Lowe and Shaw (1968): in this case bias was introduced into sales forecasts. In these examples the objectives of the managers and their subordinates were different: although the company may have had some stated objective, at the interface between the superior and subordinate the former wanted greater effort from his subordinate whilst the subordinate presumably wanted to be well thought of by his boss. As a result the subordinates deliberately distorted information to try to achieve their own personal objectives. This type of distortion has also been found experimentally by Cyert, March and Starbuck (1961). The process has also been considered as a conflict in which the parties develop 'ploys' and 'counter-ploys', see Anthony and Herzlinger (1975).

The extent to which a person can distort information in a system will obviously depend upon the environment in which the system operates, the type of activity being undertaken and the nature of the link between the person concerned and others in the system. The more routine and programmed the activity the less scope a person will generally have for distorting information about his performance. The less routine and programmed the activity the less easy it is for information about a person's activities to be checked, hence the greater the scope for senders to manipulate information to their advantage. In some spheres of activity wide discretion has to be given to the men on the spot. Tight control is not feasible when dealing in any of the fast-moving commodity markets. As some companies have learnt to their cost, unscrupulous employees have attempted to use such situations in order to manipulate information for their own personal gain. The *Daily Telegraph* (1978) noted in connection with some large losses incurred on cocoa trading by three British companies a couple of years ago: 'It is, in a way, a tale of our times. In all three instances the companies have lost substantial sums allegedly because of the wilful behaviour of executives who kept vital information from their superiors to cover up attempts to make personal fortunes with their employer's money.'

The sensible manager knows that, even though the system that provides him with information has probably many faults, he cannot operate effectively in a vacuum. He needs good reliable information regardless of whether the state of affairs being considered is 'good' or 'bad'; regardless of whether the future looks bleak or rosy, he needs the truth. Unfortunately, because of his position, he may find it difficult to obtain. Like so many powerful people have discovered to their cost: although they may buy, steal or otherwise obtain material possessions, the truth is something that often eludes them (see Lucas 1938). It is only human nature that the greater the power of a manager the more the chances that his subordinates will tell him what they think he wants to hear. Many powerful managers have found themselves out of contact with reality, their isolation from the truth becoming more complete the greater their power. Thus unless he is careful, the powerful manager may well find himself out of contact with reality (see Willmer, 1974).

Since managers can often influence decisions about an individual's promotion, hours of work, pay and bonuses, place of work, etc., it is not surprising that employees view with concern the way those in authority over them regard their activities.

Where there is scope for unscrupulous manipulation of information by subordinates every superior is vulnerable. Whatever assessment method is used for measuring performance, it is only human nature

that some employees will try to make it look as though they are bette
performers than their efforts genuinely merit. Should the superior b
deceived, the effect can be to spread disharmony amongst the sub
ordinates who learn about it, thus encouraging deviousness within th
group. This is no contemporary phenomenon; Wensley (1931), tha
great London detective of a past generation, warned some fifty year
ago about the unfortunate consequences of rewarding subordinate
unfairly in relation to a crime enquiry: 'there are men . . . with a strea
of vanity that impels them to adopt a pose at the expense of those wh
have really done .the work. They like to bask in the limelight . . . A
Chief Constable I was always on my guard against this sort of thing
and made it my business to see that credit went in the right direction
Unless kept in check it breeds resentment and checks energy.'

As far as data manipulation is concerned subordinates have show
considerable ingenuity at 'bending' or breaking the rules in order t
achieve their own objectives. It is a phenomenon that is confined to n
one country, it is worldwide:

USA – From the *Sunday Times* (1971): 'Mafia Catches out Mobil'. A
    newspaper headline introducing an article about how the oi
    company came to hire a Mafia-run firm of hoodlums in an attemp
    to break a lorry drivers' strike. Senior management, when it learn
    what had happened, stressed that scrupulous checks were carrie
    out on all suppliers. However as one official admitted: 'Some guy a
    the district marketing level was probably under tremendou
    pressure from his dealers and he decided to take a few short cuts.

    From *The Times* 1972): 'New York Police cheat on crime figure'
    An article on how senior management began to put greate
    emphasis on certain statistics and how it is believed precinc
    commanders responded by manipulating their data to show head
    quarters that they were doing a much better job of controlling crim
    than in fact they were.

USSR – With regard to the effectiveness of the railway system it ha
    been noted by Feifer (1980):
        Commandeered locomotives, I was informed, are secretly worke
        in one district desperate to fulfil its plan – while trainloads o
        fruit rot in neighbouring sidings. Other trains are driven, empty
        up and down remote lines to attain bonus-producing mileag

norms while nearby bottlenecks explode for lack of wagons.

Whole trains disappear, as did a recent one that set out from Kishinev for Odessa, 120 miles south. (While I was visiting Odessa, it was officially confirmed that a second train sent to find the first also disappeared, as did three locomotives dispatched directly from the factory.) Shipments of expensive western equipment bought with precious hard currency ... are buried because no one wants to increase his production quota by installing them.

From the manager's point of view the doubt and misapprehension that surrounds the operating position of the system under his control, P, can be divided into two components, see Figure 13.5: a component that is due to the uncertainties and ambiguities inherent in the nature of the operation and a component that is due to factors generated inside his organisation. The first component may be represented by a vector $\overrightarrow{OA}$ and the second by the vector $\overrightarrow{AP}$. The more routine and the greater the objectivity associated with the output of the process the

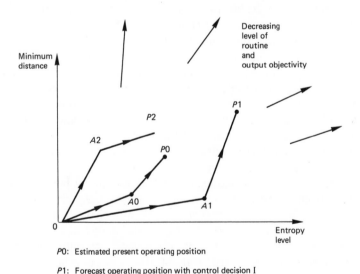

P0: Estimated present operating position

P1: Forecast operating position with control decision I

P2: Forecast operating position with control decision II

FIGURE 13.5 *Illustration of present and future operating positions*

nearer one would expect P to be to the origin. If, however, P is close to A but A is distant from O, it indicates a reliable information system in a fundamentally difficult sphere of operation.

Since Wensley's days in charge of the detectives of London, however, organisations have become much larger and senior staff more divorced from the scenes of the operations of their companies. Thus it has become more and more difficult for executives to ensure that their subordinates are fairly rewarded. As a detective Wensley was primarily interested in the pursuit of truth: his concern was with finding out what crime had been committed in London and who was responsible for it. To this end reliable information was essential. With regard to business situations, however, the problem is more complex because the method of appraising the performance of subordinates is used in a dual role: to encourage both the faithful transmission of information and to improve motivation. A manager therefore has to have a clear idea in his own mind of the states that are achievable. In order to make a realistic assessment of his organisation's potential he again needs reliable information. As in the case of the present operating position the information he obtains enables a minimum distance and an entropy level to be determined for a number of control decisions. The situation is illustrated in Figure 13.5 and the problem confronting the manager can be clearly seen: lack of knowledge about the present state of affairs and lack of knowledge about the effects of various control decisions. For routine high programmed processes where there is relatively little opportunity for subordinates to manipulate information about their activities one would expect both operating and forecast positions to be close to O. However, for non-routine processes where levels of objectivity associated with the output are low and where there is ample scope for information manipulation by subordinates one would expect the corresponding positions to be distant from O. In such cases it is clear why management control techniques based on the cybernetic paradigm such as PPBS and MBO may be unsatisfactory: because subordinates have a large measure of control over information the manager may have not only a very inaccurate picture of the true state of affairs but also he may have a false idea about the system's potential.

In view of the important role played by reliable information it is surprising to learn of leaders who 'shoot the messenger because he brings bad news'. Such phenomena occur however and a fairly modern example appears to have been the dispute between Churchill and his Director of Naval Intelligence over the success of allied anti-U-boat operations in the Second World War, if a recent analysis is to be believed (see Beesly, 1980). In this dispute it seems that the Director was determined not to allow wishful thinking to colour his intelligence reports on U-boat figures. His assessment of the situation did not please his Prime Minister and he was eventually sacked. It is also noted that he was the only British officer of his rank not to be decorated for his services to the Allied victory. Leaders are not always lucky enough to find that they have subordinates with such courage and integrity.

WHO CONTROLS WHOM?

In an organisation in which subordinates have many opportunities for manipulating information flows, who is in control? Is it the superior who has all the outward trappings of authority, who can call for data and who formally announces his decision to the workforce? Or is it a subordinate who, knowing how his superior's mind works, his weaknesses and pet theories, feeds him the information that ensures a particular decision is made? A manager may set objectives, discuss targets with his subordinates, tell them how they will be rewarded and later give them the rewards he deems appropriate. Nevertheless in many cases he has to use data supplied by the subordinates and often it is not feasible for him to carry out sufficient checks to ensure its accuracy. In such cases how useful is the cybernetic approach?

To explore this question and to give insights into the different aspects of superior/subordinate interface and the effects of various methods of performance appraisal on both the motivation of employees and the manipulation of data, the business game, 'So you think that you will make a Managing Director', was created. This game is concerned with the management of people and machines in a production environment and is played at both the superior and subordinate level. At the superior level the objective is to handle subordinates in such a way that: (i) output is increased; (ii) he is aware of the way his factories are being managed. The factories concerned specialise in the production of 'clunks' and are situated a long way from head office in unpleasant surroundings so that it is rarely convenient for the superior to visit them.

At the subordinate level each participant is asked to be the manager of one of these factories, called International Castings Ltd. His task is to become familiar with the problem of manufacturing clunks and to understand his superior. At the technical level he has to make decisions regarding the way men, money and machines are used. At the social level he has to persuade his superior that he is competent, capable and dependable. The factory, its machines and workforce, are described more fully by Willmer (1978). There are also a number of company rules which have been laid down for running the factory. However, as the superior rarely visits the factory and as the subordinate is the main source of information about how it is being run and how well it is performing, the subordinate may violate these rules without fear of immediate exposure. The extent to which production is affected by rule violations depends on which ones are broken and by how much: some violations can have both a short- and long-term effect on the state of the factory. The organisational information link is illustrated diagrammatically in Figure 13.6.

During the game the computer is programmed to represent the company and the workforce, its responses being based on assumptions and partly from analysis of data obtained from the behaviour of managers who have been participants. When the game starts each subordinate is told that his boss has believed for some time that clunk production is too low and that the previous manager had been sacked for incompetence. The game is designed, however, so that the subordinate cannot on average meet the initial aspirations of his boss by totally obeying the rules. The game is played for a number of months and each month starts by the supervisor telling the subordinate what to make his primary objective. This may be either to produce as many clunks as possible, to get as close to the agreed target as possible, or to be truthful about the number of violations made. Superior and sub-

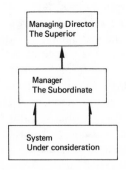

FIGURE 13.6   *The information link at International Castings Ltd*

ordinate together negotiate a target and the subordinate has to make his own decision about the running of the factory, the levels of overtime, the number of maintenance men who are asked to take on production duties, etc. He is also asked how many clunks he wants to hold over to the following months and the number of rule violations that he has committed. The recorded production figures and the number of confessions are given to the superior who assesses his subordinate's performance and gives him a rating normally between 50 and 100.

The game demonstrates clearly the conflict of objectives between the managing director and his subordinate: the boss wants the highest production and to know the state of affairs at his factories; the latter simply wants to be well thought of by his superior. The boss has nominal control over the method used to appraise performance, to reward his subordinate and to lead the negotiating process. The subordinate runs the factory and can to a significant extent determine his boss's perceptions of himself by suitably manipulating the information flow.

In the second part of the game the participant is promoted to the managing director position and the computer is programmed to act as the two subordinates, both cynical old hands who have heard many fine words in the past from other superiors. Again the computer programmes are based partly on assumptions and partly on the actual behaviour of earlier participants. By using data from people who have attended courses at the Manchester Business School the computer is now capable of handling realistically both levels regardless of whether decisions are consistent with expressed intentions. In this phase it is now the participant who selects the main objective, leads the target negotiation process and tells his subordinates what he thinks of their efforts.

The game has been played on a number of courses at the Manchester Business School with managers mainly with production experience in multinational companies as participants. When considering the responses at both levels it is helpful to bear in mind two levels of production performance suggested by Beer (1972):

1. the capability level – that which a completely efficient factory manager could achieve with the existing resources and operating under existing constraints;
2. the potentiality level – that which could be achieved by fully utilising existing resources and optimally relaxing the constraints.

In other words a demand for production above the capability level means that rules will have to be violated; a demand for production beyond the potentiality level is asking for the impossible!

It is whilst operating as the subordinate that participants are best able to develop a clear idea of both levels. Adhering firmly to the company's regulations may give valuable estimates of the capability level but such a strategy provides no guidance as to the maximum sustained production that can be obtained.

Many different strategies were pursued by subordinates when dealing with their superiors. At one extreme there were those participants who tried to satisfy their superior's requests for more production and who were strictly honest with regard to the violations they made. In contrast there were those who set out to discover how their superior made decisions and hence how to manipulate him. Sometimes they would break rules and not confess, on other occasions they would not break rules but confess to fictitious violations. They soon learnt that, to obtain a large measure of control over their superior's perceptions of their ability and performance, they had first to manipulate the information to gain a large measure of control over the target negotiation process.

One important factor in determining responses seemed to be whether or not the superior was consistent with respect to his assessment policy, i.e. did he reward his subordinate the way he said he was going to? Willmer (1980) showed that the effect of a consistent or inconsistent assessment is considerable both in regard to the subordinate's participation in the target negotiation process and on his attempts to increase production. The results also showed the complex nature of the interactions between the subordinate's responses and the inputs at the discretion of the superior.

At the superior level it is vitally important for the managing director to have an accurate understanding of the capability and potentiality levels if he is to achieve high output and an accurate knowledge of the state of affairs in his factories. If a participant's understanding of the technical aspects of the factory is accurate and thorough, he will have learnt that there are relatively few ways in which the potential level can be achieved for a sustained period. On the other hand the number of combinations of rule violations that produce an output between capability and potentiality is much greater. Research by Willmer and Berry (1976) has shown that near these extreme levels the information given to the managing director about rule violation has little effect on his uncertainty level. In between these extremes, however, the information was of considerable value, giving a significant drop in the managing director's uncertainty level. Perhaps the reason for this behaviour is that

1. when the target level is near to the capability level participants feel that a more efficient manager would not have violated the rules that they have broken. Thus they admit to fewer violations than actually have occurred.
2. when the target level is close to the potentiality level, participants feel that a more efficient manager would not have to violate as many rules as they have broken. Thus they admit to fewer violations.
3. between the extreme levels participants know that rules have to be broken even by the most efficient manager and they become less self-conscious about their behaviour and thus more willing to tell the truth.

In the experiments many different managerial styles of leadership were used and it was found that about 68 per cent followed one of the following two approaches:

1. Not mean when negotiating targets and a belief that, when honesty is the main objective, production and closeness to target encouraged lying
2. Mean when negotiating targets

The results showed a number of interesting differences between the reaction to these two approaches including several factors that were statistically significant at the 5 per cent level. However, as far as the effectiveness of the style on output was concerned there was no significant difference. On the other hand, participants who adopted Style 1 were significantly less successful in estimating the true state of affairs at the factories than those who opted for Style 2.

It was also found that the choice of main objective had a major effect on the subordinate's performance. Figure 13.7(a), (b) and (c) show a comparison between the perceived and actual operating positions of the system for each of the three objectives – output, closeness to target and honesty of information. These figures show that only in the case of output was there a sufficient number of subordinates to enable meaningful average actual operating positions to be determined at the highest production level. As regards the state of affairs at the factory, Figure 13.8 shows how the various main objectives affect the uncertainty of the managing director. When output is the main objective, increasing the production level led to a decrease in internally generated noise with a small minimum distance throughout. With 'closeness to target' as the main objective, increasing production led first to a decrease in the minimum distance and then a large increase in internally generated noise. With 'honesty' as the main objective, the minimum distance increased as the production increases.

These results are important because they show that the way subordinates are led affects the decisions they take not only with respect to the production of clunks but also with regard to their manipulation of

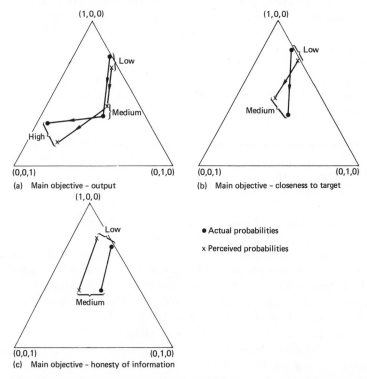

(a) Main objective – output

(b) Main objective – closeness to target

(c) Main objective – honesty of information

● Actual probabilities

x Perceived probabilities

SOURCE   M. Willmer (1978) 'System Uncertainty and Leadership Strategy', 4th European Meeting on Cybernetics and Systems Research (New York: Hemisphere Publishing).

FIGURE 13.7   *Comparison between perceived and actual operating positions of managing directors at various production levels*

information flows. Ideally, the boss or managing director would like to operate near the origin in Figure 13.8 with high production. Some methods of setting objectives, negotiating targets, rewarding performance are more likely to motivate and control subordinates than others. For instance, unless output is the main objective, high production is not likely. For low production, and with output as the main objective, internally generated noise is likely to be large. Further at medium production, there is large internally generated noise when closeness to target is the main objective and a large minimum distance when honesty is chosen.

It has also been noted that consistency of assessment can have a major effect on subordinate behaviour. However, even though a

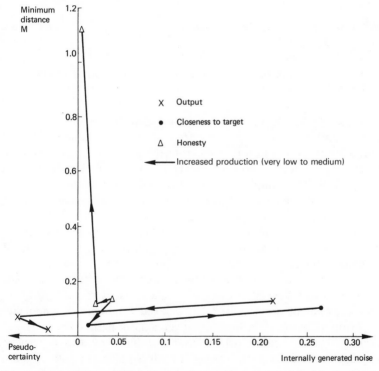

SOURCE M. Willmer (1978) 'System Uncertainty and Leadership Strategy', 4th European Meeting on Cybernetics and Systems Research (New York: Hemisphere Publishing).

FIGURE 13.8 *Comparison of actual and perceived operating positions of managing directors*

superior may wish to reward consistently it is difficult for him to be sure that his subordinates see him as doing so. Willmer (1980) examines the type of decision situation that confronts the superior when trying to pick a strategy to encourage the subordinate to become a good performer. The problem was considered as a 2 × 2 zero sum gáme and the results of game theory applied to generate a 'best' solution known as the maximin solution. When the subordinate was perceived as a poor performer it was found that the superior should

1. set a high target and make production the main objective 78 per cent of the time, and
2. set a low target and make honesty the main objective 22 per cent of the time

When dealing with a good performer, the corresponding results are

1. set a high target on 83 per cent occasions, and
2. set a low target on the remainder, and keep output as the main objective throughout.

As already noted, the computer responses to information and directives in both sections of the game are based partly on assumption and partly from information derived from the analysis of data collected from the behaviour of previous players. As more data is collected and analysed so the assumption contribution is diminished and this results in participants being asked to cope with people whose behaviour is basically similar to their own. Since this process could continue almost indefinitely the question arises as to when to stop the search for greater realism. An approach to this problem using the method of dynamic similarity is described by Willmer (1980).

Although it may never be possible to produce a completely realistic mathematical model of the complex management control problem, the development process used has allowed a number of important behavioural factors to be introduced and a meaningful framework has been produced against which the usefulness of the cybernetic approach can be assessed. Further it enables managers to learn more about the problems associated with the superior–subordinate interface and helps them to develop ways of obtaining more reliable control information. They can experience for themselves why it is that those in charge of overcentralised bureaucracies sometimes do not seem to be in control. They can learn how easy it is for the best subordinate to be passed over in favour of someone with less capability. It explains why subordinates sometimes spend more time building up their image in the eyes of their superiors than engaging in productive activity. It provides a warning to those who are tempted to put their faith in technique rather than in the judgement of people.

CONCLUSION

It was noted earlier that the less routine process with low output objectivity the greater the uncertainty of the leader was likely to be with regard to both the actual state of affairs and the potential for change and development. The power of the cybernetic approach when considering routine processes with high output objectivity is not in dispute, nor is its lack of appropriateness at the other extreme. In between its usefulness depends on the extent to which the minimum distance and the noise can be kept to a minimum both with respect to the present state of affairs and future predictions. The simulation studies have indicated that the way subordinates are handled seriously affects these parameters. The potential of the cybernetic approach to give 'finely-tuned' systems is enormous. To obtain even a major share of this potential requires effective leadership: each superior in an organisation must be a leader not just a position-holder. Furthermore, it is this quality of leadership that can extend the usefulness of techniques like PPBS and MBO. How much of this potential is realisable for a given system depends on a manager's ability to cope with the many strands of knowledge that make up the subject of management control. It is the proper application of these disciplines in nonroutine processes with low output objectivity that should be a common bond of all those who profess an interest in the subject. It is the many diverse but interrelated areas that produce the richness of the management control philosophy. Herbert Frankel (1977) once wrote of money: 'Money in itself has no character. Its character depends on what man in society breathes into it.' Similarly it may be said of the cybernetic approach to the control of human systems: the power of the cybernetic approach is derived from the leadership that managers breathe into it!

Part V

14 Organisational Effectiveness and Management Control

Tony Lowe and Wai Fong Chua

INTRODUCTION

Management control and management accounting as subjects lack a scientific language: that is to say a set of related concepts which constitute, in a relevant and coherent scientific sense, a complete and comprehensive statement of the problems to be resolved, in such a manner that it also provides a clear and definite means for indicating the general nature of the solutions to the problems at hand. Natural sciences, such as chemistry and physics, can justifiably claim to have such satisfactory scientific languages in this sense although clearly they still have unsolved problems. For instance, there is a much clearer understanding of the 'domain' of these subjects than there is for management control systems (MCS). What really is MCS about?

This chapter argues that before we can adequately define MCS and their purpose, we need first to analyse and define the concept of organisational effectiveness (OE). The purpose of control must be intrinsically coupled with the purpose and effective working of a human socioeconomic organisation. Accordingly, this chapter starts by looking at the present confusion in the MCS literature and argues that this reflects a deeper controversy surrounding the notion of effectiveness. It then reviews briefly and eclectically some of the major theories of OE and proposes a definition which is believed to aid the explanation, prediction and control of complex human social systems. Finally, from this perspective, a definition of MC is derived: MC is seen as being synomymous with organisational control and its purpose is to ensure the long-run survival of that organisation.

On management control

The lack of a coherent language in the MC literature is evidenced today by the plethora of definitions of management control (MC) and management control systems (MCS). Machin in Chapter 2 for example, defines MCS as 'the study of formal and informal systems which help a manager to control what he does with himself and other managed cost resources'. This definition focuses on the informational needs of specific, individual decision-makers and managers who, it is maintained, pass the final judgement on the effectiveness and usefulness of the system. Such a definition can be compared with that of Anthony's *et al.* (1965). He defines MC as 'the process by which managers assure that resources are obtained and used effectively and efficiently in the accomplishment of the organisation's goals'. Anthony further distinguishes between strategic planning (the definition of organisational goals) and operational control (day-to-day management decisions given specified goals and means). This second definition still sees control as the prerogative of managers and management, but brings in the wider notion of organisational goals. However, MC is seen as being a part of the total process of organisational control. Yet other definitions distinguish between MC, organisational control and planning. In the next section, we shall attempt to show that in spite of the current variety in these definitions there is a clear consensus on certain issues, such consensus providing the logical link between the purpose of MCS and the concept of OE.

Some consensus about MCS

Although there is disarray in the MCS literature and much controversy about the domain of the subject, it is useful to discover the areas of consensus as well. Too often one concentrates and exaggerates dissimilarities between different theoretical positions without paying adequate attention to the similarities between them. Three main areas of consensus will be discussed.

The first alludes to the boundary definition problem of MCS. Most researchers (see, Tannenbaum, 1968; Dalton and Lawrence, 1971; Giglioni and Bedeian, 1974) appear to agree that a MCS represents an informational or influence process or structure that operates within some defined organisational system. Whether one defines MC as being synonymous with organisational control or as the amount of power vested in the management subgroup, theorists imply a wider organisational system within which the MCS is embedded. This organisational system in turn influences and is influenced by its substantial and more general environment (see Lowe and Tinker, 1976; Rhenman, 1973). Hence, in order to understand the functioning of an MCS, one needs to model both the organisation and its environment.

The second area of consensus refers to an oft taken-for-granted assumption – that a MCS exists in order to bring about greater *effectiveness* within a organisation. Ambiguity, however, surrounds the level of analysis of this notion of effectiveness. Like the concept of MC, organisational effectiveness is a difficult construct and has been defined in a number of ways. For example, one can take either a parochial or introverted perspective, or again, in contrast, a holistic organisational–environmental level of analysis. Further not only is there disagreement about the meaning of organisational effectiveness, there is debate amongst MCS analysts as to whether *organisational* effectiveness is an appropriate criterion. Due mainly to the seemingly insurmountable barriers in defining the term adequately, some analysts have preferred to use the notion of *managerial effectiveness* or 'helping managers to do their job better' as the design criteria of a MCS (Machin, Chapter 2). We feel that the present confusion in the organisational effectiveness literature contributes to and is closely connected with the present fuzziness in the subject of MCS.

The third area of consensus concerns the notion of control. As has been pointed out by a number of MCS theorists, the word covers a wide range of possible meanings. It could mean a set of actions or plans that are necessary to attain some future outcome or that are necessary to ensure that a system operates within its survival limits. Control, unfortunately, also has pejorative implications of coercion and manipulation in a context of optimisation, such as profit-maximising behaviour, which may be falsely interpreted as representative of narrow-minded values militating against longer-run human self-interests and indeed devoid of the more human characteristics, such as grace and love. However, most theorists agree that for a system to be controlled there must exist some goal or objective function which acts as a standard against which action is being continuously compared. With a few exceptions (see Cyert and March, 1963; Silverman, 1970) the notion of *organisational* purpose and goals is generally accepted as a feasible concept that still serves as a guide for understanding what happens in an organisation. As Hall (1977) states: 'even when forgotten or ignored, the goal is still the basis for the organisation, since the means would not have developed without it in the first place'. An organisation, like a single human being, may possess internal contradictions but one does not automatically proceed to deny the existence of individual goals; why should one deny the existence and analytical usefulness of organisational goals? The dynamics of goal conflict, change and negotiation do not alter the fact that goals may still guide what happens in an organisation. Without this concept, organisational behaviour reduces to a near random occurrence, subject only to external forces and pressures. Since organisations do have continuity, do act, achieve, fail, the theoretical construct of organisational, holistic goals remains a valid explanatory and predictive tool (see Mohr, 1973; Haworth, 1959; Mandelbaum, 1955).

Disagreement, however, surrounds the meaning of organisational goals and as discussed above, the idea of organisational effectiveness. None the less the fact remains – that an understanding of organisational purpose, whatever the difficulties involved, is vital to the design and functioning of a MCS. Indeed, the word MCS presupposes some concept of organisational purpose.

We have so far argued that there are four broad areas of consensus in the current MCS literature, namely:

1. a MCS is embedded within a wider organisational system;
2. a MCS is intended to 'aid' and 'help' the working of the organisation, as seen from the value-standpoint of the intender; and thus
3. a MCS must incorporate an understanding of the values and purpose of the organisation (from some value-standpoint);
4. and therefore of the cultures and values of the society in which it is embedded.

This leads to our argument that the question of the purpose and nature of a MCS cannot be divorced from an analysis of the purpose and utility of the wider organisational system within which it exists.

Indeed, one cannot proceed to develop a theory of management control without a prior theory of organisation, organisational purpose and effectiveness. Further, we argue that the concept of *organisational* effectiveness, as opposed to interpersonal or managerial effectiveness, presents a more satisfactory MCS design criterion. This is because a partial analysis of an organisation will not enable one to explain, predict and ultimately control the organisation as a whole. This we take to be the management task. It is patently obvious that human beings almost intuitively congregate in organisations for the purpose of fulfilling their own personal objectives. And without any attempt at reification, it is clear that the behaviour of the *resultant whole* cannot be adequately explained by a partial analysis of one or several of its parts. An organisation does exist, continues and acts as an entity in itself, with outcomes and events that are properly called outcomes of the organisation and which are irreducible to the acts of specific individuals. For example, British Rail (and all other enterprises) do raise their prices by an observed amount. They do make precise amounts of investment; they do hire and fire precise numbers of employees. The organisation as a whole acts according to that decision, whatever may have been the problems in organisational analysis of how such organisational behaviour was determined. Therefore, a reductionist, pluralistic, individualistic approach that naively segments organisational analysis will not provide satisfactory knowledge of collective human behaviour.

Before we attempt to define MCS we move first to a detailed look at the concept of organisational effectiveness. The following review is necessarily selective and brief; only the major, distinctive pieces of research are discussed, as it is not the authors' intention here to launch into a close and fine-combed critique of all the organisational effectiveness literature. However, the classification scheme that is used has been developed from a careful analysis of most of the effectiveness literature that has been published in Britain and the United States over the last twenty-five years.

ORGANISATIONAL GOALS AND THE CONCEPT OF ORGANISATIONAL EFFECTIVENESS (OE)

Like the term MC, the concept of OE is complex and requires careful definition. The term is often bandied around in academic, business and professional journals with a careless assertiveness that obscures the fact that it is still a subject of controversy. As Steers (1977) pointed out, there is no generally recognised theory on the concept, no agreement on its dimensions, determinants, influences and facets. We will attempt to create a taxonomy of the research on OE as well as propose a prescriptive definition of the concept. This then leads naturally to an explication of the concept of MC.

OE theories may be classified using two main dimensions. The first differentiates descriptive theories from prescriptive ones. Descriptive theories attempt to 'reflect reality in a condensed form' (Klassen and

Schreuder, 1979). Similarly Ijiri (1975) argues that 'the basic aim of descriptive models is to represent complicated empirical phenomena by simple models without losing the essentials'. Hence descriptive theories of OE attempt to describe what the goals of an organisation *are* and how far the organisation has achieved them. They are concerned with how one might determine the extent to which given goals of an organisation have been achieved. But as we argue later, clearly no theory can be purely descriptive by its very nature. All theories must be a 'scientific' artefact of one kind or another, thus essentially all theories must be prescriptive in nature. Prescriptive theories, on the other hand, seek not to 'describe' but to prescribe the means and/or ends of human action. Such theories of OE no longer take organisational goals as given but question and evaluate them in terms of some value-based prescriptive criterion. They begin to ask questions of the following nature – given that one can identify the goals of the organisation, *should* these be the goals? Whose goals should one use as the standard against which to measure the utility of the organisation? Thus, a prescriptive approach not only questions the degree of goal achievement but the 'value' (social and individual) of the outputs of an organisation.

As Klassen and Schreuder (1979) rightly point out, the fundamental difference between descriptive and prescriptive theories is that the former tend to preserve the status quo whilst the latter are intended as tools for change. In addition, descriptive theories often imply that it is possible to construct knowledge of an 'objective', ultimate reality that is value-free, that merely and purely describes. Prescriptive theories, on the other hand, expound what 'might' be done in some ethical, value-laden sense; their value-standpoints are clear and explicit. We argue that value-neutral theory is an illusion borrowed from the natural sciences. Value judgements enter into every aspect of knowledge, in the choice of 'worthy' objectives of 'description', in the evaluation of results, in the language used to 'describe'. In this sense, even our formal distinction between descriptive and prescriptive theories grows somewhat fuzzy and unhelpful. For implicit prescription lies behind and is derived from the choice of objects for description and interpretation of descriptive 'facts'. Despite this caveat, for our purposes there may still be practical advantages to be gained from distinguishing between theories of OE that attempt to describe and those which prescribe.

The second continuum differentiates parochial theories of OE from organisational theories. The former argue for adopting the goals, objectives, needs and values of a particular participant group as the criterion against which to measure organisational effectiveness. The latter argue for evaluating OE from the standpoint of the entire organisation and thus from the society in which it is embedded. For we find that the values of 'society' will be imported into the analysis through the values and purposes of all relevant participant groups (see Lowe and McInnes, 1971; Rhenman, 1973).

A matrix is thus formed by using these two dimensions. This is shown in Figure 14.1.

Descriptive level of analysis

Within this category fall several variants of the so-called 'goal model of organisational effectiveness'. The term is unfortunate in that the concept of organisational goals has at times been equated with these approaches. Hence, inherent weaknesses in those approaches to OE have led some researchers to reject outright the notion of organisational, as opposed to group, goals. Second the oft-made distinction in the literature between a 'goal model' and a 'systems model' of OE is not helpful and tends to imply that system analysts do not consider the notion of organisational goals. The term 'a goal model of organisational effectiveness' will hence be avoided and if used will always be put in parentheses to indicate that it has a limited meaning, namely to refer solely to the official goal model, the operative goal model and the dominant coalitional goal model.

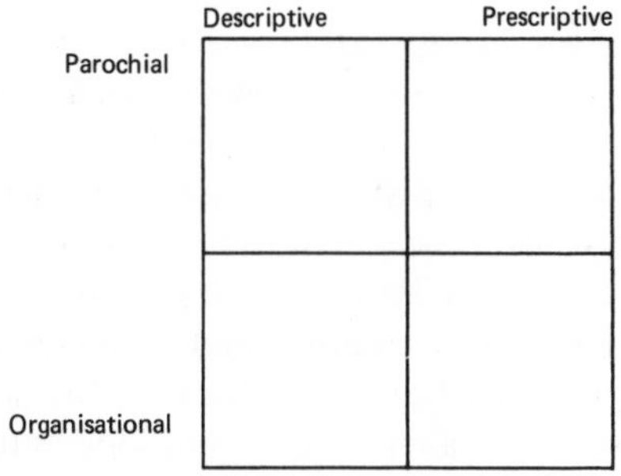

FIGURE 14.1 *A classificatory scheme for approaches to organisational effectiveness*

Descriptive, parochial approaches to OE

The legitimated authority (or official) goal model falls within this classification. It focuses on the 'general purposes of the organisation as put forth in the charter, annual reports, public statements by key executives and other authoritative pronouncements' (Perrow, 1961). Hence, it argues that OE be related to the currently stated goals of the officers within the organisation, including those contained in corporate policy statement and procedure manuals. However, these 'official' or legitimated authority statements are not very useful standards for evaluating effectiveness because they are often vague and non-operational, being subjected to a variety of interpretations. Though such statements may give some guidelines as to the objectives of an organisation, they may equally be pieces of managerial propaganda and in any case they are not representative of the goals and objectives of all organisational participants. Therefore, they can in no sense be representative of the whole organisation.

Yet another rather unsatisfactory approach which has gained some acceptance amongst organisation theorists is the dominant coalitional model. This identifies the notion of organisational goals with that of the goals of the 'dominant coalition' within an organisation. It is argued that since organisations are reified constructs, they do not have goals. What one observes is but behaviour which is indicative of the goals of the powerful individuals within the organisation, that is, the goals which are currently operational within an organisation are in reality those of this dominant subgroup.

While this concept of a dominant and influential coalition is important and useful, much empirical work remains to be done to establish that such a stable subgroup or network exists. It may be that interest and participant groups are so tightly coupled and inter-dependent that it is not possible for organisational behaviour to be fully determined by the goals of any one dominant group. It is often observed that the goals of top management are considerably modified by lower-level participants. Further, the influence of such a dominant subgroup (if it exists) could be curtailed by enviromental factors beyond its control, e.g. violent political and social change. Also in a real sense, it is the purpose of our wider view of the determinants of organisation effectiveness to answer such questions as to the extent to which a particular group is dominant with the organisation. *That question cannot be answered without a holistic system analysis of what causes what.*

However, the fundamental difficulty with parochial approaches to the study of OE is their inability to understand the organisation as a whole. In effect, they deny the concept of a holistic coalition and substitute a partial analysis for a general one. Further, highlighting the goals of particular interest groups may not adequately resolve the problem of conflicting preferences and goals amongst different interest groups. Friedlander and Pickle (1968) showed, for example, that the demands of various groups (the community, government, customers, suppliers, creditors, owners and employees) could not be concurrently satisfied and in fact some demands were negatively correlated with others. Though the dominant coalition model does attempt to incorporate some analysis of interparticipant group bargaining, there is a danger that one concentrates only on these more powerful individuals within the organisation, while neglecting the needs and goals of the 'less dominant' and 'the rest of the organisation'.

Descriptive, organisational approaches to OE

In contrast to the official, legitimated authority model, the 'operative goal model' attempts to focus on the 'ends sought through the actual operating policies of the organisation; they tell us what the organisation actually is trying to do, regardless of what the official goals say are the aims' (Perrow, 1961). This general rubric of operative goals was also to include the decisions made in choosing the priority of multiple goals and the unofficial goals pursued by various participant groups within the organisation. Hence, unlike the two approaches discussed above, this model did try to analyse organisational behaviour as opposed to the behaviour of specific groups and individuals. There was even a mention of analysing intergroup bargaining.

However, assessing what actually is going on in an organisation is an extremely difficult process. First, it assumes that there is one objective reality that will become apparent through detailed scrutiny; whereas organisational life may be more a series of subjective perceptions of reality that differ depending on the role and values of the perceiver. The activities of complex organisations are seldom clear and unambiguous. Further, as Keeley (1978) points out, this approach cannot be applied to evaluate different organisations which have different operative goals sets. It also does not resolve the question of an intraorganisational goal conflict. In summary, the evaluative quality of the approach is weak.

But even if one were able to identify what the official or operative or dominant goals of an organisation were, *should* organisational effectiveness be evaluated against these standards? This question is neither raised nor answered. These descriptive approaches merely assume that the particular goals which are observed to be operative, official or dominant at some point in time are the 'proper and correct' future goals of the organisation. These approaches ask only two questions which are of limited usefulness to organisational analysis, namely:

1. what is part of the organisation trying to do, whose interests are being operationalised?
2. to what extent are these identified goals being achieved?

What they fail to do is ask higher-order evaluative questions – *should* these be the goals of the organisation, given the resolution level of analysis? Should the organisation be doing in the future what it is now doing? Should the goals of the dominant coalition be dominant? Unfortunately, descriptive approaches to OE cannot answer these questions; merely describing how successful an organisation is in achieving what it is currently trying to do leaves little room for normative evaluation and gives precious few signposts for change. In effect, these approaches lack a feedback control device and they may elevate a description of the status quo to a dangerous normative ideal. Also, they tend to be conservative in implying that the current distribution of power, of inducements and contributions ought to prevail in the long run. Only by assuming a 'larger view' of the organisation as a whole, behaving within its environment can the important question of a societal nature be asked, thus providing a model of the determinants of the 'fate' of the particular organisation.

Prescriptive level of analysis

As discussed, prescriptive theories of OE attempt to articulate some prescriptive criterion against which organisational behaviour may be evaluated. They thus escape the weaknesses of the descriptive approach but prescriptive analysis is not without its problems. First, should social scientists attempt to prescribe organisational behaviour? Or should one leave judgements of 'what ought to be done' to participant groups within the organisation? As argued before, no theory is completely value free and even descriptive approaches to OE embrace a rather conservative philosophy. Therefore, it is necessary to articulate the value premise and assumptions of one's theoretical position. Also, it is only by having a vision of 'what ought to be' that one can induce any change that may be required into the prevailing systemic relationships and improve the collective human welfare of organisations and societies. Without such a vision, human relationships reduce to *ad hoc*, random responses that may not contribute to continued survival. Secondly, there are prescriptive approaches which are parochial and therefore are unable to predict and explain the workings of the organisation as a whole. However, prescriptive, organisational approaches to OE do also exist and they point the way forward towards a holistic theory of OE.

Prescriptive, parochial approaches to OE

These attempt to argue that the criteria, goals, values and beliefs of particular participant groups ought to be used as the standard for evaluating organisational effectiveness. Much of classical economic and accounting theory which is based on a stockholder theory of the firm falls within this category. These approaches emphasise profit-maximisation as the optimisation criterion and financial surrogates of effectiveness such as profitability, profits, return on investment, earnings per share and dividends. A similar emphasis on the goals of the 'owners' of the firm is exhibited in the work of Becker and Neuhauser (1975), who argued that it is only the owners, i.e. the holders of property rights to the total organisation, who have the right to shape and mould the organisation.

Because prescriptive approaches to OE centre on issues such as the allocation of benefits and contributions in the face of conflicting interests and the possibility of defining an optimum position on an organisational social welfare function, theorists have also (perhaps inevitably) turned to moral and ethical philosophy and welfare economics in an attempt to legitimise their particular parochial positions. Cummings (1977) for instance, argues that an effective organisation is one in which the greatest percentage of members perceive themselves free to use the organisation and its subsystems and instruments for their own ends. This clearly echoes the classical utilitarian principles of Bentham and James Stuart Mill which stress the greatest satisfaction of the greatest number. However, there are defects with this focus on the satisfaction of needs of 'as many members as possible'. First, it involves interpersonal comparisons of satisfaction with the organisation which in economics is frowned upon. Secondly, a satisfied coalition may not be a physically productive one, and clearly the concept of OE should include some notion of productivity; more to the point nor may it be conducive to the survival of the whole enterprise, upon which the survival of the satisfaction of the individual member is said to depend.

Moving from a focus on the needs of the majority, we confront the work of Keeley (1978) who argues that an effective organisation is one which maximises the satisfaction of the least advantaged participants. Arguing from Rawl's theory of justice, he maintains that a principle of minimax regret is conducive to long-run system equilibrium and is advantageous in that it does not involve cardinal or ordinal comparisons of interpersonal levels of satisfaction. However, it is doubtful whether such a criterion is conducive to long-run system survival; it is too partial in campaigning for the needs of the least advantaged and neglects to analyse the goals of other groups. Clearly these goals must also influence the stability of the whole. Also like Cummings, Keeley fails to recognise that different participants control resources which differ in terms of their strategic utility to the coalition as a whole. Hence those who at present are the most regretful members may require less attention because one must consider the needs of other dissatisfied members who possess more critical resources. In other words, if the system as a whole is to survive as a need-satisficer in the long run, then a simple blanket optimisation principle such as those advanced may not be sufficient.

As can be seen, prescriptive approaches to OE which are parochial suffer from inherent weaknesses by being parochial. That is, of not being an holistic systemic analysis which attempts to explain the behaviour of all participants in relation to one another, and also of the organisation as such.

Prescriptive, organisational approaches to OE

A theory of OE which falls rather uneasily into this section is the systems resource model of Seashore and Yuchtman (1967). They attempted to banish the concept of organisational goals and using general systems theory as their base argued that effectiveness is 'the ability of an organisation, in either absolute or relative terms, to exploit its environment in the acquisition of scarce and valued resources'. Though they did attempt to be holistic, their model is, however, theoretically weak. For instance, they fail to realise that 'valued' and 'scarce' resources can only be defined when one considers the purpose of the organisation or the valuer. Also they seem to imply that a general theory of OE is not possible since different types of organisations require different resources and hence would require different criteria of effectiveness.

However, their use of systems analysis is useful in that it focuses on the organisation as a whole and also on the organisation–environment relationship. Open systems and general systems theory stress that an organisation is a complex system of interrelated parts that needs constantly to adapt to a changing environment in order to survive. The criterion of organisational effectiveness is thus an overall goal of maintaining organisational viability, long-run survival and existence through time without depletion of its environment (see von Bertalanffy, 1968; Katz and Kahn, 1966; Lowe and McInnes, 1971; Aldrich, 1979; Pfeffer and Salancik, 1978). Flowing from this broad goal are various requirements which contribute to survival. A number of categories of these systemic needs have been provided. Parsons (1960) lists four needs: adaptation to the environment, goal attainment, integration and latency (the maintenance of cultural symbols and motivation). Caplow (1964) lists stability over time, integration of organisational components, volunteerism and achievement of organisational goals. A defect of systems analysis is that there have been few attempts to consolidate these various lists and at present, the number of systemic needs increases with each writer on the subject. None the less, systems thinking presents a powerful scientific approach to the analysis of organisations as wholes. And it is only by analysing an organisation as a whole within its societal context that one begins to understand its complexity and explain its behaviour, as such, rather than the behaviour of its participants.

Not only is the present act of survival important in assessing an organisation's effectiveness, so is *the expectation of continued survival* in the long run. And in order to remain viable in the long run the system must both adapt to changes which occur internally and externally, and initiate changes in order to create an environment suitable as a habitat. Changes in the values and beliefs of its participants, in technology or in the alternative employment opportunities of members, for instance, will all influence the costs of continued membership and the system must take cognizance of that. In effect, these changes alter an organisation's feasible set of alternative action and plans (see Tinker, 1975; Tinker and Lowe, 1977).

The F-set or feasible set of alternatives is built on the idea that each participant requires a minimum level of inducements, which reflects his opportunity cost and set of needs, before he joins a coalition. In exchange for these inducements, each participant contributes qualities that are needed by the rest of the coalition. In order for an organisation to be viable there must exist a minimum need-satisfaction level that is defined in terms of the total set of all members' opportunity costs of participation; these members being collectively necessary and sufficient for the existence of the organisation. This minimum survival level may also be defined as the minimum compensation (or sacrifice) required to maintain each and every factor (member) in its present employment in the long run. In order to survive in the long run, the system must, therefore, attempt to keep within its shifting set of feasible alternatives. These ideas, which give rise to a weak optimality condition, are shown in Figure 14.2. Here, the organisation, e.g. business enterprise, is represented by four member groups which are influenced by external environmental groups. The feasible set of alter-

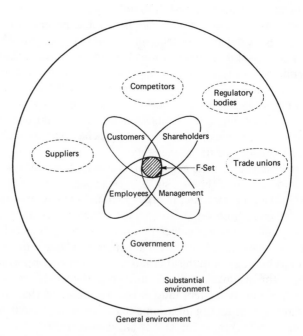

FIGURE 14.2 *The feasible set of alternatives*

natives is shown by the shaded area. The 'feasible set' defines the organisation, as such, as an entity. (The drawing of a system's boundary and the specification of a resolution level of analysis (and consequently the F-set) reflects a subjective, methodological choice on the part of the analyst.) Different resolution levels of analysis (which reflect different value positions) would, therefore, lead to different conclusions about the effectiveness of a system. The question of a/the appropriate resolution level of analysis can only be answered given the range of possible alternative resolution levels and the relative abilities of the resultant models of the system to explain, predict and control the empirical behaviour and structure of the system. The concept of resolution levels of analysis is extremely important in encouraging the analyst of complex social systems to consider all the 'direct', 'indirect' and 'relevant' influences on a system. (For a more general (i.e. general system theory) definition of 'resolution level' see Klir (1969).

Though the ideas of long-run survival and the F-set do not specify a point of optimum allocation of benefits or of optimum effectiveness, the analysis does not deny that an understanding of the processes of choice, negotiation and bargaining is essential in understanding organisational behaviour. Neither does it neglect the fact that different interest groups possess different degrees of power depending on their strategic resources and on the values of the macro-societal environment. These considerations are reflected in the opportunity costs of keeping a particular participant or group within the coalition. Lastly, it has the advantage of linking continued organisational viability to the satisfaction of the needs of members. An organisation is set up within society by particular sectors of that society for the satisfaction of human needs. If these needs are not satisfied, then in the long run the system cannot survive as members can withdraw and join alternative coalitions. In the short run, however, the system may continue to survive though it is not meeting the needs of members; due perhaps to imperfections in factor markets. But in the long run, in the absence of a slave economy, non-satisfaction of needs means an unstable and eventually non-feasible coalition.

This brief look at the OE literature is summarised in Figure 14.3. It has been argued that neither descriptive nor parochial approaches to OE will provide adequate knowledge of organisations. Further it has been proposed that organisational effectiveness be defined in terms of survival of the whole in the long run where survival is indicative of the satisfactory fulfilment of member needs. Having thus defined OE, we move to a definition of MC.

DEFINITION OF MC

Since a MCS must be related to the concept of an organisation and its effective working we define it as follows:

Management control is concerned with ensuring the achievement of a negotiated level of welfare for any organisation and its contributors consistent with maintaining boundary conditions for that enterprise, in relation to its environment, such that its long run survival is provided for.

Such a definition is wide-ranging in its application and argues that MC must be concerned with managing the organisation as a whole. Thus, we do not see MC as separate and distinct from the total process of organisational control. Neither do we feel that a difference between MC and organisational planning ought to be drawn. If plans are defined as strategies which predict and anticipate future conditions or as future states which are desired, then they logically come within our definition of MC. Thirdly, this definition could be extended to include the whole of human society itself as an 'organisation'. But if we

	Descriptive	Prescriptive
Parochial	Official goals Dominant coalition goals	Stockholder theory of the firm: Becker and Neuhauser (1975), Cummings (1977), Keeley (1978)
Organisational	Operative goals	Systems resource model Systems analysis Long-run survival The F-set

FIGURE 14.3   *A selected classification of some approaches to organisational effectiveness*

confine it to apply only to micro-socioeconomic enterprises it points out that an analysis of the environment in which the enterprise is sustained is vital. As argued before, changes in social, economic, political, legal and technological aspects of an organisation's environment leads to possible changes in the feasible set of alternatives. Hence, an integral part of a theory of MC must be to analyse the organisation and its environment holistically (Lowe and Tinker, 1976). Finally, this definition shows that the subject of MC must necessarily be interdisciplinary due to the variety of aspects to be considered in arriving at a satisfactory understanding of the relationships between the inducements and contributions pertaining to any particular factor, which is necessary to the social and economic survival of any enterprises.

In essence our argument is that any positive account of MC as a systemic feature of socioeconomic organisations must explain the specific function of MC in assuring long-run survival. Further, the value of MC seen normatively and from a particular resolution level must be measured in terms of its contribution to (i) the continued satisfaction of the F-set of needs of the coalition and (ii) the long-run survival of the system as defined from the same resolution level of analysis.

Notes on the Contributors

ANTHONY J. BERRY is Lecturer in Management Control at the Manchester Business School in the University of Manchester. He graduated from the University of Bath (BSc Eng), University of London (M Phil), where he was also President of the Union, and the University of Manchester (Ph D in financial management). He worked in the British and American aircraft industries before concentrating upon management control. He was editor of the journal, *Management Education and Development* (1978–80). In 1979–81, he was Director of the International Teachers Programme and is currently Director of the MBA programme at Manchester Business School.

WAI FONG CHUA is a Lecturer in Accounting and Financial Management in the Division of Economic Studies at the University of Sheffield. She graduated from Sheffield University in 1978 in accounting and financial management. From 1978 to 1980 she was a Junior Research Fellow in Organisational Behaviour in the Business Studies Section. In 1981 she joined the Accounting Section as a lecturer and is currently engaged in teaching and research in the fields of accounting methodology and epistemology, new forms of organisational performance assessment and management control systems. She has published papers on these subjects as well as on the relationship of organisational control theory to accounting.

KENNETH P. GEE, B Sc, Ph D, is Professor of Accountancy and Chairman of the Department of Business and Administration at the University of Salford. He is the author of two books and more than thirty papers in accounting and management journals. He is the past winner of the Sir Frederick Hooper, Walter Taplin and Reed Executive Essay Awards, and is active as a consultant to a number of companies.

TREVOR M. HOPPER is Director of Postgraduate Courses in Accounting and Financial Management at the University of Sheffield.

He graduated in business administration from the University of Bradford in 1967, and obtained his M Phil from the Management Centre of the University of Aston in 1978. Prior to holding his present position he worked as a cost accountant in a large food manufacturing company and as a lecturer in a Polytechnic. His current research and teaching is in the area of management control – in particular the application of contemporary work in organisation theory to management accounting.

TONY LOWE spent a number of years as a chartered accountant in practice before obtaining a first-class degree at the London School of Economics. During this early period of working life, after several years of junior professional training and national service, he helped found a provincial practice for a London firm and subsequently became managing clerk of a City of London professional practice and secretary of a London Stock Exchange quoted company.

He has been Professor at Sheffield since 1971, before which he was at the University of Leeds, the Bradford University Management Centre and the Manchester Business School. He has also held visiting appointments at the Massachusetts Institute of Technology School of Management, Harvard Business School, the University of California (Berkeley) and the University of British Columbia. He has been Chairman of the Council of Departments of Accounting Studies and the Association of University Teachers in Accounting, and his consulting work includes both the academic (the design of a Polytechnic's Business and Computing Studies degree and the development, organisation and teaching of an MBA programme at the University of Nairobi) and the industrial (including financial analysis regarding a capital project in an Arabian Gulf state and work for the British Steel Corporation). He is joint editor and chairman of the *Journal of Enterprise Management*.

His research interests are very wide, and he has published extensively in the field of management control, organisation theory, systems theory, internal auditing, financial management and business forecasting. He is a member of the Institute of Chartered Accountants in England and Wales, the Institute of Chartered Secretaries and Administrators, the American Accounting Association, the Institute of Management Sciences, and in the past has been involved with the British Institute of Management.

JOHN L. J. MACHIN was educated at London, Oxford and Harvard

Universities. After qualifying as an interpreter in Mandarin Chinese he studied philosophy, politics and economics before undertaking managerial training in a UK-based multinational. His subsequent first-hand experience of helping in the company's change from a centralised to a decentralised management philosophy and of observing the consequential alteration to the managerial control systems in use within the organisation led him to develop a desire to research and design such systems.

A founder-member of the Durham University Business School, he led the research team which invented and developed the management systems and training methods known collectively as the 'expectations approach' (EA). The involvement of more than 2500 managers from over forty organisations in the development of EA testifies to his belief that the best way of producing simple, relevant, useful and *used* systems is to put control of the design process in the hands of the intended user of the system wherever possible.

He was Dean of the Faculty of Social Sciences in the University of Durham and is Managing Director of the Centre for Management Control and Communication. He is a Fellow of the British Institute of Management and the Association of Certified Accountants. He is the author of a number of articles on ways of improving managerial effectiveness through the use of better management systems and training methods, and of two books: *The Expectations Approach: Improving Managerial Communication and Performance* and *Toward Managerial Effectiveness.*.

EUGENE McKENNA, M Sc, Ph D, DIA, ABPsS, ACIS, is an occupational psychologist and Head of the Department of Business Studies at North East London Polytechnic. He was educated at the Universities of Bradford, Lancaster and Surrey. Before taking up his present position in 1979 he was a Principal Lecturer in Organisational Behaviour at Birmingham Polytechnic and a Visiting Lecturer at the Universities of Aston and Birmingham. His academic and research interests embrace the behavioural aspects of accounting, executive stress and behavioural implications of microtechnology. Among his publications is *The Management Style of the Chief Accountant*, which is based on his doctoral thesis. Before entering education in 1969 he worked as an organisation analyst in a management consultancy unit, and early in his career received training in professional accountancy. He is a member of the Undergraduate Studies Board and the Research Subcommittee (Committee for Business and Management Studies) of the Council for National Academic Awards; the Business Studies Board of the Business Education Council; and the Membership Subcommittee of the British Psychological Society.

DAVID T. OTLEY is a Lecturer in the Department of Accounting and Finance at the University of Lancaster. He spent 1981–2 as Visiting Associate Professor in the Department of Accounting at Michigan State University. After taking his first degree in theoretical physics at Churchill College, Cambridge, he worked with the Operational Research Executive of the National Coal Board, where he became interested in the behavioural effects of management control systems. He developed this interest by following the doctoral programme at Manchester Business School, where his thesis research studied the relationship between budgetary control and managerial performance. He is the author of *ICAEW Accountants' Digest on Behavioural Aspects of Budgetary Control* and of a number of articles in journals including the *Journal of Accounting Research*, *Accounting, Organisations and Society* and *Accounting and Business Research*. He is also a member of the Editorial Board of the *Journal of Business Finance and Accounting* and of *Accounting, Organisations and Society*.

SUZANNE RICHBELL worked in the Civil Service for five years and then took her undergraduate and research degrees at University College, Cardiff, and since 1971 has been a Lecturer in Industrial Relations at Sheffield University. She is currently involved in teaching and research and has acted in an advisory capacity to various organisations. Her main research interests include worker participation and the development of industrial relations policy within the firm.

CHARLES H. S. TAI, M Sc, Ph D, is the Organisation Development Director of the Soon Seng group of companies, a Malaysian conglomerate with forty wholly-owned subsidiaries in industrial manufacturing (steel and building materials), primary extractive (tin, rubber and oil palm) and tertiary (insurance, hotel, house-building and finance) trade sectors.

His postgraduate and doctoral research was centred on management control. For his M Sc he concentrated on the development of the expectations approach managerial planning and control system in a subsidiary of a multinational. His doctoral research focused on the development of effective relationships between main board directors

and subsidiary company directors in multinationals. Prior to undertaking extensive field work in three such organisations, he developed
two new models with which to explore and link the effectiveness of the
multinational as a whole and the effectiveness of interpersonal interactions between main board and divisional board members.

ANDREW P. THOMAS is a social science graduate of the Open
University and a Fellow of the Association of Certified Accountants.
He is currently Lecturer in Accounting at the University of Birmingham. Before taking up his appointment at Birmingham he was a
senior lecturer in a college of higher education, and has worked in
both industry and accountancy practice. His main research interests
relate to the behavioural and organisational aspects of accounting.

CHARLES WILKINSON is a graduate chemical engineer who carried
out his doctoral work at the University of Lancaster School of
Management and Organisational Sciences. His doctoral research was
concerned with issues of management control in process and manufacturing industries. He has worked on a number of consultancy
assignments in those industries and in the field of information
technology, and is currently Managing Director of MIPAC Services –
a firm offering consultancy services in the field of managerial
planning and control.

MICHAEL A. P. WILLMER graduated in mathematics from
Imperial College, London University, and later studied aeronautical
engineering at the College of Aeronautics. On joining the Royal
Aircraft Establishment in 1956 he carried out theoretical studies in
rotary wing aerodynamics. In the early 1960s he became involved in an
operational research study to determine the optimum type of heli-
copter for anti-submarine warfare duties in the following decade. In
1962 he became a member of a small OR team engaged in problems
connected with the flow of aircraft in and out of airports as well as
along the international airways. He went to the Home Office in 1964
to become one of the first members of a 'think tank' set up to study
new methods of preventing and detecting crimes. In 1967 he was
elected to a Research Fellowship at Nuffield College, Oxford, where
he developed a new approach to crime and police work based on the
systems used by criminals for choosing, planning and executing crimes
and the systems used by the police for preventing and detecting them.
In 1971 he became Reader in Operational Research at the Manchester

Business School, Manchester University. His current research interests include the study of the ways in which information can become lost and distorted in both business and social systems, small business 'start-up' operations and the re-employment of redundant managers and professionals. The nature of his work and his main research findings are described in over seventy publications.

Bibliography

Ackoff, R. L. (1971) 'Towards a System of Systems Concepts', *Management Science*, vol. 17, no. 11, July.

Adams, J. S. (1963) 'Towards an Understanding of Inequity', *Journal of Abnormal and Social Psychology*, vol. 67, no. 5, pp. 422–36.

Adams, J. S. (1976) 'The Structure and Dynamics of Behaviour in Organisational Boundary Roles', in M. D. Dunette (ed.), *Handbook of Industrial and Organisational Psychology* (New York: Rand-McNally).

Aguren, S., Hansson, R., Karlsson, K. G. (1976) *The Volvo Kalmar Plant*, The Rationalisation Council (Stockholm: SAF-LO Publication).

Aldrich, J. E. (1979) *Organisations and Environments* (Englewood Cliffs, NJ: Prentice-Hall).

Aldrich, H. (1971) 'Organisational Boundaries and Inter-Organisational Conflict', *Human Relations*, vol. 24, no. 4, pp. 279–93.

Aldrich, H. and Mindlin, S. (1978) 'Uncertainty and Dependence: Two Perspectives on Environment' in L. Karpic (ed.), *Organisation and Environment* (London: Sage).

Aldrich, H. and Pfeffer, J. (1976) 'Environments of Organisations', *Annual Review of Sociology*, pp. 79–105.

Allen, S. A. (1979) 'Understanding Reorganisations of Divisionalised Companies', *Academy of Management Journal*, vol. 22. no. 4, pp. 641–71.

Allport, G. W. (1937) 'The Functional Autonomy of Motives', *American Journal of Psychology*, vol. 50, pp. 141–56.

Amey, L. R. (1975) 'Tomkins on Residual Income', *Journal of Business Finance and Accounting*, vol. 2, no. 1, Spring, pp. 55–68.

Amey, L. R. (1979) *Budget Planning and Control Systems* (London: Pitman).

Amigoni, F. (1978) 'Planning Management Control Systems', *Journal of Business Finance and Accounting*, pp. 279–91, Autumn.

Anderton, R. (1978) 'Systems in the Seventies: An Emerging Discipline?', *Journal of Applied Systems Analysis*, vol. 5, no. 2, pp. 149–56.

Anthony, R. N. (1965) *Planning and Control Systems: A Framework for Analysis*, Division of Research (Boston: Harvard Graduate School of Business).

Anthony, R. N. and Dearden, J. (1976) *Management Control Systems: Text and Cases* (Homewood, Ill.: Irwin).

Anthony, R. N., Dearden, J. and Vancil, R. F. (1965) *Management Control Systems, Cases and Readings* (Homewood, Ill.: Irwin).

Anthony, R. N. and Herzlinger, R. (1975) *Management Control in Non-Profit Organisations* (Homewood, Ill.: Irwin).

Archer, S. (1981) 'Towards a Characterisation of Management Control:

Contributions from Decision Theory and Information Economics', Discussion Paper, Lancaster University, UK.

Argenti, J. (1974) *Systematic Corporate Planning* (Sunbury-on-Thames: Nelson).

Argyris, C. (1952) *The Impact of Budgets on People* (Ithaca, N. Y.: The Controllership Foundation).

Argyris, C. (1953) 'Human Problems With Budgets', *Harvard Business Review*, vol. 31, no. 1, January/February, pp. 97–110.

Argyris, C. (1964) *Integrating the Individual and the Organisation* (New York: Wiley).

Ashby, W. R. (1956) *An Introduction to Cybernetics* (London: Chapman and Hall).

Ashby, W. R. (1964) *Introduction to Cybernetics* (London: Methuen).

Atkinson, J. W. (1964) *An Introduction to Motivation* (New Jersey: Van Nostrand).

Bankerhoff, D. W. and Kanter, R. M. (1980) 'Appraising the Performance of Performance Appraisal', *Sloan Management Review*, vol. 21, no. 3, Spring.

Barrett, C. K. (1966), *Commentary on Paul: 1st Epistle to the Corinthians* (London: A. & C. Black).

Bass, B. M. and Leavitt, H. (1963) 'Some Experiments in Planning and Operating', *Management Science*, no. 4, pp. 574–85.

Bateson, G. (1973) *Steps to an Ecology of Mind* (London: Paladin).

Becker, S. W. and Neuhauser, D. (1975) *The Efficient Organisation* (New York: Elsevier).

Beer, S. (1966) *Decision and Control* (New York: Wiley).

Beer, S. (1967) *Cybernetics and Management* (London: English University Press).

Beer, S. (1970) *The Law and the Profits*, the Sixth Frank Newsam Memorial Lecture, Police College, Bramshill, 29 October 1970.

Beer, S. (1972) *Brain of the Firm* (London: Allen Lane).

Beer, S. (1974) *Designing Freedom* (New York: John Wiley).

Beer, S. (1975) *Platform for Change* (New York: Wiley).

Beesly, P. (1980) *Very Special Admiral* (London: Hamish Hamilton).

Bell, D. W. (1979) *Industrial Participation* (London: Pitman).

Beresford Dew, R. and Gee, K. P. (1973) *Management Control and Information* (London: Macmillan).

Berlyne, D. E. (1960) *Conflict, Arousal and Curiosity* (New York: McGraw-Hill).

Bertalanffy, L. von (1968) *General Systems Theory: Foundations, Development Applications* (New York: Braziller).

Blau, P. M. and Schoenherr, R. (1971) *The Structure of Organisations* (New York: Basic Books).

Blau, P. M. and Scott, W. R. (1962) *Formal Organisations: A Comparative Approach* (London: Routledge and Kegan Paul).

Boulding, K. E. (1956) 'General Systems Theory – The Skeleton of Science', *Management Science*, vol. 2, no. 2, pp. 197–208.

Boussard, D. (1979) 'A Scheme on Dimensions of Accounting', *Workshop Paper: EIASM* (Stockholm).

Bower, J. F., (1970) *Managing the Resource Allocation Process* (Boston:

Harvard Graduate School of Business, Division of Research).

Brannen, P., Batstone, E. Fatchett, D. and White, P. (1976) *The Worker Directors* (London: Hutchinson).

Brewster, C. J., Gill, C. G. and Richbell, S. (1981) 'Developing an Analytical Approach to Industrial Relations Policy', *Personnel Review*, vol. 10, no. 2, pp. 3–10.

Brookes, W. L., Garside, M. C., Machin, J. L. J., McCormack, L. F. and Seabury, J. D. (1982) 'Annotated Bibliography of Expectations Approach Literature', *Expectations Approach Working Paper 01*, 5th edn (Durham University Business School, Mill Hill Lane, Durham, UK).

Brown, W. (1972) *Participation* (Bradford: MCB Management Decision Monograph).

Bruns, W. J. and Waterhouse, J. H. (1975) 'Budgetary Control and Organisation Structure', *Journal of Accounting Research*, pp. 177–203, vol. 13, no. 2, Autumn.

Buckley, W. (1968) 'Society as a Complex Adaptive System', in W. Buckley, (ed.), *Modern Systems Research for the Behavioural Scientist* (London: Aldine).

Buckley, A. and McKenna, E. (1972) 'Budgetary Control and Business Behaviour', *Accounting and Business Research*, vol. 2, no. 6, Spring, pp. 137–50.

Bullock, A. (1977) *Report of the Committee of Inquiry on Industrial Democracy* (London: HMSO).

Burchell, S. *et al.* (1980) 'The Roles of Accounting in Organisations and Society', *Accounting, Organisations and Society*, vol. 5, no. 1, pp. 5–27.

Burns, T. and Stalker, G. M. (1961) *The Management of Innovation* (London: Tavistock).

Burrell, G. and Morgan, G. (1979) *Sociological Paradigms and Organisational Analysis* (London: Heinemann).

Caplan, E. H. (1971) *Management Accounting and Behavioural Science* (Reading: Addison-Wesley).

Caplow, T. (1964) *Principles of Organisation* (New York: Harcourt, Brace).

Carlson, R. E. (1969) 'Degree of Job Fit as a Moderator of the Relationship Between Job Performance and Job Satisfaction', *Personnel Psychology*, vol. 22, pp. 159–70.

Carter, E. E. (1971) 'Project Evaluation and Firm Decisions', *Journal of Management Studies*, October.

Caspari, J. A. (1976) 'Wherefore Accounting Data – Explanation, Prediction and Decisions', *The Accounting Review*, vol. L1, no. 4.

Chandler, A. (1962) *Strategy and Structure* (Cambridge, Mass: MIT Press).

Channon, D. F. (1973) *The Strategy and Structure of British Enterprise* (London: Macmillan).

Checkland, P. B. (1972) 'Towards a Systems-Based Methodology for Real-World Problem Solving', *Journal of Systems Engineering*, vol. 3, no. 2, Winter.

Checkland, P. B. (1976) *The Third European Meeting on Cybernetics and System Research*, proceedings of a conference held in Vienna (New York: Hemisphere).

Checkland, P. B. (1979a) 'The Shape of the Systems Movement', *Journal of*

Applied Systems Analysis, vol. 6, pp. 129–35.

Checkland, P. B. (1979b) 'Review of Lilienfeld, R., "The Rise of Systems Thinking: An Ideological Analysis"', in *Journal of Enterprise Management*, vol. 2, no. 1, pp. 114–15.

Checkland, P. B. (1981) *Systems Thinking, Systems Practice* (London: John Wiley).

Checkland, P. B. (forthcoming) 'Problem Formulation for Systems Analysis', draft chapter for IIASA *Handbook of Systems Analysis*, vol. i (London: Wiley) in press.

Child, J. (1973) 'Predicting and Understanding Organisation Structure', *Administrative Science Quarterly*, vol. 18, no. 2, pp. 168–85.

Child, J. (1977) *Organisation, A Guide to Problems and Practice* (London: Harper & Row).

Child, J. (1978) 'Industrial Participation in Israel', *Working Paper Series*, no. 42 (University of Aston in Birmingham).

Child, I. L. and Whiting, J. W. M. (1954) 'Determinants of Level of Aspiration: Evidence from Everyday Life', in H. Brand (ed.), *The Study of Personality* (New York: Wiley).

City comment (1978) *The Daily Telegraph*, 30 November.

Clegg, S. and Dunkerley, D. (1980) *Organisation, Class and Control* (London: Routledge & Kegan Paul).

Coch, L. and French, J. R. P. (1948) 'Overcoming Resistance to Change', *Human Relations*, vol. 1, no. 4, pp. 512–32.

Cohen, M. D., March, J. G. and Olsen, J. P. (1972) 'A Garbage Can Model of Organisational Choice', *Administrative Science Quarterly*, vol. 17, no. 1, pp. 1–25.

Cosyns, J., Leveridge, R. and Child, J. (1980) 'Micro-Electronics, Organisation and the Structuring of Employment in Retailing'. Paper presented to the EGOS/SSRC Colloquium on *Organisational Innovations in the 1980s*, Strathclyde Business School, Glasgow, 29 March–2 April, 1980.

Craven, D. L. (1981) 'Working towards more effective identification and recognition of working relationships', ch. 6, pp. 88–102, in *Toward Managerial Effectiveness*, eds John Machin, Rosemary Stewart and Colin Hales (Farnborough: Gower).

Crawford, D. M., Huntzinger, B. C. and Kirkwood, C. W. (1978) 'Multi-objective Analysis for Transmission Conductor Selection', *Management Science*, vol. 24, no. 16, December, pp. 1700–9.

Crozier, M. (1964) *The Bureaucratic Phenomenon* (London: Tavistock).

Cummings, L. L. (1977) 'Emergence of the Instrumental Organisation', in Goodman, P. X., Pennings, J. J. M. and Associates (eds) *New Perspectives on Organisational Effectiveness* (San Fransisco: Jossey-Bass).

Cyert, R. M., March J. G. and Starbuck, W. M. (1961) 'Two Experiments on Risk and Conflict in Organisational Estimation', *Management Science*, vol. VII.

Cyert, R. M. and March, J. G. (1963) *A Behavioural Theory of the Firm* (Englewood Cliffs, N. J.: Prentice-Hall).

Dalton, G. W. and Lawrence, P. R. (1971) *Motivation and Control in Organisations*, (Homewood, Ill.: Irwin).

Dalton, M. (1950) 'Conflicts Between Staff and Line Managerial Officers',

American Sociological Review, vol. 15, pp. 342–51.

Daniel, W. W. and McIntosh, N. (1972) *The Right To Manage* (London: Macdonald).

Davis, K. (1967) *Human Relations at Work – The Dynamics of Organisational Behaviour* (New York: McGraw-Hill).

Dennison, W. E. (1970) 'Management Developments in Government Resource Allocation: The Example of The Rise and Fall of PPBS (Planning-Programming-Budgeting System)', *Journal of Management Studies*, vol. 16, no. 3, October.

Dollard, J. and Miller, N. E. (1950) *Personality and Psychotherapy: An Analysis in Terms of Learning, Thinking and Culture* (New York: McGraw-Hill).

Donaldson, L. (1976) 'Woodward, Technology, Organisational Structure and Performance – A Critique of the Universal Generalisation', *Journal of Management Studies*, vol. 13, no. 3, pp. 255–73.

Downey, H. K. and Slocum, J. W. (1975) 'Uncertainty: Measures, Research and Sources of Variation', *Academy of Management Journal*, vol. 18, no. 3, pp. 562–77.

Dubin, R. (1976) 'Organisational Effectiveness: Some Dilemmas of Perspective', in S. L. Spray (ed.), *Organisational Effectiveness* (Kent State University).

Duck, R. E. V. (1972) 'The Use of Management Accounting Techniques in Industry', *Journal of Management Studies*, vol. 8, no. 3, pp. 355–9.

Duncan, R. (1972) 'Characteristics of Organisational Environment and Perceived Environmental Uncertainty', *Administrative Science Quarterly*, vol. 17, no. 3, pp. 313–27.

Edstrom, A. and Galbraith, J. R. (1977) 'Transfer of Managers as a Co-ordination and Control Strategy in Multi-national Organisations', *Administrative Science Quarterly*, vol. 22, no. 2, pp. 248–63.

Edwards, E. D. and Bell, P. W. (1961) *The Theory and Measurement of Business Income* (University of California Press).

Eilon, S. (1975) 'Seven Faces of Research', *Operational Research Quarterly*, vol. 26, no. 2.

Emerson, R. E. (1962) 'Power-Dependence Relations', *American Sociological Review*, pp. 31–41.

Etzioni, A. (1961) *A Comparative Analysis of Complex Organisations* (New York: Free Press).

Evan, W. M. (1966) 'The Organisation Set: Toward a Theory of Inter-organisational Relations', in J. D. Thompson (ed.), *Approaches to Organisational Design* (University of Pittsburg).

Fayol, H. (1949) *General and Industrial Management* (London: Pitman).

Feifer, G. (1980) 'Moscow's Angry Silence', *The Sunday Times*, 20 July 1980.

Feyerabend, P. (1975) *Against Method* (London: NLB).

Flanders, A. (1964) *The Fawley Productivity Agreements* (London: Faber and Faber).

Follett M. P. (1956) see Homans, G., *The Human Group*.

Foran, M. F. and DeCoster, D. R. (1974) 'An Experimental Study of the Effects of Participation, Authoritarianism and Feedback on Cognitive Dissonance in a Standard Setting Situation', *Accounting Review*, pp. 751–

763, October.

Ford, C. H. (1979) 'MBO: An Idea Whose Time Has Gone?', *Business Horizons*, vol. 22, no. 6, December.

Fox, A. (1966) 'Industrial Sociology and Industrial Relations', Research Paper No. 3, Royal Commission on Trade Union and Employers Association (London: HMSO).

Fox, A. (1974) *Beyond Contract: Work, Power and Trust Relations* (London: Faber and Faber).

Frankel, S. M. (1977) *Money: Two Philosophies* (Oxford: Basil Blackwell).

French, D. and Saward, H. (1977) *Dictionary of Management* (London: Pan Books).

French, J. R. P., Israel, J. and As, D. (1960) 'An Experiment on Participation in a Norwegian Factory', *Human Relations*, vol. 13, no. 1, pp. 3–19.

Freud, S. (1943) *An Outline of Psychoanalysis* (New York: W. W. Norton).

Friedlander, R. and Pickle, H. (1968) 'Components of Effectiveness in Small Organisations', *Administrative Science Quarterly*, vol. 13, no. 2, pp. 289–304.

Fromm, E. (1942) *Fear of Freedom* (London: Routledge & Kegan Paul).

Galbraith, J. R. (1977) *Organisation Design* (Reading, Mass.: Addison-Wesley).

Gee, K. P. (1977) *Management Planning and Control in Inflation* (London: Macmillan).

Gee, K. P. (1979) 'A Note on the Estimation of Replacement Cost for a Job', *Journal of Business Finance and Accounting*, vol. 6, no. 1, Spring, pp. 37–43.

Gee, K. P. (1980) 'Multiattribute Utility and Capital Budgeting: An Indirect Review', *Journal of Enterprise Management*, vol. 2, no. 2, pp. 201–10.

Gerwin, D. (1979) 'Relationships Between Structure and Technology at the Organisational and Job Levels', *Journal of Management Studies*, vol. 16, no. 1, pp. 70–9.

Giglioni, G. B. and Bedeian, A. G. (1974) 'A Conspectus of Management Control Theory: 1900–1972', *Academy of Management Journal*, vol. 17, no. 2, pp. 292–305.

Goldthorpe, J. H. *et al.* (1970) *The Affluent Worker* (Cambridge University Press).

Gordon, L. A. and Miller, D. (1976) 'A Contingency Framework for the Design of Accounting Information Systems', *Accounting, Organisations and Society*, vol. 1, no. 1, pp. 59–70.

Gouldner, A. W. (1953) *Patterns of Industrial Democracy* (Glencoe, Ill.: The Free Press).

Gouldner, A. W. (1955) *Patterns of Industrial Bureaucracy* (London: Routledge & Kegan Paul).

Gouldner, A. W. (1967) *Enter Plato* (London: Routledge & Kegan Paul).

Gowler, D. and Legge, K. (1978) 'Participation in Context: Towards a Synthesis of the Theory and Practice of Organisational Change, Part 1', *Journal of Management Studies*, vol. 15, pp. 149–75.

Guest, D. and Fatchett, D. (1974) *Worker Participation: Individual Control and Performance* (London: Institute of Personnel Management).

Hackman, J. R. and Oldham, G. R. (1975) 'Development of the Job

Diagnostic Survey', *Journal of Applied Psychology*, vol. 60, no. 2, pp. 159–70.

Hagg, I. (1974) 'Reviews of Capital Investments', in S. Asztely (ed.), *Budgeting Och Redovisning Som Instrument for Styrning* (Stockholm: P. A. Norstedt).

Hall, D. T. and Nougaim, K. E. (1968) 'An Examination of Maslow's Need Hierarchy in an Organisational Setting', *Organisational Behaviour and Human Performance*, vol. 3, pp. 12–35.

Hall, R. H. (1963) 'Intra-organisational Structural Variation: Application of the Bureaucratic Model', *Administrative Science Quarterly*, vol. 7, no. 2, pp. 295–308.

Hall, R. H. (1972) *Organisations: Structure and Process* (Englewood Cliffs: NJ: Prentice-Hall).

Hall, R. H. (1977) *Organisations: Structure and Process*, 2nd edn, (Englewood Cliffs, NJ: Prentice-Hall).

Haworth, L. (1959) 'Do Organisations Act?', *Ethics*, vol. 70, no. 1, pp. 59–63.

Hayes, D. (1977) 'The Contingency Theory of Management Accounting', *Accounting Review*, January, pp. 22–39.

Hayes, D., Wolf, F. and Cooper, D. J. (1979) 'Accounting and Organised Anarchies: An Explanation of the Budgetary Process' (unpublished paper).

Helms, G. (1975) 'Texas Instruments' OST System for Managing Innovation', *Management by Objectives*, vol. 1, no. 4, pp. 11–19.

Herbst, P. B. (1976) *Alternatives to Hierarchies* (Leiden: Nijhoff).

Herzberg, F. (1966) *Work and the Nature of Man* (London: Staples Press).

Hickson, D. J., Hinings, C. R., Lee, C. A., Schneck, R. E. and Pennings, J. M. (1971) 'A Strategic Contingencies Theory of Intra-Organisational Power', *Administrative Science Quarterly*, vol. 16, no. 2, pp. 216–29.

Hickson, D. J., Pugh, D. S. and Pheysey, D. C. (1969) 'Operations Technology and Organisation Structure: An Empirical Reappraisal', *Administrative Science Quarterly*, vol. 14, no. 2, pp. 378–97.

Hinrichs, J. R. and Mischkind, L. A. (1967) 'Empirical and Theoretical Limitations of the Two-Factor Hypothesis of Job Satisfaction', *Journal of Applied Psychology*, vol. 51, no. 2, pp. 191–200.

Hofstede, G. H. (1968) *The Game of Budget Control* (London: Tavistock).

Hofstede, G. H. (1978) 'The Poverty of Management Control Philosophy', *Academy of Management Review*, July.

Homans, G. C. (1951) *The Human Group* (London: Routledge & Kegan Paul).

Hopper, T. (1979) 'Role of Management Accountants and Their Organisational Context'. A discussion paper presented at the Management Control Workshop held at the Management Centre, University of Aston, January 1979.

Hopwood, A., (1974) *Accounting and Human Behaviour* (London: Haymarket).

Hopwood, A. G. (1978) 'Editorial', *Accounting, Organisations and Society*, vol. 3, no. 2.

Horngren, C. T. (1977) *Cost Accounting: A Managerial Emphasis* (Englewood Cliffs, NJ: Prentice–Hall).

House, R. J. and Wigdor, L. A. (1967) 'Herzberg's Dual Factor Theory of Job Satisfaction and Motivation: A review of the evidence and a criticism', *Personnel Psychology*, vol. 20, no. 4, pp. 369–89.

Hulin, C. L. and Blood, M. R. (1968) 'Job Enlargement, Individual Differences And Workers' Responses', *Psychological Bulletin*, vol. 69, no. 1, pp. 41–55.

Ijiri, Y. (1972) 'The Nature of Accounting Research', *Research Methodology in Accounting*, ed. R. R. Stevling (Houston: Scholars Books Co.).

Inland Revenue (1980) *Stock Relief: A Consultative Document*, 14 November.

Jackson, J. H. and Morgan, C. P. (1978) *Organisation Theory: A Macro Perspective for Management* (Englewood Cliffs, NJ: Prentice-Hall).

Jacobs, D. (1974) 'Dependency and Vulnerability: An Exchange Approach to The Control of Organisations', *Administrative Science Quarterly*, pp. 45–59. March.

Jacobson, W. B. (1972), *Power and Interpersonal Relations* (Belmont, Ca.: Wadsworth Publishing Company).

Jaques, E. (1976) *General Theory of Bureaucracy* (London: Heinemann).

Kast, F. E. and Rosenzweig, J. E. (1974) *Organisation and Management: A Systems Approach* (New York: McGraw-Hill).

Katz, D. and Kahn, R. L. (1966) *The Social Psychology of Organisations* (New York: John Wiley).

Katz, D. and Kahn, R. L. (1978) *The Social Psychology of Organisations*, 2nd edn (New York: John Wiley).

Keeley, M. (1978) 'A Social-Justice Approach to Organisational Evaluation', *Administrative Science Quarterly*, vol. 23, no. 2, pp. 272–92.

Keeney, R. L. and Raiffa, H. (1976) *Decisions with Multiple Objectives: Preferences and Value Tradeoffs* (New York: John Wiley).

Khandwalla, P. N. (1977) *Design of Organisations* (New York: Harcourt Brace Jovanovich).

Kimberley, J. R. (1976) 'Organisational Size and the Structuralist Perspective', *Administrative Science Quarterly*, vol. 21, no. 4, pp. 571–97.

Klaassen, J. and Schreuder, H. (1979) 'Accounting Research: The Unhappy Marriage of Rule-Making and Tool-Making', unpublished discussion paper, Free University of Amsterdam.

Klir, G. J. (1969) *An Approach to General Systems Theory* (New York: Litton Educational Publishing).

Kuhn, T. S. (1970) *The Structure of Scientific Revolutions* (Chicago University Press).

Lawrence, P. R. and Lorsch, J. W. (1967a) 'New Management Job: The Integrator', *Harvard Business Review*, November/December, pp. 142–51.

Lawrence, P. R. and Lorsch, J. W. (1967b) *Organisation and Environment: Managing Differentiation and Integration* (Graduate School of Business Administration, Harvard University, Boston, Mass.).

Lazarus, R. S. (1971) *Personality* (Englewood Cliffs, NJ: Prentice-Hall).

Lee, W. W. (1977) *When Values Conflict: An Application of Multiattribute Decision Analysis to Marine Sand and Gravel Mining*, Doctoral Dissertation, Massachusetts Institute of Technology, unpublished.

Leifer, R. and Huber, G. P. (1977) 'Relations Among Perceived Environmental Uncertainty, Organisation Structure, and Boundary Spanning

Behaviour', *Administrative Science Quarterly*, June, pp. 235–47.

Levinson, H. (1970) 'Management by Whose Objectives?', *Harvard Business Review*, vol. 48, no. 4.

Levinson, H. (1970) 'Appraisal of *What* Performance?', *Harvard Business Review*, July/August.

Lewin, K. (1964) 'The Psychology of a Successful Figure', in H. S. Leavitt and L. R. Pondy (eds), *Readings in Managerial Psychology* (University of Chicago Press) pp. 25–31.

Likert, R. (1961) *New Patterns of Management* (New York: McGraw-Hill).

Lilienfeld, R. (1978) *The Rise of Systems Theory: An Ideological Analysis* (New York: Wiley).

Littler, C. R. (1978) 'Understanding Taylorism', *British Journal of Sociology*, vol. 29, no. 2, pp. 185–202.

Lowe, E. A. and McInnes, J. M. (1971) 'Control of Socio-economic Organisations: A Rationale for the Design of Management Control Systems (part 1)', *Journal of Management Studies*, vol. 8. no. 2, pp. 213–27.

Lowe, E. A. and Puxty, A. G. (1979) *The Problems of a Paradigm: A Critique of the Prevailing Orthodoxy in Management Control*, University of Sheffield, Division of Economic Studies, Working Paper.

Lowe, E. A. and Shahin, I. (1980) 'Internal Audit of the Budgetary Function and the Propensity for Information Bias', *Managerial Finance*, vol. 5, no. 2.

Lowe, E. A. and Shaw, R. W. (1968) 'An Analysis of Managerial Biasing: Evidence from a Company's Budgeting Process' *Journal of Management Studies*, vol. V, no. 3, pp. 304–15, October.

Lowe, E. A. and Tinker, A. M. (1976) 'The Architecture of Requisite Variety: An Empirical Application of Managerial Cybernetics to the Organisation of Socio-Economic Enterprise and their Information-for-Control Systems (part 1)', *Kybernetes*, vol. 5, no. 1, pp. 145–54.

Lowe, E. A. and Tinker, A. M. (1977) 'New Directions for Management Accounting', *OMEGA*, vol. 5, no. 2.

Lucas, F. L. (1938) *The Delights of Dictatorship* (Cambridge: W. Heffer & Sons).

Lupton, T. (1963) *On the Shop Floor* (Oxford: Pergamon).

Lupton, T. (1966) *Management and the Social Sciences* (London: Hutchinson).

Lynch, B. P. (1974) 'An Empirical Assessment of Perrow's Technology Construct', *Administrative Science Quarterly*, vol. 19, no. 3, pp. 338–56.

McClelland, D. C. (1967) *The Achieving Society* (New York: The Free Press).

McClelland, D. C. (1975) 'Good Guys Make Bum Bosses', *Psychology Today*, December, pp. 69–70.

McCosh, A. M. (1978) 'Paper from sub group: Management Control Systems and Future of Research', Manchester Business School.

McCosh, A. M. (1980) 'Review of L. R. Amey, "Management Planning and Control Systems"', in *Accounting and Business Research*, pp. 341–2, Summer.

McDougall, C. (1973) 'How Well Do You Reward Your Managers?', *Personnel Management*, pp. 38–43, March.

McGregor, D. (1960) *The Human Side of Enterprise* (New York: McGraw-

Hill).

McKenna, E. F. (1978) *The Management Style of the Chief Accountant* (Farnborough: Saxon House).

McKenna, E. F. (1980) 'Stress: What Causes It Among White-Collar Workers?', *Occupational Safety and Health*, vol. 10, no. 3, April, pp. 8–14.

Machin, J. L. J. (1973) 'Measuring the Effectiveness of an Organisation's Management Control Systems', *Management Decision*, vol. 11, no. 5, pp. 260–79, Winter.

Machin, J. L. J. (1977) 'Using the Expectations Approach to Improve Managerial Communication and Organisational Effectiveness', *Management Decision*, vol. 15, no. 2, pp. 259–77, Spring.

Machin, J. L. J. (1979) 'A Contingent Methodology for Management Control', *Journal of Management Studies*, vol. 16, no. 1, pp. 1–29, February.

Machin, J. L. J. (1980), *The Expectations Approach: Improving Managerial Communication and Performance* (New York: McGraw-Hill).

Machin, J. L. J. (1982) 'Expectations Analysis: A New Tool for On-The-Job Training', Chapter 23 in B. Taylor and G. I. Lippett (eds), *Management Development and Training Handbook*, 2nd edn (New York: McGraw-Hill).

Machin, J. L. J. (1983) 'Developing Communication Profiles of Managerial Jobs', in Osmo A. Wiio and Lee Thayer (eds), *Dimensions of Organisational Communication* (New York: ABLEX).

Machin, J. L. J. (1983) 'Studying the Contents, Volume and Direction of Interpersonal Communication in Senior Management Groups', in Osmo A. Wiio and Lee Thayer (eds), *Dimensions of Organisational Communication* (New York: ABLEX).

Machin, J. L. J. and Kokkalis, J. N. (1979a) 'A Model of the Management Control Cycle', *Journal of Enterprise Management*, vol. 1, no. 3, pp. 245–51.

Machin, J. L. J. and Kokkalis, J. N. (1979b) 'An Experiment to Test the Effect of Improved Communication on the Management Control Process', *Journal of Enterprise Management*, vol. 1, no. 3, pp. 253–61.

Machin, J. L. J. with Stewart, R. (1981) 'Directions for Future Research into Managerial Effectiveness', Chapter 9 in J. L. J. Machin, R. Stewart and C. Hales, (eds), *Toward Managerial Effectiveness* (Farnborough: Gower) pp. 148–60.

Machin, J. L. J., Stewart, R. and Hales, C. P. (1981) *Toward Managerial Effectiveness: Applied Research Perspectives on the Managerial Task and its Effective Performance* (Farnborough: Gower).

Machin, J. L. J. and Tai, C. H. S. (1979) 'Senior Managers Audit Their Own Communication', *Journal of Enterprise Management*, vol. 2, no. 1, pp. 75–89.

Machin, J. L. J. and Wilson, L. (1979) 'Closing the Gap Between Planning and Control', *Long Range Planning*, vol. 12 no. 2, pp. 16–32, April.

Machin, J. L. J. and Wilson, L. (1981) 'Plans and People', Paper 5 in C. J. Ragg (ed.), *Practical Issues for Planners in the Eighties* (London: The Society for Long Range Planning).

Machin, J. L. J., Woolley, A. and Seabury, J. (1981) *Expectations Approach*

User Manual (University of Durham, UK) pp. 1–81.

Mandelbaum, M. (1955) 'Societal Facts', *British Journal of Sociology*, pp. 305–17.

March, J. G. (1976) 'The Technology of Foolishness', in J. G. March and J. P. Olsen (eds), *Ambiguity and Choice in Organisations* (Universitetsforlaget).

March, J. G. and Simon, H. A. (1958) *Organisations* (New York: Wiley).

Maslow, A. H. (1954) *Motivation and Personality* (New York: Harper and Row).

Maslow, A. H. (1965) *Eupsychian Management* (Homewood, Ill.: Dorsey).

Mason, R. O. and Mitroff, I. I. (1973) 'A Programme for Research on Management Information Systems', *Management Science*, vol. 19, no. 5.

Menzies, I. E. P. (1970) *The Functioning of Social Systems as a Defence Against Anxiety* (Centre for Applied Social Research, Tavistock Institute of Human Relations).

Merton, R. K. (1949) *Social Theory and Social Structure* (Glencoe, Ill.: The Free Press).

Merton, R. K., Gray, A. P., Hockey, B. and Selvin, H. C. (1957) *Reader in Bureaucracy* (Glencoe, Ill.: The Free Press).

Meyer, M. W. (1975) 'Organisational Domains', *American Sociological Review*, vol. 40, no. 5, pp. 599–615.

Michael, D. (1973) *On Learning to Plan and Planning to Learn* (London: Jossey Bass).

Milani, K. (1975) 'The Relationship of Participation in Budget Setting to Industrial Supervisor Performance and Attitudes: A Field Study', *The Accounting Review*, pp. 274–84, April.

Milgram, S. (1963) 'Behavioural Study of Obedience', *Journal of Abnormal and Social Psychology*, vol. 67, October.

Miller, E. J. and Rice, A. K. (1967) *Systems of Organisation* (London: Tavistock).

Mintzberg, H. (1973) *The Nature of Managerial Work* (London: Harper and Row).

Mintzberg, H. (1979) *The Structuring of Organisations* (Englewood Cliffs, N. J.: Prentice-Hall).

Mohr, L. B. (1973) 'The Concept of Organisational Goal', *American Political Science Review*, vol. 67, no. 2, pp. 470–81.

Morgan, G. (1979) 'Cybernetics and Organisation Theory: Epistomology or Technique', Working Paper, Department of Behaviour in Organisations, University of Lancaster, May.

Mulder, M. (1971) 'Power Equalisation Through Participation', *Administrative Science Quarterly*, vol. 16, no. 1, pp. 31–8.

Naughton, J. (1979a) 'Functionalism and Systems Research: A Comment', *Journal of Applied Systems Analysis*, vol. 6, pp. 69–73.

Naughton, J. (1979b) 'Review of Lilienfeld (1978)', *Futures*, vol. 11, no. 2.

Nelson, E. G. and Machin, J. L. J. (1976) 'Management Control: Systems Thinking Applied to the Development of a Framework for Empirical Studies', *Journal of Management Studies*, vol. 13, no. 3, pp. 274–87, October.

Nicholls, T. (1969) *Ownership, Control and Ideology* (London: Allen &

Unwin).

Otley, D. T. (1977) 'Behavioural Aspects of Budgeting', *Accountants Digest*, ICAEW, no. 49, Summer.

Otley, D. T. (1978a) 'Budget Use and Managerial Performance', *Journal of Accounting Research*, Spring.

Otley, D. T., (1978b) 'Strategies for Research in Studying the Use Made of Accounting Information in Organisational Control', Workshop Paper, EIASM, September.

Otley, D. T. (1979) 'Towards a Contingency Theory of Management Accounting: A Critical Assessment', unpublished paper, University of Lancaster.

Otley, D. T. (1980) 'The Contingency Theory of Management Accounting: Achievement and Prognosis', *Accounting, Organisations and Society*, vol. 5, no. 4, pp. 413–28.

Otley, D. T. and Berry, A. J. (1977) 'Control and Organisation'. Paper presented at Information and Control Systems Workshop, European Institute for Advanced Studies in Management, Brussels.

Otley, D. T. and Berry, A. J. (1980) 'Control, Organisation and Accounting', *Accounting, Organisations and Society*, vol. 5, no. 2, pp. 231–46.

Ouchi, W. F. (1977) 'The Relationship Between Organisational Structure and Organisational Control', *Administrative Science Quarterly*, vol. 22, no. 1, pp. 95–113.

Parker, L. (1976) 'Goal Congruence: A Misguided Accounting Concept', *Abacus*, June, pp. 3–13.

Parker, L. (1977) 'A Reassessment of the Role of Control in Corporate Budgeting', *Accounting and Business Research*, pp. 135–43. Spring.

Parker, L. D. (1979) 'Participation in Budget Planning – The Prospects Surveyed', *Accounting and Business Research*, pp. 123–37, Spring.

Parsegian, V. L. (1972) *This Cybernetic World* (New York: Doubleday).

Parsons, T. (1956) 'Suggestions for a Sociological Approach to the Theory of Organisations', *Administrative Science Quarterly*, pp. 63–85, June.

Parsons, T. (1960) *Structure and Process in Modern Societies* (New York: The Free Press).

Pask, G. (1961) *An Approach to Cybernetics* (London: Hutchinson).

Pearce, F. T. (1976) 'Business Intelligence Systems: The Need, Development and Interpretation', *Industrial Marketing Management*, vol. 5.

Pennings, J. M. (1975) 'The Relevance of the Structural Contingency Model for Organisational Effectiveness', *Administrative Science Quarterly*, pp. 393–411, September.

Perrow, C. (1961a) 'The Analysis of Goals in Complex Organisations', *American Sociological Review*, vol. 26, pp. 854–66.

Perrow, C. (1961b) *Organisational Analysis: A Sociological View*, (London: Tavistock).

Perrow, L. (1967) 'A Framework For The Comparative Analysis of Organisations', *American Sociological Review*, vol. 32, no. 2, pp. 194–208.

Perrow, L. (1979) *Complex Organisations: A Critical Essay*, 2nd (Glenview, Ill.: Scott, Foresman).

Pettigrew, A. M. (1973) *The Politics of Organisational Decision-Making* (London: Tavistock).

Pfeffer, J. (1978) *Organisational Design* (Arlington Heights, Ill.: A. H. M. Publishing Company).

Pfeffer, J. and Salancik, G. R. (1978) *The External Control of Organisations: A Resourse Dependence Perspective* (New York: Harper and Row).

Phillips, D. C. (1977) *Holistic Thought in Social Science* (London: Macmillan).

Pollard, S. (1965) *The Genesis of Modern Management* (Harmondsworth, Middlesex: Penguin).

Pondy, L. R. and Mitroff, I. I. (1979) 'Beyond Open System Models of Organisation', in L. M. Staw (ed.), *Research in Organisational Behaviour, Vol. I* (Greenwich, Conn.: JAI Press).

Porter, L. W. and Lawler, E. E. (1968) *Managerial Attitudes and Performance* (Homewood, Ill: R. D. Irwin).

Porter, L. W., Lawler, E. E. and Hackman, J. R. (1975) *Behaviour in Organisations* (New York: McGraw-Hill).

Pratt, V. (1978) *The Philosophy of the Social Sciences* (London: Methuen).

Prévost, P. (1976) ' "Soft" Systems Methodology, Functionalism and the Social Sciences', *Journal of Applied Systems Analysis*, vol. 5, no. 1, pp. 65–73.

Pugh, S. and Hickson, D. J. (1976) *Organisational Structure in its Context: The Aston Programme I* (Westmead, Farnborough: Saxon House).

Rathe, A. W. (1960) 'Management Controls in Business', in D. G. Malcolm and A. J. Rowe (eds), *Management Control Systems* (New York: Wiley).

Reid, A. R. (1980) 'A Study of the Performance Appraisal Process as a Contributor to Managerial Effectiveness'. Unpublished M Sc Dissertation, Durham University Business School.

Reilly, P. A. (1979) *Participation, Democracy and Control*, Management Survey Report No. 45 (London: British Institute of Management Publication).

Revans, I. (1980) *Action Learning* (London: Blonde and Brigg).

Revans, R. W. (1969) 'The Structure of Disorder', in J. Rose (ed.), *Survey of Cybernetics* (London: ILEFFE).

Rhenman, E. (1973) *Organisation Theory for Long-Range Planning* (London: Wiley).

Rice, A. K. (1963) *The Enterprise and Its Environment* (London: Tavistock).

Richbell, S. (1976) 'Participation and Perceptions of Control', *Personnel Review*, vol. 5, no. 2, pp. 13–19.

Richbell, S. (1979) 'Participative Design and Organisational Sub-Groups', *Industrial Relations Journal*, vol. 10, no. 1, pp. 40–50.

Roethlisberger, F. J. and Dickson, W. J. (1939) *Management and the Worker* (Harvard University Press).

Rosenberg, J. M. (1978) *Dictionary of Business and Management* (New York: Wiley).

Ross, E. C. (1957) 'Role Specialisation in Supervision', unpublished Ph D thesis, Columbia University.

Rumelt, R. P. (1974) *Strategy, Structure and Economic Performance*, (Division of Research, Graduate School of Business Administration, Boston, Mass.).

Salaman, G. (1979) *Work Organisations* (London: Longman).

Sartre, J. P. (1957) *Being and Nothingness* (London: Methuen).

Sayles, L. R. (1957) 'Research in Industrial Human Relations', *Industrial Relations Research Association* (New York: Harper and Row).

Sayles, L. R. and Chandler, M. K. (1971) *Managing Large Systems: Organisations for the Future* (New York: Harper and Row).

Schiff, M. and Lewin, A. J. (1970) 'The Impact of People on Budgets', *The Accounting Review*, vol. 45, no. 2, pp. 259–68, April.

Schoderbek, P. P., Kefalas, A. G. and Schoderbek, C. G. (1975) *Management Systems: Conceptual Considerations* (Dallas, Texas: Business Publications Inc.).

Seashore, S. E. and Yuchtman, E. (1967) 'Factorial Analysis of Organisational Performance', *Administrative Science Quarterly*, vol. 12, no. 3, pp. 377–95.

Selznick, P. (1966) *T. V. A. and the Grassroots* (New York: Harper Torchbooks).

Shannon, C. E. and Weaver, W. (1949) *The Mathematical Theory of Communication* (University of Illinois Press).

Shaw, A. (1967) 'How to Make Productivity Pacts', *Management Today*, August.

Silverman, D. (1970) *The Theory of Organisations* (London: Heinemann).

Silverman, D. and Jones, J. (1973) 'Getting In: The Managed Accomplishment of "Correct" Selection Outcomes', in J. Child (ed.), *Man and Organisation* (London: Allen and Unwin).

Simon, H. A. (1976) *Administration Behaviour*, 3rd edn (New York: Free Press).

Skinner, B. F. (1973) *Beyond Freedom and Dignity* (Harmondsworth: Penguin).

Smyth, D. S. and Checkland, P. B. (1976) 'Using a Systems Approach: The Structure of Root Definitions', *Journal of Applied Systems Analysis*, vol. 5, no. 1, pp. 75–83.

Spencer, H. (1873) *The Study of Sociology* (London: Kegan Paul, Trench & Co).

Starbuck, W. H. (1971) *Organisational Growth and Development* (Harmondsworth: Penguin Books).

Stead, P. J. (1957) *The Police of Paris* (London: Staples Press).

Stedry, A. C. (1960) *Budget Control and Cost Behaviour* (Englewood Cliffs, NJ: Prentice-Hall).

Stedry, A. C. and Kay, E. (1964) *The Effects of Goal Difficulty on Performance: A Field Experiment*, Sloan School of Management (Cambridge, Mass.: MIT Press).

Steers, R. M. (1975) 'Problems in the Measurement of Organisational Effectiveness', *Administrative Science Quarterly*, vol. 18, no. 4, pp. 546–58.

Steers, R. M. (1977) *Organisational Effectiveness. A Behavioural View* (Santa Monica, California: Goodyear Publishing Co.).

Tai, C. H. S. (1975) 'A Systems and Expectations Approach to Planning and Control in an Industrial Subsidiary', unpublished M Sc dissertation, University of Durham, pp. 1–214.

Tai, C. H. S. (1979) 'The Inter-Dependence of Corporate and Divisional

Expectations: An Empirical Investigation of Managerial Nexus Based on a Contingency Perspective', vol. 1, pp. 1–381, vol. 2, pp. 1–281, unpublished Ph D Thesis, University of Durham.

Tannenbaum, A. S. (1962) 'Control in Organisations: Individual Adjustment and Organisational Performance', *Administrative Science Quarterly*, vol. 7, no. 2, pp. 236–57.

Tannenbaum, A. S. (1968) *Control in Organisations* (New York: McGraw-Hill).

Tannenbaum, A. S. and Allport, F. H. (1956) 'Personality Structure and Group Structure: An Interpretative Study of Their Relationship Through an Event–Structure Hypothesis', *Journal of Abnormal and Social Psychology*, vol. 53, no. 3, pp. 272–80.

Tannenbaum, A. S. and Kahn, R. L. (1957) 'Organisation Control Structure: A General Descriptive Technique as Applied to Four Local Unions', *Human Relations*, vol. 10, no. 2, pp. 127–40.

Tannenbaum, R. and Massarik, F. (1963) 'Participation by Subordinates in the Managerial Decision Making Process', in R. L. Sutermeister (ed.), *People and Productivity* (New York: McGraw-Hill).

Tawney, R. H. (1920) in the foreword to C. L. Goodrich, 'The Frontier of Control: A Study of British Workshop Politics, (London: Bell).

Taylor, F. M. (1947) *Scientific Management* (New York: Harper and Row).

Thomason, G. F. (1973) 'Workers' Participation in Private Enterprise Organisations', in C. D. Balfour, (ed.), *Participation in Industry* (London: Croom Helm).

Thompson, J. D. (1967) *Organisations in Action* (New York: McGraw-Hill).

Thompson, J. D. and McEwen, W. J. (1958) 'Organisational Goals and Environment: Goal Setting as an Interaction Process', *American Sociological Review*, pp. 23–31, February.

Thompson, V. A. (1961) 'Hierarchy, Specialisation and Organisational Conflict', *Administrative Science Quarterly*, vol. 5, no. 4, pp. 485–521.

The Times, 16 May 1972.

Tinker, A. M. (1975) 'An Accounting Organisation for Organisational Problem-Solving', unpublished Ph D thesis, University of Manchester.

Tinker, A. M. and Lowe, E. A. (1977) 'Regulating 'Jumpy' F-Sets', paper presented at the International Conference on Applied General Systems Research, SUNY, Binghampton, New York.

Tocher, K. (1970) 'Control', *Operational Research Quarterly*, pp. 159–80, 21 June.

Tomkins, C. (1973) *Financial Planning in Divisionalised Companies* (London: Haymarket).

Tomkins, C. (1975) 'Residual Income – A Rebuttal of Professor Amey's Arguments', *Journal of Business Finance and Accounting*, vol. 2, no. 2, pp. 161–8.

Tosi, H. (1970) 'A re-examination of Personality as a Determinant of the Effects of Participation', *Personnel Psychology*, vol. 23, pp. 91–9.

Tricker, R. I. (1979) 'Research in Accounting – Purpose, Process and Potential', *Accounting and Business Research*, Winter.

Trist, E. L. and Bamforth, K. W. (1951) 'Some Social and Psychological Consequences of the Longwall Method of Coal-Getting', *Human*

Relations, vol. 4, no. 1, pp. 3–38.

Turner, A. N. and Lawrence, P. R. (1965) *Industrial Jobs and the Worker* (Cambridge, Mass.: Harvard University Press).

Umstot, D. D., Bell, C, H, and Mitchell, T. R. (1976) 'Effects of Job Enrichment And Task Goals On Satisfaction And Productivity: Implications For Job Design', *Journal of Applied Psychology*, vol. 61, no. 4, pp. 379–94.

Urwick, L. F. (1947) *The Elements of Administration* (London: Pitman).

Van de Ven, A. H. and Delbecq, A. L. (1976) 'Determinants of Co-ordination Modes Within Organisations', *American Sociological Review*, vol. 41, no. 2, pp. 322–38.

Veroff, J. (1953) 'Development and Validation of a Projective Measure of Power Motivation', *Journal of Abnormal and Social Psychology*, vol. 55, pp. 1–8.

Vickers, G. (1965) *The Art of Judgement: A Study of Policy Making* (London: Chapman and Hall).

Vickers, G. (1967) *Towards a Sociology of Management* (London: Chapman and Hall).

Vroom, V. H. (1960) *Some Personality Determinants of the Effects of Participation* (Englewood Cliffs, NJ: Prentice-Hall).

Vroom, V. H. (1964) *Work and Motivation* (New York: Wiley).

Vroom, V. H. and Yetton, P. W. (1973) *Leadership and Decision-Making* (University of Pittsburgh Press).

Walker, K. F. (1975) 'Workers' Participation in Management: Concepts and Reality', in B. Barrett, E. Rhodes and J. Beishon (eds), *Industrial Relations and the Wider Society: Aspects of Interaction* (London: Collier Macmillan in Association with the Open University Press).

Walker, K. F. (1974) 'Workers' Participation in Management – Problems, Practice and Prospects', *Bulletin of the International Institute of Labour Studies*, no. 12, pp. 4–8.

Wall, T. D. and Lischeron, J. A. (1977) *Worker Participation: A Critique of the Literature and some Fresh Evidence* (New York: McGraw-Hill).

Wallace, M. E. (1966) 'Behavioural Considerations in Budgeting', *Management Accounting*, vol. 47, pp. 3–8.

Walton, R. E. and McKersie, R. B. (1965) *A Behavioural Theory of Labour Negotiations* (New York: McGraw-Hill).

Warmington, A., Lupton, T. and Gribben, C. (1977) *Organisational Behaviour and Performance* (London: Macmillan).

Waterhouse, J. H. and Tiesson, P. (1978) 'A Contingency Framework for Management Accounting Systems Research', *Accounting, Organisations and Society*, vol. 3, no. 2, pp. 65–76.

Watts, R. and Zimmerman, J. L. (1979) 'The Demand for and Supply of Accounting Theories: The Market for Excuses', *The Accounting Review*, April.

Weber, M. (1947) *The Theory of Social and Economic Organisation* (New York: Free Press).

Weick, K. E. (1969) *The Social Psychology of Organising* (Reading, Mass.: Addison-Wesley).

Weick, K. E. (1979a) *The Social Psychology of Organising*, 2nd edn (Reading,

Mass.: Addison-Wesley).

Weick, K. E. (1979b) 'A Behavioural Scientist's Overview, With Reference to the 1971 Conference', in T. J. Burns (ed.), *Behavioural Experiments in Accounting II*, (Columbia, Ohio: College of Administrative Science, Ohio State University).

Weiner, N. (1948) *Cybernetics* (Cambridge, Mass.: MIT Press).

Wells, H. C. (1976) 'A Revolution in Accounting Thought', *Accounting Review*, July.

Wensley, F. P. (1931) *Detective Days* (London: Cassell & Co.).

Wernimont, P. (1966) 'Intrinsic and Extrinsic Factors in Job Satisfaction', *Journal of Applied Psychology*, vol. 50, no. 1, pp. 41–50.

White, R. W. (1960) 'Competence and Psychosexual Stages of Development', in M. R. Jones (ed.), *Nebraska Symposium on Motivation* (Lincoln: University of Nebraska Press) pp. 97–141.

Wildavsky, A. (1975) *Budgeting: A Comparative Analysis of the Budgetary Process* (Boston: Little, Brown).

Williamson, D. E. (1964) *The Economics of Discretionary Behaviour: Managerial Objectives on a Theory of a Firm* (Englewood Cliffs, NJ: Prentice-Hall).

Willmer, M. A. P. (1970) *Crime and Information Theory* (Edinburgh University Press).

Willmer, M. A. P. (1974) 'The Priest and the President', *Management in Action*, vol. 5, no. 60, September, pp. 21–3.

Willmer, M. A. P. (1976a) 'The Third European Meeting on Cybernetics and System Research, Vienna, 1976', *Kybernetes*, vol. 5, p. 248.

Willmer, M. A. P. (1976b) 'Optimising Pilfering Control', *Security Gazette*, vol. 18, no. 12, December, pp. 424–5.

Willmer, M. A. P. (1977) 'Information Theory and Organisation Structure', *Kybernetes*, vol. 6, pp. 277–87.

Willmer, M. A. P. (1978) 'System Uncertainty and Leadership Strategy', Proceedings of the European Meeting of Cybernetics and Systems Research, Linz, 1978, *Progress of Cybernetics and Systems Research*, vol. III (Washington D. C.: Hemisphere Publishing Corp.).

Willmer, M. A. P. (1980) 'Subordinate Behaviour and Management Control', *5th European Meeting on Cybernetics and Systems Research*, Vienna (New York: Hemisphere Publishing).

Willmer, M. A. P. and Berry, A. J. (1976) 'Managerial Performance and System Uncertainty', *3rd European Meeting on Cybernetics and Systems Research*, Vienna, (New York: Hemisphere Publishing).

Wisdom, (1956), 'The Cybernetic Hypothesis', *General Systems Theory I*.

Wispe, L. G. and Lloyd, K. E. (1955) 'Some Situational and Psychological Determinants of the Desire For Structured Interpersonal Relations', *Journal of Abnormal and Social Psychology*, vol. 51, pp. 57–60.

Woodward, J. (1965) *Industrial Organisation: Theory and Practice* (London: Oxford University Press).

Woodward, J. and Rackham, J. (1970) *Industrial Organisation: Behaviour and Control* (London: Oxford University Press).

Yetton, P. (1979) 'The Efficiency of a Piecework Incentive Payment System', *Journal of Management Studies*, vol. 16, no. 3, October.

Subject Index

311

Author Index